ABSENT CITIZENS:
DISABILITY POLITICS AND POLICY IN CANADA

Disability exists in the shadows of public awareness and at the periph-ery of policy making. People with disabilities are, in many respects, missing from the theories and practices of social rights, political par-ticipation, employment, and civic membership. *Absent Citizens* brings to light these chronic deficiencies in Canadian society and emphasizes the effects that these omissions have on the lives of citizens with dis-abilities.

Drawing together elements from feminist studies, political science, public administration, sociology, and urban studies, Michael J. Prince examines mechanisms of exclusion and inclusion, public attitudes on disability, and policy-making processes in the context of disability. *Absent Citizens* also considers social activism and civic engagements by people with disabilities and disability community organizations, highlighting presence rather than absence and advocating both inquiry and action to ameliorate the marginalization of an often over-looked segment of the Canadian population.

MICHAEL J. PRINCE is Lansdowne Professor of Social Policy in the Faculty of Human and Social Development at the University of Victoria.

MICHAEL J. PRINCE

Absent Citizens

Disability Politics and Policy in Canada

UNIVERSITY OF TORONTO PRESS
Toronto   Buffalo   London

© University of Toronto Press Incorporated 2009
Toronto Buffalo London
www.utppublishing.com
Printed in Canada

ISBN 978-0-8020-9939-6 (cloth)
ISBN 978-0-8020-9630-2 (paper)

Library and Archives Canada Cataloguing in Publication

Prince, Michael John, 1952–
    Absent citizens : disability politics and policy in Canada / Michael J. Prince.

    Includes bibliographical references and index.
    ISBN 978-0-8020-9939-6 (bound) – ISBN 978-0-8020-9630-2 (pbk.)

    1. People with disabilities – Canada.   2. People with disabilities – Govern-
ment policy – Canada.   3. People with disabilities – Legal status, laws, etc. –
Canada.   I. Title.

    HV1559.C3P75 2009   305.9'080971   C2008-908153-6

This book has been published with the help of a grant from the Canadian
Federation for the Humanities and Social Sciences, through the Aid to
Scholarly Publications Program, using funds provided by the Social Sciences
and Humanities Research Council of Canada.

University of Toronto Press acknowledges the financial assistance to its
publishing program of the Canada Council for the Arts and the Ontario Arts
Council.

University of Toronto Press acknowledges the financial support for its
publishing activities of the Government of Canada through the
Book Publishing Industry Development Program (BPIDP).

Contents

Preface

Struggles over the meaning and practice of citizenship feature in contemporary societies and nowhere more so than for people with mental and physical disabilities. Equality and inclusion are principles evoked by individuals, families, community groups, social movement organizations, and coalitions to legitimate claims for human rights, social acceptance, public participation, and an array of material benefits. Overcoming the marginalization of persons with disabilities requires a politics of cultural recognition, a politics of economic redistribution, and a politics of political representation. All three are essential for advancing toward full citizenship for all members of society. This is the challenge and the promise of disability inquiry and political action.

As a field of inquiry in Canada, studying disability is coming of age. In universities there are now undergraduate and graduate programs in disability studies at Brock, Manitoba, Ryerson, and York, alongside older programs in rehabilitation studies at Calgary, Queen's, and University of British Columbia, among others. There are courses on disability in anthropology, child and family studies, education, geography, law, nursing, political science, sociology, social work, and women's studies. In 2004 the Disability Studies Association was formed by a network of Canadian researchers, advocates, academics, and policy officials. In government agencies at Aboriginal, federal, provincial, territorial, and municipal levels increasing interest in disability is apparent in strategies, organizational reforms, and program developments. As a movement, the disability community is working hard to encourage a new period of innovative social policy development for advancing the citizenship of persons with disabilities.

Disability issues, despite these developments and efforts, have a relatively low profile in Canadian political life. This is not to suggest that disability policy and practice lacks controversy or struggle. Court cases over autism treatments; heated debates over closing (and reopening) institutions of persons with developmental disabilities or mental health challenges; issues over euthanasia, mercy killing, and selective non-treatment; bio-medical techniques of genetic testing for predisposition to impairments; the murder of Tracy Latimer by her father Robert Latimer and his two trials and requests for parole, all illustrate the intense and crucial issues of disability at stake in Canada.[1] All too often, however, such issues are in the shadows of public awareness, on the margins of Canadian politics, and the periphery of policy making. And too often, persons with disabilities are treated as dependents and personal tragedies in schools and workplaces or left out altogether from cultural and media representations. Persons with disabilities are, in many respects, missing from the theories and practices of social rights, political participation, employment, and civic membership. They are absent citizens.

A statement on terminology is in order. Kathryn Church and her colleagues (2007) cogently outline some basic conceptual choices and issues involved in this field of inquiry and action:

> People with disabilities? Or disabled people? There are ongoing and unresolved debates about ways to talk about disability. It is common practice to use what is called 'people first' language. This is the result of arguments made by some disability scholars/activists that 'we are people first, and disabled only incidentally.' The strategy here is to use language to dislodge bodily difference, 'impairment' and/or limitation as a 'master status' in defining how people are perceived and treated. We are comfortable with this terminology but we are also aware of arguments made recently by other scholars/activists that 'disability' is not only such a primary but such a valued aspect of identity (and also of social perception) that it is not possible or even advantageous to push it to the periphery. From this perspective 'disabled' does not signify 'damaged' identity. Instead, it is a differently legitimate form of personhood that can be fully incorporated into a valued self. (2)

Mostly I use the expression 'people with disabilities,' the phrase widely used within the Canadian disability movement, recognizing that some authors and advocates, in Canada and especially in the United Kingdom, prefer the term disabled people (Barnes and Mercer 2003; Devlin and Pothier 2006; Titchkosky 2001). Even this brief discussion on terminology indicates the significance of discourse to political activism and citizenship.

Absent Citizens extends the growing body of academic literature in Canada and internationally on disability. It develops from key texts such as Bickenbach (1993) on physical disability and social policy, Rioux and Bach's (1994) collection on new research paradigms on disability, and the analysis by Enns (1999) on the Tracy Latimer case and the general status of people with disabilities as 'voices unheard.' As well, the book builds on the case studies by Boyce and colleagues (2001) on the role of persons with disabilities and their organizations in Canadian policy making processes.

In this book, I also build upon analysis from works by Cameron and Valentine (2001) and Puttee (2002) on federalism, democracy, and disability policy in Canada and other countries, as well as by Enns and Neufeldt (2003) and by Stienstra and Wight-Felske (2003) on advocacy and the pursuit of equality by disability groups in Canada and abroad. Titchkosky (2003a, 2007) has written two significant books, blending theory and everyday experience that consider texts on disability, the embodied self, and society. Other important recent works are by McColl and Jongbloed (2006) on disability and Canadian social policy, Pothier and Devlin (2006) on critical disability theory and their notion of 'dis-citizenship,' Panitch (2007) on how and why mothers with children with disabilities became 'accidental activists' in fighting against exclusion and for human rights, Lord and Hutchison (2007) on pathways to creating an inclusive civil society, and Moss and Teghtsoonian (2008) on processes and practices of contesting illnesses. Many of these works are edited collections spanning a range of topics on disability law, philosophy, meanings of disablement, and issues of service provision.

Another stream of Canadian literature illustrates the narrative form in disability studies. This includes oral histories and stories of men and women's embodied experiences living with blindness, spinal cord injury and other impairments, chronic illness, disease, trauma, psychiatric hospitals and survivors, and community mental health intersecting with age, social class, race, language and place, among other social markers (Capponi 1992; Church 1995; Crooks 2007; Dale-Stone 2007; Doe 2003; Dossa 2005, 2008; Driedger, Crooks, and Bennett 2004; Driedger and Owen 2008; Krause 2005; Matthews 1983; Michalko 1999, 2002; Moss and Dyck 2002; Overboe 2007; Raoul et al. 2007; Reaume 2000; Shimrat 1997; Titchkosky 2003a; Tremblay, Campbell, and

Hudson 2005). In making sense of illness and identity, this body of work acknowledges human agency and gives voice to groups of people marginalized and forgotten. Employing biographical and other research methods, these works underline the capacity of people with disabilities in negotiating notions of self, building networks of support, and resisting governing health and social practices. At times, powerful and heart-wrenching stories of people with disabilities appear in public documents, such as the Senate report on mental health, mental illness, and addiction (Kirby 2006). All such stories, and accompanying analyses, are important in influencing public aware-ness and social theory, motivating disability movement activism at local and extra local levels, and affecting policy development.

An extensive international literature, particularly American and British, is useful for comparisons and theoretical insights, though not always a close fit with Canadian experiences. Political activism by the Canadian disability movement has garnered some academic attention, mostly from the disability studies field itself, with relatively little analysis from political science or policy studies.

In addition to the literature and documents cited, I draw on my own location and experiences within the Canadian disability community as an academic, consultant, and participant. In relation to the analysis and interpretation of events and issues in this book, I am at times an 'outsider' and at other times an 'insider,' roles that inevitably overlap creating insights as well as tensions. I am an 'insider' in the disability rights movement in that I work closely with key national disability organizations as well as frequently advise federal and provincial levels of Canadian government and Parliament on disability issues and other social policy topics. Since 2004, I have served as a board member of the British Columbia Association of Community Living, a province-wide federation that advocates for children, youth, and adults with devel-opmental disabilities and their families to ensure justice, rights, and opportunities in all areas of their lives. And, I am an 'outsider' writing as an academic reflecting on the development and absences of policies and programs. For example, in chapter 9, when discussing key reform ideas put forward by national disability organizations, I was involved in writing some of those action plans and generating some of the reform options.

I am, at present, a non-disabled person, working as an ally, col-league, and friend of people with disabilities and the movement. In that context, I am not a neutral observer. As an outsider, I perform a role as a 'public intellectual,' conducting research on policy and social issues of our times, conveying findings through the media and in presentations to community groups, legislative committees, and administrative officials. As an insider, I perhaps perform a role akin to a 'movement intellectual' (Haluza-Delay 2003), an academic working collaboratively with social movement organizations in developing policy plans, designing reforms, and monitoring trends.

Absent Citizens adopts a broad understanding of politics and policy in the Canadian context. As a specialist in social policy, political science, and public administration, and as someone who participates in the Canadian disability movement, I write this book from a sociological and political perspective. Instead of taking a bio-medical or worthy poor approach, the book focuses on several kinds of disability activism and engagements with the state. It relates disability policy issues and programs to theoretical issues of power, social inequalities, urbanization, and city life. It is perhaps the first book to apply a general political sociology approach to disability issues and disabling processes in Canada. The book offers a multi-dimensional analysis of citizenship, demonstrating in concrete terms what citizenship for people with disabilities can and does mean in practice, including its contested nature. I draw on ideas, theories, and lines of inquiry from feminist research, political science, public administration, social policy, sociology, and urban studies.

This book's contributions are in three areas. First, the book makes the case for greater attention to disability in social theory and research, and the need to link the politics of identity and difference with the politics of social stratification and inequality. As a dimension of social division, disability is usually overlooked in public policy studies and other social science fields. The book also looks at material and symbolic aspects of social stratification. Second, the book adopts a broad conception of citizenship, arguing that who belongs and who does not, on what terms and conditions entails multiple elements and levels: civil, legal, political, economic, and discursive elements of individual and group rights and responsibilities. Third, the book points out how the state constructs roles and orders social relationships through the design and provision of services, rules, and benefits, as well as through attitudinal and built environments in urban life.

My primary purpose in this book is to describe and understand the citizenship of persons with disabilities in contemporary Canada using a political and social policy analysis. Citizenship rights and duties are not above politics; they are embedded within and an expression of politics whether understood as competing claims, interpreting needs, allocating resources, reconciling diverse values, or people relating to one another.

Attention focuses on power relationships, societal trends and inequalities, as well as to viewing persons with disabilities as political actors and the disability community as a political entity in its own right. My focus is on experiences in the Canadian context since the 1980s when disability issues received international and national awareness as a social issue and recognition as a policy field in itself. My objective is to provide an introduction to vital policy issues and political questions of our age that concern the struggles of people living with disabilities.

A related purpose is to contribute to the up-and-coming field of disability studies, a field that is multi-disciplinary in its origins, methodologies, and perspectives. I am guided by socio-political ideas on disability, rather than by a charitable outlook or a bio-medical model of disability. From this perspective, disability is seen as a social issue not a personal trouble or an individual's defect. Disability as a public issue requires individual and community responsibility, social change, policy reforms, and cultural changes. Alongside historical tendencies of medical care, individual treatment, and professional assistance, I emphasize inclusion and self-determination. I further aim to present conceptual ideas and theoretical propositions pertaining to social inclusion, new policy techniques, and innovative approaches to service provision.

Disability studies is part of a larger movement in contemporary societies in which fundamental issues of identities and rights for several groups – Aboriginal peoples, ethnic groups, women, and members of sexual minorities, among others – are actively debated and in some cases help effect new governance arrangements. In this book, I examine the organizational and political nature of Canada's disability movement and its relations with the state and social policy. In our age of globalization, the authority of states remains essential to citizenship. Canadian disability groups look to federal and provincial governments, along with city governments, as defenders of human rights, providers of public services, and enablers of social inclusion. In this vein, chapters that follow examine policy and administrative practices, electoral system reforms, revitalized roles for governments, accessible urban public spaces, and a national act for persons with disabilities.

The main political outlook of the disability movement, I suggest, is a version of social liberalism and I outline key features of this perspective, comparing it to the ever-present discourse of neo-liberalism. Without doubt, these two perspectives collide, generating ideological sparks in disability policy making. I also conclude that the Canadian disability community, while a diverse social institution, has forged an agenda of national priorities and achieved some progress in furthering community inclusion.

Absent Citizens will appeal to students and instructors in disability courses and related courses examining identities and social change. Activists, self-advocates, and members of disability organizations and those in other social movements are another intended audience. A third group that should find this book of interest include policy analysts, decision makers, administrators, and practitioners in governments and other public sector bodies committed to tackling exclusion and advancing social inclusion. I share French social theorist Alain Touraine's belief 'in the possibility of a collective movement that can enhance the capacity for action on the part of social categories that are dominated but not completely alienated' (2001: 4), and the vision of Canadian disability activist Jim Derksen that 'we are helping to awaken humanity to the reality that all people are flawed and yet beautiful, and each one limited in his or her unique way and yet powerful' (quoted in Driedger 1989: 115).

For support of various kinds in completing this book I wish to acknowledge the following organizations: British Columbia Association for Community Living, Canadian Association for Community Living, Council of Canadians with Disabilities, and the Canadian Disability Studies Association. I gratefully acknowledge the Roeher Institute to use material previously published by them in chapters 1 and 7, and to the *Disability Studies Quarterly* that published a version of chapter 2. For their influences on my thinking, acting, and writing over the past years, I also acknowledge the following people: Michael Bach, Laurie Beachell, Laney Bryenton, Cam Crawford, Jim Derksen, Harvey Lazar, Yvonne Peters, Jessica Prince, Kathleen Prince, Karen Wallace-Prince, Allan Puttee, John Rae, Marcia Rioux, Zuhy Sayeed, Deborah Stienstra, Sherri Torjman, Deborah Tunis, Fraser Valentine, Traci

Walters, and Marie White. Special thanks are also due to anonymous University of Toronto Press academic reviewers who offered useful comments on the manuscript, making the final document a better one. Above all, I wish to thank Karen, Jessica, and Kathleen for invaluable editorial advice and their incomparable love.

Michael J. Prince
Oak Bay
January 2009

ABSENT CITIZENS:
DISABILITY POLITICS AND POLICY IN CANADA

Introduction: Disability, Politics, and Citizenship

Approaching disability as a socially significant and politically contested domain, *Absent Citizens* examines citizenship, the state, federalism, and relationships between governments and communities. The general purpose of this book is to investigate the precarious status and practice of citizenship for persons with disabilities in Canadian society. To do so, I consider disability in connection to power relations in and around both state and social institutions. In addition to consideration of the functional limitations and capacities of individuals or their families, an adequate understanding of disability requires consideration of social structures. The major issues of disability are not merely problems of individual capacity or health condition, but rather questions of community commitments or neglects, in short, matters of power relations at many levels and segments of communities. Struggling for 'full citizenship' is the paradigmatic form of political action by groups representing persons with physical disabilities, intellectual disabilities, and mental health conditions.

The central argument of the book is that as a social group Canadians with disabilities are absent citizens. Compared to persons without disabilities, persons with disabilities experience significant cultural, material, and political disadvantages. This is evident in higher rates of poverty and unemployment, and inaccessible built environments in towns, suburbs, and cities. Persons with disabilities cope with public ambivalence, in the form of pride and prejudice, as to their needs for inclusive policy actions. They confront persistent barriers to participation in politics, education, the labour market, and other realms of community living. Citizenship is much more than a political concept and legal status, though these too are crucial dimensions. Citizenship entails cultural, economic, and social dimensions. In one or more of these dimensions, many Canadians with disabilities are effectively absent, lacking full enjoyment of liberty of the person, or freedom of expression and communication.

Frequently, Canadians with disabilities struggle to participate as voters, campaign workers, candidates, and elected representatives in democratic processes. Mainstream classrooms and other regular learning opportunities exclude large numbers of children and youth with disabilities. Adults with disabilities wishing to work are unemployed or discouraged altogether from pursuing gainful employment with decent wages in a supportive work setting; others labour in sheltered workshops. Issues around the living conditions of persons with disabilities and their families are recurrently absent from academic disciplines, social theories, and public attitudes. Access to a basic level of essential public services, including adequate income, is a problem for upwards of two million Canadians with disabilities across all age groups and types of impairments (Canada 2006; Statistics Canada 2002, 2007). As a consequence, most persons with disabilities in Canada do not experience full substantive citizenship (Bonnett 2003; Lord and Hutchison 2007; Rioux and Valentine 2006); they do not, in the words of T.H. Marshall (1964: 74), 'live the life of a civilised being according to the standards prevailing in the society.'

So, how does the general public understand disability? What are the attitudes of Canadians toward the adequacy of social programs and the distribution of responsibilities for meeting needs and advancing the inclusion of citizens with disabilities? How does existing theory and social science research treat disability as a dimension in Canadian urban society? Where is the Canadian state in the distribution of social inclusions and exclusions? How do public programs structure the status of people with disabilities? What kinds of politics do people with disabilities and organizations of the disability community practise? What does political representation and community engagement mean? What are the implications for citizenship of neo-liberalism and its main alternative in Canada, social liberalism? These are basic questions for understanding the uncertain status of persons with disabilities in this country. This introduction sets out the analytical foundation and main concepts of the book – disability and inclusion; political struggles for recognition, redistribution, and representation; and, enabling citizenship. Given the centrality of citizenship in theory and in politics, the introduction describes five elements of citizenship as they relate to disability.

Disability Perspectives: Contesting Identity and Inclusion

With many diagnoses, experiences, and meanings, disability is the subject of assorted perspectives, interests, and debates. Table 1 lists no less than a dozen different ways of understanding disability, touching on attitudinal outlooks, personal and societal aspects, political dimensions, and policy perspectives. A functional view of disability, represented in personal and professional assessments of having difficulty with daily living activities or having a physical or mental condition or a health problem that reduces the kind of activity that an individual can do is a dominant perspective of disability. Such difficulties and limitations prevent or restrict a person's ability to participate fully in society. This is the conventional Canadian definition of who is a person with a disability and what makes him or her disabled. It is rooted in biological and medical ways of understanding disablements (Jennissen, Prince, and Schwartz 2000). The Canadian Human Rights Act, for example, defines disability as any previous or existing mental or physical disability and includes disfigurement. Previous or existing dependence on alcohol or a drug is also included in this statutory definition of disability. Other federal and provincial laws define disability in terms of a range of impairments: physical, sensory, neurological, learning, intellectual or developmental, psychiatric or mental disorder. In this context, disability is a thing – whether temporary or permanent, stable or episodic, mild or severe – that is located in the person.

A second perspective is the social rights or the socio-political model in the disability studies literature. Here, disability is part of the fabric of Canadian society, something that all individuals experience in one way or another and from which everyone can learn (Titchkosky 2003a). Attention focuses especially to attitudes, beliefs, body identities, and social values, as well as to issues of human rights, prejudice, and stigma. Moreover, disability is an assemblage of socio-economic, cultural, and political disadvantages resulting from an individual's exclusion by society. Disability exists or occurs when a person with impairment encounters barriers to performing everyday activities of living, barriers to participating in the societal mainstream, and/or barriers to exercising his or her human rights and fundamental freedoms. Here, disability is understood as a social process more than as some individual condition.

Work in recent decades by the World Health Organization conceptualizes disability as the relationship between body structures and

Table 1
What is disability?

- Bio-medical conditions, functional restrictions, and individual impairments
- Personal misfortunes, bad luck, and tragedy
- Objects of pity and charity and/or fear and dread
- Phenomenon that many people believe affects only a small minority of a population
- Legal concepts in Canadian constitution, legislation, regulations, and court decisions
- Formal administrative categories in program design and delivery systems
- Historically layered and fragmented policy field of divergent programs and practices
- Research areas across various disciplines and professions
- Market sector for business activities and transactions
- Social construct of cultural, societal, and economic factors and relationships
- Issues of social oppression, power(lessness), and political will
- Community movement of actors, service groups, advocacy coalitions, and associations

functions, daily activities and social participation, and environmental factors. Today, most Canadian policy related disability research tends to interpret disability in this way. For instance, Catherine Frazee, Joan Gilmour, and Roxanne Mykitiuk (2006: 226) see disability as 'embracing both the politics of social and cultural disablement and the material reality of embodied impairment.' Whether at the level of the individual, family, group, or social movement, the nature of disability is neither a fixed nor a uniform phenomenon. This observation immediately admits realities of diversity, changes, and contradictions. Through different claims of experiences and different types of knowledge, disability is socially constructed, administratively negotiated, and politically contested. Far from being a monolithic entity, disability is a multi-dimensional set of differential life experiences ignored or

responded to in various imperfect ways in particular contexts. Following those in the disability movement, I adopt a position that views disability as part of human diversity and the general human condition,
and as an environmental outcome, a social consequence of actions and
inactions, more than a personal condition (Enns and Neufeldt 2003).

A significant disjuncture exists between this socio-cultural perspective and much of Canadian public policy and service provision. Most
programs and delivery systems embody aspects of other perspectives
on disability: a bio-medical, charitable, and worthy poor welfare viewpoint (Lord and Hutchison 2007; Rioux and Prince 2002; Valentine and
Vickers 1996). Traditionally, and still today, most public policy on disability focuses on a person's functional limitations due to disease,
injury, or chronic illness as the cause or a major explanation for relatively low levels of formal educational attainment, employment, and
income. An image of people with disabilities still common is of a
person who suffers from an affliction, accidental or biological, thus to
be pitied or feared. 'There are times when nondisabled people "see us"
and take this opportunity to "thank" God that they are not like us'
(Michalko 2002: 165). Disability politics is about choices over whether
the priority in policy and practice should relate to body structures and
functions, daily activities and social activities, or environmental and
cultural factors requiring adaptation and transformation.

Federal, provincial/territorial, and local governments are slowly
reorienting their conceptions of disability and the place of people with
disabilities in Canadian society. Everyday language, terminology in
legislation, and the conceptual underpinnings of public policy receive
considerable attention by disability advocates, their organizations, and
government decision makers (Titchkosky 2007). Disability offices issue
guidelines to educate the public and media on the use of terms about
people with disabilities that are respectful and descriptive. As recently
as 2007, provincial laws contained such terms as 'idiot' and 'moron' to
describe people with mental health conditions. Law reforms can mod-
ernize language as well as legislation of concern to Canadians with
disabilities. Such reforms represent a reordering of the symbolic fabric
of citizenship.

As cultural scripts, policy documents communicate certain values,
cast specific roles, and convey particular models of people and communities. Over the last generation, governmental and disability organization papers have adopted citizenship as the central organizing principle and benchmark in policy advocacy, analysis, and agreements. For

example, federal, provincial, and territorial ministers responsible for social services released in 1998, a policy framework for disabilities. *In Unison: A Canadian Approach to Disability Issues* is the first substantial consensus among governments, except the government of Quebec, on a national vision for disability policy. The shared vision states:

> Persons with disabilities participate as full citizens in all aspects of Canadian society. The full participation of persons with disabilities requires the commitment of all sectors of society. The realization of the vision will allow persons with disabilities to maximize their independence and enhance their well-being through access to required supports and the elimination of barriers that prevent their full participation. (Canada 1998: 1)

The vision embraces values of equality, inclusion, and independence, plus the principles of rights and responsibilities, empowerment, and participation. At a rhetorical level, these are the dominant ideas in disability policy and politics. These ideas concern individual liberty (self-determination and competence), stability in social relations (the critical issue of managing stable transitions across life stages), equality and inclusion (citizenship), as well as equity and fairness (reasonable accommodation, among other practices). Table 2 shows the planned changes in approach to disability issues endorsed by Canadian governments.

These desired changes promise a notable shift for disability policy and practice. Within and across political jurisdictions, changes along these lines are in varying states of amendment and transformation. The most progress to date in policy directions is in emphasizing the employability of working age persons with disabilities. Linked to that, is the intended shift in the portrayal of Canadians with disabilities as independent participants endowed with skills and experiences. Nonetheless, tensions between the old and new approaches remain a basic problematic in advancing progressive changes in disability policy and practice.

Contending understandings of inclusion are a key feature of contemporary disability politics and policy. The concept of 'social inclusion' is a rhetorical device of the movement to mobilize collective action; it is a desired state of community affairs suggesting the absence of barriers and discrimination, purportedly endorsed by governments; and it is an idea with which disability groups organize their mandates

Table 2
Canadian government planned changes in approaches to disability issues

Old	New
Recipients	Participants
Passive income support	Active measures to promote employment in addition to providing necessary income support
Dependence	Independence
Government responsibility	Shared responsibility
Labelled as unemployable	Work skills identified
Disincentives to leave income support	Incentives to seek employment and volunteer opportunities
Insufficient employment supports	Opportunities to develop skills and experience
Program-centred approach	Person-centred approach
Insufficient portability of benefits and services	Portable benefits and services
Multiple access requirements	Integrated access requirements

Source: Canada. (1998). *In Unison: A Canadian Approach to Disability Issues.* Report by the Federal/Provincial/Territorial Ministers Responsible for Social Services. Ottawa: Supply and Services Canada.

and represent their activities and tactics. For all these reasons, inclusion is an idea that merits critical reflection to illuminate assumptions and power relations.

Marcia Rioux and Fraser Valentine (2006) argue that a basic contradiction exists between the vision of inclusion as held by governments and the vision understood by disability groups. Canadian governments, Rioux and Valentine suggest, downplay a rights-based approach to inclusion and citizenship; instead, governments emphasize selective services, discretionary programs, and, through social insurance contributions, earned benefits. For some time now, governments have stressed spending limitations, viewing public programs as expensive responses to social needs. Their preference is to promote social partnerships, which means other sectors of society are to play a significant role in tackling obstacles to participation. Most government activities and programming emphasize bio-medical and functional approaches to disability. Whereas governments interpret inclusion in terms of equality of opportunity, Rioux and Valentine argue that most Canadian disability groups emphasize equality of treatment and a human rights approach.

Disability groups appreciate the importance of social partnerships, but look to governments to play a strong leadership role in tackling exclusions. Public expenditures in the form of general entitlements, the disability movement regards as essential investments in advancing access and equality. The preferred approach to disability, by the community, is to socio-political and environmental approaches. This difference between disability groups and governments in interpreting what inclusion means 'creates a circle of tension and confusion' (Rioux and Valentine 2006: 48), resulting in inconsistent messages, inadequate processes for dialogue, and an incoherent policy context.

Analytical Approach: Critical Policy and Institutional Studies

Critical policy studies (Orsini and Smith 2007a; Rioux and Prince 2002; Wharf 1992) and an institutional approach (Coleman and Skogstad 1990; Rice and Prince 2000) inform my methodological approach. *Absent Citizens* examines a non-traditional domain of policy and a set of issues not given a central place in political science or public administration studies. Further, the book is about a social group still largely excluded from the governance structures and processes of policy making in Canada. Critical policy studies is an informative perspective for disability studies because of the explicit connection between power, politics, and social life; the location of individuals, families, and groups within larger societal contexts; and a consideration of the interplay in agency and capacity between actors and structures. Unlike some works in political sociology that focus on elites and those with considerable authority and influence, I focus on the marginal and the forgotten, those with relatively little in society (Tyjewski 2006; Wilton 2006). Among other qualities, having a critical perspective 'means being able to see beyond the status quo, looking beyond symptoms and labels, seeing the reality of people's situations, and understanding how they are linked to attitudes, policies, and systems' (Lord and Hutchison 2007: 14). Accordingly, I endeavour to present some of the perspectives and concerns of persons with physical disabilities and mental disabilities, and to indicate how different social markers of identity intersect (Orsini and Smith 2007b).

Drawing on concepts from several academic disciplines, my analysis focuses on power relations in and between societal and state institutions as important factors in shaping policy and practice. In regard to the politicization of citizenship, I consider the role of neo-liberalism and its interplay with social liberalism, and in addressing the theme of citizens and democracy, I examine the issues of civic engagement by individuals; rights, litigation, and the courts; and modes of representation by organized interests in the disability community. On the themes of difference, discourse, and knowledge, I look at disability mainstreaming, the significance of public attitudes toward inclusion and access, and the production of policy related research. In *Absent Citizens*, I examine the 'official public sphere' of politics as well as the 'unofficial community sphere' of politics to capture a wider range of citizenship practices and issues. Throughout, I take issue with key concepts such as citizenship, inclusion, and disability. In Canada, the state and society are institutions with contradictory effects for the status of persons with disabilities.

Disability Politics in Canada:
Recognition, Redistribution, Representation

Canadian disability politics plays out through struggles over absences and actions constituted by cultural, economic, and political structures. The main contours of disability activism concern the pursuit of respectful inclusion, adequate social security, and an authentic democratic voice. Contrary to some analyses, contemporary disability politics in Canada has not marked a shift from a politics of socio-economic redistribution toward a politics of cultural recognition to the point of actually displacing redistribution as the goal of political struggle (Fraser 1989, 2000). Other commentators, following on the work of Ronald Inglehart across several countries, describe a long-term shift in political values from materialist concerns of economic security and personal safety to post-materialist concerns of identity, belonging, esteem, and dignity. This proposition is too simplistic an interpretation of new social movements in Canadian politics (James 2006; Mulvale 2001).

While disability theorists and activists understand disability as an identity in group terms, they conceptualize disability as a social construction, a concept more nuanced in content and wider in scope than a cultural construction of identity. For understanding the matrix of oppressions and opportunities, the social construction approach by design forges close linkages to political and economic structures. As well, while disability theorists and activists are attentive to discursive aspects of disability, they emphasize material dimensions of struggles for justice and equality. Likewise, the framework on disability issues formulated by federal, provincial, and territorial governments, discussed earlier, highlights problems of employment, personal supports, and income benefits for Canadians with disabilities.

In contemporary Canada, issues of recognition and of redistribution are central features of activism by the disability movement and analysis by disability studies. Claims-making by the movement includes a politics of representation that encompasses traditional concerns of citizen participation and voting, and, more recently, the practices of deliberative democracy and community dialogue (Laforest and Phillips 2007). Overall, Canadian disability politics comprises three forms of struggle for social change and justice: the comparatively new politics of cultural recognition and identity interacting with the long-established politics of redistribution of material goods, and a politics of representation that combines conventional and alternative modes of decision making.

Analytically, these three forms of political struggle correspond to distinct institutional domains: the politics of recognition to the cultural order of society, the politics of redistribution to the market economy and welfare state, and the politics of representation to the political system and civil society. An observation by Matt James on the interests of equality-seeking social movements in Canadian politics neatly captures the presence of these three forms of politics and their interconnections in practical terms: 'to enjoy security in human society, people must also enjoy a measure of respect. When members of disrespected groups interact with more powerful groups, they tend to experience problems of political voice that make them exceedingly vulnerable to the decisions and inclinations of others' (2006: 112). Like other social movements, policy priorities of the disability community in Canada include a mixture of symbolic, material, and political concerns. Fundamental obstacles to full participation by Canadians with disabilities include their non-recognition as full persons in prevailing cultural value patterns; the mal-distribution of resources in the form of income, employment, housing, and other material resources; and their misrepresentation or marginal voice in elections, policy development, and decision-making processes.

Using this line of analysis the book is structured into a two-part conceptual focus on Canadian disability politics and policy development. One part focuses on absences; the ambiguous status of persons with disabilities within Canadian society and the state, the role of disability as a basis for stratification, and inequality in urban life.[1] In the words of one scholar, 'disabled people are still excluded from the public role and from societal structures of power. Disability is still in collusion with the underside of appearance and with the established' (Michalko 2002: 165). Looking at Canadian society, Richard Devlin and Dianne Pothier observe that 'not all share equally in the good life, or feel adequately included. Among those who face recurring coercion, marginalization, and social exclusion are persons with disabilities' (2006: 1). Absences include the reverse of social rights of citizenship: the 'dis-welfares' of exclusion and discouragement, the 'invisible other,' the ill-being of persistent poverty and other social wrongs of society (Bryson 1992; Tyjewski 2006). For the experience of unequal citizenship by Canadians with disabilities, in both formal status and substantive practice, Devlin and Pothier give the name a 'regime of dis-citizenship'; that is to say, 'a form of citizenship minus, a disabling citizenship' (2006: 1–2). In these neo-liberal political times in which we live, issues of social exclusion often appear in a way that those groups and practices doing the excluding and reproducing the barriers are not in the spotlight (Aronson and Neysmith 2001). In this sense, the absent citizens are not those struggling on the social margins but those living in the 'mainstream,' a place taken for granted as supportive and caring, thus obscuring the privileges and power relations in broader social systems.

The second part addresses actions by individuals and groups of persons with disabilities and their allies in obtaining, defending, and extending the rights of inclusion and participation in modern life. Such actions include potential and actual measures by state or societal organizations involving persuasion, research, expenditures, taxation, service provision, or laws and regulations. Both parts draw attention to different forms of disability politics and aim to foster positive change in raising the citizenship claims of Canadians with disabilities. (See table 3.)

This framework captures only a select number of social issues, political processes, and institutional relationships; of course, I could add

Table 3
Analytical focus for *Absent Citizens*

Absences created through:

- Public attitudes on disability and social inclusion
- Ableism and stigma, especially toward people with mental health challenges and people with developmental disabilities
- Cities with inaccessible built environments
- Social inequalities in economic, legal, and cultural aspects
- Programs with a provision/division dynamic that are segregating and stratifying

---

Actions for citizenship:

- Create national indicators on social inclusion and well-being
- Apply disability lens for policy analysis and disability-related budget reports
- Advocate, litigate, research, and change attitudes/culture with policy initiatives
- Outreach to electors with special needs to promote participation as voters, campaign workers, and candidates
- Network, form partnerships, and mobilize through organizations
- Enable disability as a distinct domain of policy and a dimension of other program areas
- Politicize citizenship encouraged through intersectional analyses
- Legislate reform: national disability act, refundable disability tax credit, investments in supports, inclusive infrastructure

---

others. There are sufficient items, though, to demonstrate the contention underlying the framework; namely, that the often marginal status of Canadians with disabilities and legitimate aspirations for full citizenship take place in relation to the interplay between absences and actions centred in both the state and society. Social status and personal/political struggle shape the citizenship role of Canadians with disabilities. Victims there are to be sure, but also at times victories. With this conceptual framework, I intend neither to ignore oppression nor to exaggerate accomplishments, but rather to combine the ideas of absences and actions. Both are crucial to a realistic understanding of the concerns of individuals with disabilities and their families as well as the myriad activities of the disability movement.

Enabling Citizenship

In modern disability politics, citizenship is a leading term of discourse and a central target of policy reform. Disability groups are seeking to achieve equality of status through full citizenship as well as alter the language of the social policy community and wider society. Ideas such as citizenship are linking actions, processes, and structures across micro, meso, and macro levels of human society exemplified by the disability movement's watchword, 'nothing about us without us' (Charlton 1998).

The story of citizenship for people with disabilities differs from conventional accounts in liberal democracies. This is not a simple story of the continual and steady extension of rights and responsibilities over many decades or centuries. The status of full citizenship is a relatively recent struggle for people with disabilities, a struggle mixed with considerable rhetoric, setbacks, and frequent delays, a few major successes, and many marginal gains. Thus, for Canadians with disabilities the promise of inclusion and equal status has in practice meant absent citizens and the struggle for citizenship by instalments.

A turn to citizenship in the past generation relates to a number of factors. In the face of persistent inequalities and numerous forms of discrimination, issues of disability emerged in the 1970s and 1980s or were reframed as a challenge to the ideal of citizenship. Among the most vulnerable of Canadians at risk of poverty and exclusion, persons with disabilities have organized to gain recognition of barriers to equality and demand supportive actions by governments and other institutions. The 'worthy poor' perspective of disability policy was historically and is still today a double-edged sword for people with disabilities. Under this long-established approach, people with disabilities are the object of charity, but often at the cost of basic citizenship rights. Considered incompetent to function in society, authorities established systems of segregation for people with disabilities, such as asylums, special schools, and sheltered workshops. In this outlook, disability is an individual impairment of pathology and persons with disabilities are deemed to be unemployable. Today, issues of disability are more frequently discussed in the vocabulary of citizenship. As the Council of Canadians with Disabilities (CCD) expresses it:

> When we represent ourselves as equal citizens, it means we're no longer 'the less fortunate,' 'the deserving poor,' or 'the chronically unemployed'; it means we now must be related to non-traditionally, with no preconceptions as to limitations. Best of all, governments have had lots of experience relating to this handy mental construct of the citizen. Unlike 'the disabled' of old, citizens pay taxes, always demand their full due, are unexceptional, and can never be safely disregarded. (1999, 1–2)

International developments have influenced the turn to citizenship in disability politics. Following on the civil rights movement for blacks, the women's liberation movement, and the disability rights campaign in the United States, and paralleling similar movements for Aboriginal peoples in Canada, disability advocates embrace the concepts and tactics of rights-seeking minority groups. The World Program of Action Concerning Disabled Persons, passed by the UN General Assembly in 1982, marked the shift from the medical and worthy poor perspectives to the philosophy that persons with disabilities are citizens of communities with rights. Passage of the UN Convention on the Rights of Persons with Disabilities in 2006 reaffirmed this citizen-oriented perspective.

Domestically, legislative and constitutional reforms are decisive developments in Canadian politics for persons with disabilities. Such reforms include amendments to federal and provincial human rights laws through the 1970s and 1980s, the entrenchment of the Charter of Rights and Freedoms in 1982 with a section providing for equality rights for persons with mental and physical disabilities, and the federal Employment Equity Act, passed in 1985 and extended in 1996. The Charter, in particular, bestows a highly significant constitutional status on persons with disabilities, encouraging disability groups to express their interests in the language of equality rights and to seek clarification of these rights and others through tribunals and the courts.

Framing disability issues as matters of citizenship is potentially a powerful strategy for the disability movement. It challenges old images and stereotypical beliefs about disability, calling for the re-examination of medical definitions and approaches in consultation with disability groups. It calls forward new ways of thinking about and serving people with disabilities, their families, and communities

(Lord and Hutchison 2007). It offers a normative benchmark for eval- uating existing services and benefits in terms of enabling or restricting the dignity and self-determination of persons with disabilities, and thus, by extension, advocating for reforms. It places responsibility on governments to respond to claims for equal status in the democratic community by committing public resources for promoting and pro- tecting human rights. It argues for consulting with persons with dis- abilities as citizens on a host of policy areas, and for supporting a vibrant network of disability organizations at the national and local levels. It can draw these issues to the attention of wider publics and connect them to other equality seeking groups. At the same time, however, framing matters of disability in terms of citizenship can allow governments to claim a consensus with disability groups over the policy direction and ultimate ends, giving the policy agenda a halo of democratic virtue, even while there is dispute over the pace and means of change.

Five Elements of Citizenship

For Canadian disability policy and politics, five elements of citizenship are particularly significant. These are the discourse of citizenship, legal and equality rights, democratic and political rights, fiscal and social entitlements, and economic integration. These elements correspond to certain sections of the Charter of Rights and Freedoms, as well as actual domains of public policy. Each element is a sphere of policy action with a particular blend of ideas, programs, and institutions, and with connections to the other elements. The discourse of citizenship points to the rhetorical and symbolic nature of much of our 'policy talk' these days, and to the growing prominence of citizenship lan- guage in advocacy work, government vision statements, and strategic plans. Popular culture and the mass media are other important insti- tutions for the discursive side of citizenship. Citizenship as legal and equality rights, and as democratic and political rights, contain some of the oldest rudiments of citizenship, accentuating the official meaning of membership within a state. Institutions here include the legal system and judiciary, the Charter of Rights and Freedoms, the electoral system, the legislative, executive, and administrative branches of gov- ernment, and disability organizations. The concept of social citizen- ship is associated with programs and benefits in education, equaliza- tion, and other transfer payments, health care, housing, income security, social services, and tax assistance. Citizenship as economic integration refers to participation and mobility within the paid labour market.

Each of these elements of citizenship has a formative period of development that, for Canadians with disabilities, clusters around the last thirty years. At the same time that the Canadian and other governments were under assault by ideas of downsizing the state, disability groups were asserting their claims for inclusion in the public domain. These contradictory agendas help to explain why the pace of change in achieving full citizenship for disability groups has been partial, slow, and incomplete.

Citizenship as disability discourse arose in the 1970s, but only became a dominant theme in authoritative statements since the 1990s. Legal and democratic rights, in theory, have been available to people with disabilities for as long as most other Canadians. In practice, though, for many people with disabilities to realize meaningfully their legal rights or democratic right to vote has been a struggle that manifested in a series of court cases and legislative reforms in the last decade. Some public programs that can be said to contribute to social citizenship for persons with disabilities trace back to the early part of the twentieth century, such as workers' compensation and veterans' benefits. Others, notably income support and vocational rehabilitation, were introduced in the 1950s and 1960s. Tax assistance at the federal level for Canadians with disabilities is largely a policy trend of the 1990s. The formulation of citizenship as economic integration was a central part of the 1991 to 1996 national strategy for persons with disabilities and has received emphasis since then in reforms to the Canada Pension Plan (CPP) Disability Benefit, and the introduction of the employability assistance measures in the 1990s and early 2000s.

Citizenship is a bundle of rights, duties, programs, and entitlements. As discourse, it is also a bundle of reasoning, declarations, promises, and expectations. Much more than the political right to speak in public places, citizenship as discourse refers to cultural, rhetorical, and symbolic practices which *construct the notion of citizenship itself* and thus help to define membership in society. Citizenship concerns the way politicians, officials, disability organizations, and other stakeholders talk about disability issues – current problems and needs, desired public goals, and preferred policy instruments. It involves the use of language to make things happen by using persuasive terms, creating new ways of thinking, telling stories and presenting arguments.

Legal rights are the first generation of citizenship rights in that they were the initial ones enacted by governments. By many decades or centuries, legal rights preceded widespread political rights and social entitlements. For Canadians with disabilities, however, legal rights are under continuing debate and development. This ongoing interpretation of basic civil rights through judicial forums is contributing to a 'legalization' of citizenship, a process in Canadian politics not unique to people with disabilities, but one central to their struggle for full membership. The disability community's agenda seeks to ensure that law making and the administration of justice account for the concerns of people with disabilities. For example, a change to the Criminal Code in 1994 added the matter of an aggravated offence when the crime is motivated by the vulnerability of the victim as a result of her or his disability. Amendments made to the Criminal Code and the Canada Evidence Act in 1998 improved the access of people with disabilities to criminal and civil proceedings and other justice matters under federal jurisdiction. After many years of lobbying by the disability community, the Canadian Human Rights Act was amended in 1998, adding a 'duty to accommodate' to ensure that federal employers and service providers are accessible to persons with disabilities. The Supreme Court has since altered the legal test for an employers' defence of valid occupational requirements by eliminating the distinction between direct discrimination and adverse effect discrimination. The Canadian Human Rights Tribunal has reported an increase in the number of disability cases they handle.

A review in 2000 of the Canadian Human Rights Act, the first comprehensive appraisal of the law since its passage in 1977, raised issues of particular interest to the disability community. The review panel examined whether the Act should be amended to prohibit discrimination arising out of the results of genetic testing. The panel reported that,

> Genetic testing may show individuals carry a gene putting them at greater risk of contracting a particular disease. They may have a predisposition, but not necessarily ever develop it. This raises the issue of whether the Act should prohibit discrimination in employment and services based on the predisposition of a disability. It also raises the related question of whether discrimination based on the perception of a disability should be prohibited. (Canada 2000a, 17: 1)

The Canadian Human Rights Act defines disability as any previous or existing mental or physical disability and includes disfigurement and previous or existing dependence on alcohol or a drug. To clarify and strengthen the law, the Council of Canadians with Disabilities (CCD) pushed for adding perceived disability and predisposition to having a disability in the future to the definition of disability. The panel agreed in part, recommending that the definition of disability in the Act be expanded to include 'the predisposition to being disabled.' At the time of writing, however, this amendment is absent.

Under section 15 of the Canadian Charter of Rights and Freedoms, people with disabilities are specifically included and guaranteed a set of equality rights. Section 15(1) states: 'Every individual is equal before and under the law and has the right to the equal protection and equal benefit of the law without discrimination and, in particular, without discrimination based on race, national or ethnic origin, religion, sex, age or mental and physical disability.' This equality section applies to the administration and enforcement of law, the substance of legislation, together with the procedurally fair provision (and non-provision) of benefits, be they regulations, transfer payments, or public services.

Litigation is a strategic tool for seeking to advance the rights of citizenship of Canadians with disabilities. Litigation can be a social movement's political activity, readily seen as the advocacy of interests through judicial means. As well, litigation can be a constitutional reform process, aptly understood as affirming or altering fundamental legal norms of the country. Results in litigating for disability rights and against discrimination vary by type of disability and by area of law or public policy. There are a number of legal victories for individuals with disabilities or disability groups. Successful legal challenges 'reflect a shift towards ensuring the well-being of people with disabilities; their self-determination; participation in decisions that affect their person and their life; and equality with others regardless of differences' (Bach and Rioux 1996: 322). In cases ranging from a local school board, the federal correctional services, to provincial health care services, the Supreme Court of Canada has held that employers have a duty under section 15 to make reasonable accommodations to the needs of a person with a mental or physical disability (Hogg 2007). Accommodations, however, may not be as generic in programming as disability advocates or family members want, nor are legal victories promptly implemented throughout the institutions of government or the private sector.

Political citizenship includes rights to vote, stand for, and hold elected office and participate in social activities supported by the fundamental freedoms of expression, association, and assembly. Electoral systems, parliamentary government, and other forms of governance, interest groups, and social movements institutionally express these rights and freedoms. For many Canadians with disabilities, their right to vote or to have guaranteed access to the electoral system did not exist until the 1990s. Fraser Valentine and Jill Vickers observe of the federal government's overdue response to guarantee full political rights to people with disabilities:

> It was only in 1991, after the disability rights movement challenged the *Canada Elections Act* in the courts and won, that people with mental disabilities gained the federal franchise. For people with physical disabilities, full access to the franchise was guaranteed only in 1992 when the architectural accessibility of polling stations became mandatory. (Valentine and Vickers 1996: 173)

In fact, the process of securing the right to full access continues. Further amendments were made to the federal electoral law and administrative practices in 1993, 1996, and 2000. Furthermore, Elections Canada has sponsored a series of articles on the electoral participation of people with disabilities (Davidson and Lapp 2004; D'Aubin and Stienstra 2004; Leclerc 2004; Prince 2004a) and funded research examining outreach services for electors with special needs – a category that includes people with low literacy skills, homeless people, and persons with disabilities – with the aim of increasing voter turnout and related forms of electoral participation. In general, a finding running through this work is that despite some advances, active democratic citizenship for many people with disabilities in Canadian society remains behind barriers (McColl 2006a; Stienstra and D'Aubin 2006). Chapter 6 examines in more detail the electoral participation of Canadians with disabilities.

Income security programs and the tax system can be concrete expressions of social citizenship. For people with disabilities, fiscal and social benefits are especially critical for overcoming obstacles in achieving membership and participation within Canadian society. At the national level, three major income programs relate expressly to disability: the CPP Disability Benefit, veterans' disability benefits, and the sickness benefit under the Employment Insurance (EI) program. CPP and EI are social insurance programs based on previous employment and contributions and provide incentives for claimants to return to work, an objective that has received greater policy and administrative attention in recent years. Chapter 3 discusses the CPP program more fully. Veterans' disability benefits have a distinctive purpose of offering societal recognition and financial reparations. Given these eligibility criteria, persons with disabilities make applications as individuals with employment- or military-related claims, and all three programs involve some form of medical assessment of the disability or sickness. Citizenship, therefore, is not the entrée to these income benefits, although the administration of the programs does emphasize the rights and responsibilities of claimants, and include mechanisms for the review and appeal of decisions.

In Canada's income tax system several major disability-related programs deal with income support and tax relief, as well as promoting independent community living, education, employment, family support, and care giving (Prince 2001a). The federal system includes several measures of disability-related tax support through the personal income tax system. These include the Disability Supports Deduction, Caregiver Tax Credit, Child Disability Benefit, Disability Tax Credit, and the Infirm Dependant Credit. The tax system is a frequent instrument for disability policy making because of court decisions, sustained lobbying efforts by disability groups, the personal interests of Finance ministers, and the active support of parliamentary committees.

Tax assistance for persons with disabilities has both advantages and disadvantages. Tax relief is a relatively straightforward policy instrument for the federal government to select in regard to disability issues, though it is not necessarily the most needed or most beneficial reform for individuals and families. On one hand, tax supports serve a welfare function of recognizing human needs and influencing in a positive manner the income, goods, and services available to persons with disabilities and their families. Tax assistance is a way for government to respond visibly to group claims and to connect directly with citizens with disabilities across the country. On the other hand, increasing use of the tax system for delivering disability benefits adds complexity, possible inequities, and information challenges to clients in accessing the system. For national disability groups, tax related reforms are not always a high priority. Such measures place groups in an awkward position of deciding whether to loudly oppose, publicly support, or just quietly accept these incremental reforms.

As a capitalist society, the economic element of citizenship in Canada tends to be a market-oriented conception of individual belonging and contributing. In this perspective, citizenship is associated with employment, with the individual portrayed as a productive member of the economy. This suggests a move away from a state-centred understanding of citizenship, stressing legal and political status, toward an emphasis on partnerships with the private and voluntary sectors for promoting the employability of persons with disabilities. At times called the investment view of social policy, economic citizenship is strongly apparent in contemporary government documents on disability issues in Canada. Employment is one of the building blocks for achieving full citizenship, and the objectives agreed to by federal, provincial, and territorial governments are: to reduce reliance on income support programs, to promote access to the training programs available to all Canadians, to increase the availability of work-related supports, to encourage employers to make appropriate job/workplace accommodations, and to promote work and volunteer opportunities for persons with disabilities.

Attention to employment – a prominent aspect of the politics of socio-economic redistribution – by advocates and others is understandable in light of changing ideas about disability, and the fact that the unemployment rate among Canadians with disabilities is about double the national average. Furthermore, research studies suggest that with various attitudinal and environmental barriers removed, more than half of working age persons with disabilities could enter paid employment on a part-time or full-time basis.

Multiple Frames of Citizenship

This stocktaking of dimensions of citizenship to understand the status of disabled Canadians is by no means a complete one. Beyond this admittedly state-oriented conception, other notions of citizenship discussed in disability studies and other fields include: biological citizenship, domestic (or intimate) citizenship, ecological citizenship, gender citizenship, global citizenship, indigenous citizenship, multicultural citizenship, urban citizenship, and, of course, the ubiquitous 'full citizenship' (Baubock 2003; Cairns 1995; Kivisto and Faist 2007; Lister

1997; Man Ling Lee 2006; Moss and Teghtsoonian 2008). Vast gaps exist and debates ensue over the theoretical and empirical basis of these types of citizenship: what each means, how they interrelate, and with what consequences for individuals and identities or for social policies and practices. In one sense, multiple visions suggest multiple memberships, a democratization of public identities. In another sense, it raises questions about the ideas and interests behind each notion of citizenship claimed and the resistance that accompanies any claim. Each citizenship claim seems based on a distinctive form of knowledge, public discourse, and relations of power. Each seems to imply different kinds of collective action and policy responses on recognition, redistribution, and representation. For the disability movement and for individual advocates, a strategic issue entails estimating the advantages and disadvantages of pressing for rights through any particular one or combination of these citizenship frames.

While multiple frames of citizenship vie for attention, neo-liberalism as the pre-eminent political frame in our present age certainly conditions which approaches to citizenship are encouraged and which discouraged by governments and other institutions. In a study on home care in Ontario, for example, Jane Aronson and Sheila Neysmith conclude that the marginalization of the elderly and persons with disabilities 'is deepened by neo-liberal conceptions of citizenship that prize self-sufficiency and independence, disparage need and dependence and, thus, permit receding state intervention and greater privatization of care' (Aronson and Neysmith 2001: 153). With privatization and contracting-out of formerly public services, comes 'a consumerist, market-oriented conception of citizenship rights in which the citizen is transformed into a customer' (Lister 1997: 206). Neo-liberalism promotes additional troubling notions of citizenship. The personal tragedy, charitable, and medical-oriented notions of citizenship converts Canadians with disabilities, respectively, into citizens with spoiled identities, as supplicants and as sick patients.

The political project of enabling citizenship for all persons with disabilities therefore requires disrupting the benign aura of neo-liberalism. As shown in later chapters, the disability movement in Canada offers a form of 'social liberalism' with a relatively broader and deeper vision of citizenship, one that calls for a renewed role for governments in tackling discriminatory values, extending core services and income benefits, and engaging with community groups in governance and policy matters.

Structure of the Book

Chapters in *Absent Citizens* arrange into three parts. Following this introduction, part 1 centres on ambiguities, exclusions, and divisions in the study and practice of disability. The focus is on Canadian society since the 1980s, the contemporary age of disability activism. Chapters 1, 2, and 3 deal with various absences of the presence and voice of persons with disabilities in relation to public opinion, social inquiry, and social policy. These three chapters correspond roughly to the three broad forms of political struggles today by the disability movement for recognition, representation, and redistribution. Part 2 of the book then examines capacities, engagements, and inclusions. Chapters 4, 5, 6, and 7 all deal with the agency and activities of disability organizations and coalitions to tackle obstacles and establish the conditions for full participation in community, the economy, and political affairs. In part 3, chapters 8 and 9 offer concluding observations on citizenship politics and present leading reform ideas for advancing the inclusion and the symbolic, material, and political well-being of Canadians with disabilities.

Concerning part 1, chapter 1 presents evidence on the nature and scope of consensus for public action on disability issues. There is a set of shared values, to a degree, on various issues. There are limits, however, to that shared support for tackling barriers to access and promoting inclusion of persons with disabilities in all segments of Canadian life. Access and inclusion are ideas marked with doubts and qualifications and, therefore, political uncertainties in terms of public policy action. There is far from complete consensus on the nature, priority, or the means for advancing the full citizenship of Canadians with disabilities. In recent times, advancements in inclusion and citizenship have been irregular, insecure, and changeable.

Chapter 2 examines how disability and differences relate to urban societies. Writings by Ignatieff and Young serve to consider relationships among strangers in cities and the possibilities of building more inclusive public spaces in communities. Although the city is under-theorized by disability studies, the chapter draws several themes from that field of inquiry on the implications of urbanism for social cohesion, inclusion, and diversity. Canadian cities are critical sites for struggles over disabling features of society and for popular efforts at developing what citizenship means in practice.

The theoretical and practical intentions of chapter 3 are threefold: first, to stimulate more serious attention to social stratification and social inequality, certainly in public policy analysis and social policy studies; second, to emphasize disability as a lived experience and social and historical construction, as a core dimension of inequality that ought to be routinely included in sociological research and texts; and, third, to insert the welfare state more centrally into mainstream examinations of stratification and how, through a range of technologies, state agencies and officials structure enabling and/or disabling environments for marginalized social groups.

In part 2, chapters examine various organizational relations and process tools and policy techniques for incorporating the interests of persons with disabilities into policy development and for advancing the political participation of Canadians with disabilities. Chapter 4 explores strategic cross-government reforms, such as an overall index on social inclusion and a disability budget, for enhancing focus and action on disability issues. As an overarching policy framework, full citizenship remains an emergent approach to disability issues in federal and provincial governments. To incorporate this approach more centrally into decision making, this chapter argues for adopting a general index on inclusion for all Canadians with specific measures on a range of disability-related issues. Chapter 5 surveys the organizational boundaries and composition of the disability community in Canada. The community comprises five arenas: a sector of diverse service agencies; a new social movement; a constitutional category of citizens with Charter rights and freedoms; a knowledge and research network; and a policy community with interest groups and advocacy coalitions. Chapter 6 examines a fundamental aspect of conventional political participation in liberal democracies – the involvement of persons with disabilities in electoral systems as voters, campaign workers, and candidates. Chapter 7 examines another aspect of political participation at the structural level of engagement by disability organizations and coalitions in public policy development processes.

In part 3, chapter 8 looks at how the activities of disability groups are politicizing the idea and practice of citizenship. I suggest that disability activism, in the Canadian context, is a form of social liberalism that emphasizes not only individual self-development but also community and the rights of groups. Lastly, chapter 9 offers a broad assessment of the Canadian record on disability reform over the last decade, and then reviews leading reform ideas currently under consideration by various political and community interests, including the concept of a national disability act for Canada.

Canadian disability politics hook up with society, the economy, and state, often loosely, at times uneasily, but undeniably so. Disability issues and policies are relevant to debates about federal-provincial relations, the nature of citizenship, the respective responsibilities of the state, market economy, communities, and families. Furthering the status of persons with disabilities as full and equal members requires a decline in the tragedy/charity model, a careful definition of the role of the medical model, and a vigorous expansion of the citizenship model of disability politics and policy making. In the chapters that follow, I suggest there is some likelihood of this coming about, although developments of rights and responsibilities for people with disabilities are uneven, with distinctive features in different policy areas and across different provincial and territorial jurisdictions. Conceptualizing disability requires contextualizing disablement. This means acknowledging diverse experiences, perspectives, and identities; recognizing complex interplay of biological and social processes; and situating disability in relation to gender, ethnicity, age, and other social divisions and their intersections. Matters of impairments, handicaps, mental health, and physical and developmental limitations are among the central issues of the human condition.

PART ONE

Ambiguities, Exclusions, and Divisions

1 Pride and Prejudice: Canadian Ambivalence towards Inclusion

Questioning societal assumptions of normalcy and challenging common beliefs about impairments are the daily stuff of disability struggles and a politics of recognition. On the fundamental importance of recognition and respectful interaction, Charles Taylor writes: 'Our identity is partly shaped by recognition or its absence, often by the misrecognition of others, and so a person or group of people can suffer real damage, real distortion, if the people or the society around them mirror back to them a confining or demeaning or contemptible picture of themselves' (Taylor 1992: 25). For persons with disabilities, what images and identities does society mirror back to them? What attitudes do Canadians hold on who they think of as disabled, on what they understand to be a disability, and on which institutions in society are responsible for advancing the inclusion of persons with disabilities? Taking up these questions, this chapter examines the Canadian government's 2004 benchmark survey and focus group results on Canadian attitudes toward disability issues. This survey and focus group study are the first systematic national effort by the Government of Canada to measure and explore the attitudes, beliefs, and perceptions of the general population on issues of disability.

The main argument of this chapter is that prevailing cultural values in Canada toward disability are not overwhelmingly negative and nor are they generally positive. Public thinking on issues of disability is marked by contending attitudes toward people with disabilities, and by feelings of hesitancy and uncertainty over solutions for their social inclusion. Most Canadians hold an affirmative image of their own views towards and experiences with people with disabilities; and they believe progress has occurred over the last decade in the inclusion of people with disabilities in community life. At the same time, most

Canadians believe that discriminatory attitudes and behaviours toward people with disabilities are still widespread. Canadians are also inclined to think of disability in terms of a specific image: visible physical disabilities rather than mental health, developmental, and learning disabilities. The resulting public opinion environment is one of pride and prejudice. This ambivalence is complex and contradictory, undoubtedly challenging to governments as well as community groups committed to enhancing the citizenship of persons with mental and physical disabilities.

The chapter proceeds as follows: first, the impetus for the national survey and focus groups are discussed, along with the techniques themselves, thus highlighting the goals and methods for the research. Second, a range of findings from the survey and focus groups is presented and critically discussed. Third, the chapter considers how the federal government and national disability organizations are using these research results. Finally, the chapter raises issues facing governments and the disability rights community in advancing recognition and inclusion. Given the ambivalence surrounding public attitudes and beliefs regarding people with disabilities, cultural work is required to improve the understanding of disability issues, to interrogate existing models or ideologies of disablement, and to mobilize public and political interest in improving the well-being of people with disabilities.

Impetus for a National Study of Public Attitudes on Disability

After a period in the 1990s when it seemed the federal government was withdrawing from the disability policy field, prompting strong political reaction by the community and a response by the Chrétien government, the federal government and parliamentary committees began articulating a more explicit role on disability issues. Among activities is the production of a federal agenda on future directions, intergovernmental agreements on employment measures for people with disabilities, various tax measures, reports on key activities and outcome measures in selected policy areas, and the generation of statistical information on disability (Canada 2006). Disability as a public issue endures, often finding expression by policy makers, yet overshadowed by other issues, never attaining a high priority for transformative initiatives. Much of disability policy making continues to be a hit-and-miss affair of piecemeal actions and struggles (Prince 2001b, 2004b, 2008a).

Canada has been assembling a national data base on disability through a number of survey instruments since the mid-1980s, with the Health and Activity Limitation Survey in 1986 and 1991, succeeded by the Participation and Activity Limitation Survey of 2001 and 2006. In addition to these disability-specific surveys that focus on the experience of people with different types and severity of disability, the federal government collects information on disability in other major surveys, including the Survey of Labour and Income Dynamics and the National Population Health Survey. Despite this growing source of statistical information, a gap exists in knowing the attitudes and beliefs of Canadians, those with and without disabilities, toward issues of disability. A national survey specifically on Canadian attitudes toward disability issues has the potential of shedding light on the puzzle as to why the disability file is never at the top of the agenda – always a bridesmaid, never the bride.

A few enterprising federal policy analysts recognized that a national survey on attitudes, by assessing public opinion, could be a useful input to inform strategic thinking and for shaping policy options within government policy structures and processes. In making the results freely available (Environics Research Group 2004a), the national survey and focus groups represent a public good that the disability rights movement and others can use with a prospect of shaping the attention given to disability issues on societal and governmental agendas.

The Office for Disability Issues in Social Development Canada commissioned Environics Research Group to undertake a national study of public awareness and attitudes toward disabilities, in two stages, one a qualitative study using focus groups and the second stage a quantitative study using a telephone survey. Eight focus groups were conducted, two each in Halifax, Montreal, Toronto, and Lethbridge. Both focus groups in Montreal were conducted in French while the others were carried out in English. Focus groups ranged between five to eight participants, with forty-nine participants overall. In the main, participants did not identify themselves as having a disability.[1] The quantitative research phase of the study used the method of telephone surveys, the standard technique in polling the opinions of population groups on public affairs. The questionnaire design is unique, developed specifically for this study by officials in the Office for Disability

Issues in conjunction with the Environics Research Group, along with input by some specialists in the disability community.

As is usual with telephone surveys, nearly all of the fifty-eight questions were closed-ended, with just three open-ended questions dealing with conceptions of disabilities, beliefs on barriers to fuller participation, and beliefs on important solutions to stop discrimination against persons with disabilities. Overall, the questionnaire is an ambitious, innovative research tool aimed at measuring general opinions and specific attitudes. More than an opinion poll on current events, the survey collected information on enduring attitudes of Canadians and illuminates something of their core beliefs and values regarding disability, normality, and human dignity.

The survey occurred over a three-week period in January and February 2004 with a representative sample of 1,843 Canadians, of whom 521 respondents reported a self-defined disability as reflected in responses to specific questions.[2] The completion rate was 22 per cent (1,843 completed interviews from 8,562 qualified respondents contacted), which is within the range common for telephone surveys (Mendelshon and Brent 2001).

The research objectives were multiple and intricate, seeking to obtain a more in-depth understanding about numerous issues pertaining to disabilities and attitudes toward persons with disabilities. The workshops and the national survey aimed at dealing with the following topics:

• What the term 'disability' means to Canadians (for example, as a medical/health versus rights/citizenship versus human capital/economic issue);
• Attitudes and perceptions of disabilities by severity and type;
• The degree of acceptance versus rejection of persons with disabilities in various settings (educational, workplace, community) and in various roles;
• Personal experience with disabilities, either first- or second-hand, and how this experience influences attitudes and perceptions;
• General opinions about prejudice and discrimination against persons with disabilities and their role in society;
• Awareness and opinions about the barriers to inclusion created by disabilities (for example, physical access, social isolation, economic obstacles, absence of social supports);
• What barriers are perceived, and how they are managed or not managed now;

- Awareness of and knowledge about existing sources of support available to persons with disabilities;
- The range of beliefs about the appropriate roles for different sources of support for persons with disabilities (for example, government, non-governmental organizations [NGOs], families, local communities); and
- How awareness and attitudes vary, if at all, by population segment such as by region, demographic characteristics such as age, and by extent of experience with disabilities (Environics Research Group 2004b: 3–4).

Using mixed methods of quantitative and qualitative research, the telephone survey generates statistically valid and measurable results of the topic, while the focus groups offer an understanding into people's experiences, interpretations, and perceptions, as well as elicit their questions and beliefs in greater depth than is possible in the survey. Findings from the focus groups also augment the national survey in providing concrete narratives and local textures to issues.

The Findings: A Critical Overview

Key findings emerge along the lines of the national study itself, first outlining results from the qualitative research of the focus groups and then the quantitative research from the telephone survey. Table 1.1 summarizes major findings from the focus groups in terms of main themes from the responses of the forty-nine participants in the workshops. The pride and prejudice of Canadians is apparent in their attitudes and perceptions of disabilities, especially by type and severity of disabilities. In terms of pride, focus group interactions showed that most participants 'like to think of themselves as being open to the idea of integration of persons with disabilities into their day-to-day activities' and that they 'want to behave toward a person with disabilities in a kind and sympathetic manner. They don't want to appear uncaring or unsympathetic' (Environics Research Group 2004b: 9–10).

At the same time, focus group participants revealed certain biased preconceptions; for example, 'many [participants] were uncomfortable with some aspects involved in developing relations or communications with those who have various types of disabilities.' In the blunt words of one participant from Toronto, with some post-secondary education: 'I don't mind being around anyone with a disability as long as it is visible and not ugly' (Environics Research Group 2004b: 34).

Table 1.1
Canadian pride and prejudice: Attitudes and themes emerging from 2004
national Environics focus group workshops

Attitudes
- Disabilities and disability-related issues not 'top-of-mind awareness' for most participants
- Tendency to think of 'disability' in terms of visible and physical limitations, especially by people with little contact with persons with disabilities
- Confusion as to whether a disability is an illness or sickness
- Agreement that people with visible disabilities experience discrimination in schools, workplaces, and in social settings
- Belief, in general, there has been important progress in accepting people with physical disabilities into various spheres of mainstream community life
- Belief that funding and support is likely insufficient to help people with disabilities live with comfort and dignity
- Belief that families (immediate or extended) should be the first resource for people with disabilities, along with provincial health care systems and non-profit agencies

Themes
- Awareness and knowledge of actual supports available to persons with disabilities is low
- Most common suggestion for improving the status of Canadians with disabilities is for raising public awareness through education and information
- First Nations persons with disabilities living off-reserve face 'double discrimination' and a jurisdictional maze of elusive service responsibilities

---

Source: Summarized from Environics Research Group, *Canadian Attitudes toward Disability Issues, A Qualitative Study, Final Report.* Prepared for Government of Canada (2004b: 7–45).

Similarly, as the final report on the focus groups states: 'Many thought visible disabilities easier to "assess" than invisible disabilities, including cognitive limitations and mental illness. Many admitted that they are made very uncomfortable by behaviour that doesn't seem "normal"' (9). In the words of a Halifax focus group participant:

People tend to fear them, if you can't communicate with someone, a lot of people with cerebral palsy and that type of thing, they can't communicate properly. I've got to get away from them. Then, there are those that are not right, somehow – you will see people in malls and stores who are talking to themselves and stuff. What do we do? We get right away from them too. (9–10)

On interacting with a physically impaired person, a Montreal participant said: 'Il y une couples d'années, quand on voyait un handicape on baissait les yeux' [A couple of years ago, when one saw a handicapped person one lowered their eyes]; or if the person was disfigured in the face, a Toronto participant admitted, 'I just feel more self-conscious and it shouldn't be that way but I just do' (Environics Research Group 2004b: 29). These statements graphically illustrate the striking observation of Canadian society by Frazee, Gilmour, and Mykitiuk of 'the pervasive cultural toxins of shame, pity, and charity that mask the social oppression of disabled people' (2006: 225).

Canadians' ambivalent attitudes further arise in the degree of acceptance of persons with disabilities, the awareness and opinions about barriers to inclusion, and suggestions for improving the status quo for persons with disabilities. While participants felt people with disabilities deserve the same opportunities as other citizens to participate in social, economic, and public affairs to the fullest, some participants expressed concern that the integration of people with disabilities in workplaces could negatively affect the rights of those who do not have disabilities to participation in the labour market (Environics Research Group 2004b: 9–10; also see Burge, Ouellette-Kuntz, and Lysaght 2007). Greater concern emerged in focus groups about the integration of children with various 'special needs' into regular classrooms. The mix of beliefs is obvious in this summary statement of participants' views:

Some argue that it is important for people to become familiar with people who have either physical or mental disabilities. Some argue that class sizes are now larger and that teachers are stretched; integrating children with special needs into classes in the mainstream may compromise the quality of education. Some felt that if there is a way to 'categorize' physical and mental disability, then it might be possible to integrate some students with disabilities and to offer special segregated opportunities to others [such as for children with learning and behavioural disabilities]. (Environics Research Group 2004b: 10)

Here we see age-old habits of thinking and therapeutic practices in assessing and classifying people by their differences, then segregating certain types of people with certain kinds of impairments away from the mainstream.

On suggestions for improving the present situation for persons with disabilities, many focus group participants disclosed being 'particularly uncomfortable with the idea of integration of those with mental illness into mainstream, work, and school. These participants feel almost "ashamed" of themselves for not knowing how to respond or how to behave in the presence of someone with behaviour that is out of their "normal" experience' (Environics Research Group 2004b: 43).

As with the focus groups, the national survey found Canadians tend to think of disability first in terms of physical handicaps and that some people then think of mental, learning, and developmental disabilities. The survey revealed that the type of disability under consideration matters as to what is seen to be a disability, people's experiences and feelings being around persons with disabilities, their support for integrated classrooms for children with different kinds of 'special needs,' and their beliefs about people with disabilities experiencing discrimination.

On the question of does the respondent personally know someone with a disability, 75 per cent of the sample said, yes they did. This does not necessarily mean, though, that most Canadians have 'fairly wide, if not extensive' experience with people with disabilities. Survey results show that the person with a disability who the respondent has direct contact with is most likely either a family member (48 per cent) or a friend (43 per cent). However, the results also show that these family members 'are most likely to be someone outside of the immediate family, such as an uncle or cousin,' and that of 'those Canadians who have a family member with a disability, only 11 per cent report that this individual is currently living with them in their home' (Environics Research Group 2004c: 14). Comparatively few Canadians say that the person with a disability whom they know is a classmate or co-worker (9 per cent) or an acquaintance (6 per cent). The actual nature and extent of contact seems more akin to 'a silent relation between us,' or at its best, a 'solidarity among strangers' mediated through an assemblage of public and private services (Ignatieff 1984: 10).

When Canadians encounter someone they do not know well who has an obvious disability, what is their reaction? Do they feel awkward or afraid of the person, sorry for the person, indifferent towards the person, or feel admiration for the person? Table 1.2 presents the results of Environics Research Group's survey. To be clear, these results

Table 1.2
Canadian pride and prejudice: Personal reactions to someone with an
obvious disability
(percentages)

Reaction	Often	Occasionally	Rarely	Never
Admiring	45	31	8	9
Sorry	21	33	17	24
Awkward	5	26	22	43
Indifferent	6	12	19	58
Afraid	*	4	13	80

* Less than one per cent.
Note: Rows do not add up to 100 because non responses have been
omitted.
Source: Environics Research Group, *Canadian Attitudes toward Disability
Issues: 2004 Benchmark Survey, Final Report.* Prepared for the Office for
Disability Issues, Social Development Canada (2004c: 16).

measure how Canadians *think* that they and others *ought to respond* to
these items, rather than measure how they actually would behave in
specific situations. I would also add to these caveats that the items in
this question do not include any emotional responses that relate to
understanding disability in terms of human rights, citizenship, or economics – feelings, say, of solidarity toward the person or equality with
the person. Indeed, I could argue that the choices available reflect
aspects of the personal tragedy, charitable, and medical viewpoints of
disability (Rioux and Prince 2002; Valentine and Vickers 1996).

The survey data, augmented by the focus group results, suggest
that much of the explanation Canadians hold for the exclusion of
people with disabilities is in cultural factors situated in society at
large and personal factors situated in the individual, rather than systemic factors located in structural conditions or in the absence or
inadequacies of public policies (Stienstra and Wight-Felske 2003).
Marginalization and isolation of people with disabilities is thought by
much of the general public to reside largely in attitudinal and personal factors, whether these factors are understood as intolerance and
stereotyping, severe medical problems, physical restrictions of mobility, the lack of basic skills, or low self-esteem (Burge, Ouellette-Kuntz,
and Lysaght 2007).

When asked what they thought to be important barriers facing people with disabilities, the most common responses by Canadians dealt with attitudinal barriers (49 per cent), followed by architectural barriers such as physical obstacles (29 per cent). The next most commonly cited barriers focused on the persons with the disability, limited capabilities (17 per cent) and lack of self-confidence (15 per cent). The lack of government programs (13 per cent) and financial barriers (11 per cent) were identified by only a small number of respondents as the principal barrier to inclusion by disabled Canadians, even though in response to another question three-quarter of respondents recognized that people with disabilities face difficulties in achieving financial security, having access to reliable transportation services, and raising a family (Environics Research Group 2004c: 21). So, while most Canadians see themselves as comfortable in the presence of people with disabilities, they believe that prejudice on the part of other Canadians is the most significant barrier facing people with disabilities.

An associated dichotomy in beliefs is that 83 per cent of Canadians believe there has been at least 'some progress' attained in improving the social inclusion of people with disabilities over the last decade, yet an almost identical number (82 per cent) believe that discrimination against people with disabilities still takes place in our society. This mixture of beliefs may be explained partly by the vagueness of the phrases 'somewhat included' and 'some progress' yielding majority responses in the survey from both people with and without disabilities. Ambivalence is apparent as well in perceptions and beliefs about workplace opportunities for persons with disabilities. Most Canadians strongly (40 per cent) or somewhat (24 per cent) agree that their workplace is accessible to employees with visible and non-visible disabilities. There is, however, a notable difference in views between persons without disabilities (65 per cent) and persons with disabilities (51 per cent) on this question of equal access to employment. Furthermore, a slender majority of Canadians agrees (54 per cent) they would hide a non-visible disability such as dyslexia or depression from their employer and co-workers, a finding that illustrates a widely perceived negative status and social stigma associated with these disabilities, among others no doubt.

What do Canadians think need to be done in furthering social inclusion and tackling discrimination? The national survey responses divide into three realms of actions. First, 62 per cent believe *personal awareness* through education efforts in schools and general information campaigns is the primary solution to addressing discrimination and stigma, advancing inclusion, and enhancing the self-confidence of people with disabilities. Second, 30 per cent point to what we can call *community acceptance* as the main solution, involving such measures as the fuller integration of children with special needs in schools, better accessibility to public facilities, and continued efforts to improve the employment of adults with disabilities in the labour force. Third, just 9 per cent indicate *government action* as the preferred solution to addressing barriers to inclusion for disabled Canadians through public programs, laws and regulations, benefits, and services. This low identification of government action as the favoured strategy seems congruent with still another finding that only a few Canadians associate the term 'disability' as an economic issue of employment or as a human rights issue of citizenship (Environics Research Group 2004c: 8). This last finding appears to expose a profound difference between the general public's attitude and the dominant rights discourse of disability advocacy groups. A review of international and domestic initiatives similarly reveals a lack of consensus on the desired approaches, through legislation or judicial decisions, for addressing issues of equality and citizenship for persons with disabilities (Rioux and Valentine 2006).

A related survey question asked Canadians which of the following they feel plays the most essential role in helping disabled persons participate fully in society: disabled persons themselves, families of disabled persons, governments, voluntary organizations, religious organizations, or more than one is most important. Table 1.3 shows the results. For many Canadians, primary responsibility for social inclusion of those living with disabilities is on disabled people themselves and their families, revealing what some observers call 'an individualist and essentializing conception of disability' (Devlin and Pothier 2006: 12). That is to say, from this perspective disability is a personal misfortune rooted in biological impairments and functional limitations. The problem largely resides in and with the disabled person, so, apparently, should responsibility for being able to participate in the social world. Such sentiments align with core ideas of neo-liberal thinking on a limited role for governments and public services while promoting personal responsibility in meeting needs.[3]

Public opinion on responsibilities for helping people with disabilities with social participation recognizes the pluralistic nature of the provision of benefits and allocation of resources for all sorts of groups,

Table 1.3
Canadian pride and prejudice: Most important role in helping people with disabilities participate fully in society (percentages)

Families of the persons with the disability	31
Voluntary organizations	22
Disabled persons themselves	16
Governments	16
Religious organizations	5
More than one is most important	9
Don't know	2

Source: Environics Research Group, *Canadian Attitudes toward Disability Issues: 2004 Benchmark Survey, Final Report.* Prepared for the Office for Disability Issues, Social Development Canada (2004c: 32).

with multiple sectors and groups involved in a mixed economy of welfare. This result raises questions that go well beyond the survey or the scope of this chapter about the actual capacity of various groups to undertake these tasks and the quality and equity in the provision of help, among other issues (Rice and Prince 2000: 119–23). A more detailed question on the roles for supporting people with disabilities generates results that indicate a public consensus on the primacy of government in several areas of life and less so in others. As table 1.4 shows, results to a question of supporting the needs of people with disabilities reveal three profiles of the place of governments vis-à-vis other institutions and actors.

In obtaining good health care, accessing reliable transportation, providing specialized equipment (such as hearing aids or wheelchairs), and getting a good education, Canadians see governments as playing the primary role over all other groups. Second, for the areas of finding adequate housing and achieving financial security, Canadians identify governments more frequently than the other groups as a leading player, but not in a dominant sense of majority support. Third, in the areas of maintaining stable employment, having opportunities for recreation, and raising a family, Canadians mention other groups as playing the most important role, namely, employees, voluntary agencies, and families of the disabled respectively.

No unequivocal consensus exists among Canadians as to which level of government is best able to provide supports and services for

Table 1.4
Canadian pride and prejudice: Most important role in supporting the needs of Canadians with disabilities in specific areas (percentages)

Areas of Life	Governments	Employees	Voluntary agencies	Families of the disabled	Disabled themselves
Health care	71	3	5	10	8
Transportation	61	3	14	15	5
Specialized equipment	60	3	15	11	7
Education	54	3	5	19	16
Housing	47	3	13	16	14
Financial security	40	14	4	16	20
Stable employment	28	28	7	16	16
Recreation opportunities	28	5	33	16	15
Raising a family	15	6	7	38	28

Source: Environics Research Group, *Canadian Attitudes toward Disability Issues: 2004 Benchmark Survey, Final Report.* Prepared for the Office for Disability Issues, Social Development Canada (2004c: 33).

individuals with disabilities. Results reflect the 'federal condition' of the country, and the intergovernmental nature of civil society and political discourse, as well as governmental arrangements (Cameron and Valentine 2001; Puttee 2002; Smiley 1987). Canadians are divided as to whether the provinces/territories (37 per cent), the federal government (34 per cent), or municipal government (14 per cent) is the best level to provide supports. Just 10 per cent expressed the opinion that it is all or some combination of these levels. Perhaps on disability issues Canadians hold more of a classical view of federalism of two independent orders of senior governments exercising their jurisdictions than a view that stresses the interconnections of responsibilities across levels.

Most Canadians acknowledge they know very little about legislation and policies in place for people with disabilities; only 21 per cent claim to be aware of such state activities. This is a low civic literacy on disability-related public policies and programs. Perhaps because of this low awareness, 77 per cent of respondents believe governments are supportive in helping the needs of people with disabilities. These mixed feelings and conflicting values point to challenges in the politics of recognition for disability equality and inclusion.

Applications of Public Opinion Results

The Environics Research Group's findings are in circulation inside the federal government, provincial governments, and some national and provincial community groups in the disability policy and mental health sectors. The Office for Disability Issues staff have presented the survey and focus group results to federal officials and some of the findings have found their way into briefings to senior executives and ministers. The limitations of this type of survey must be recognized. As a cross-sectional study, it is a snapshot picture of a single point in time. To better describe and explain cultural value patterns in a dynamic manner, longitudinal research methods such as time series research, panel studies, or cohort studies are worth consideration by governments and foundations. No firm plan or decisions have been made in the responsible federal department, Human Resources and Skills Development Canada, for a follow-up survey.

The research findings appeared in the 2004 edition of *Advancing the Inclusion of Persons with Disabilities*, the Government of Canada's accountability report to the public and Parliament on federal goals, actions, and outcomes on the disability agenda (Canada 2004). In addition to meeting accountability commitments of federal activities and plans, other purposes of this report, of which this is the second in the series, are to stimulate interest and dialogue on disability issues, to showcase or promote topics that warrant greater analysis, and to lever research and policy agendas. In *Advancing the Inclusion*, the federal government describes the 2004 national survey of Canadian attitudes toward disabilities as a major information source that, along with other recent surveys and reports exploring concepts and program definitions of disability (Canada 2003a), contributes 'to our knowledge base on disability and our efforts to better understand disability and inclusion' (Canada 2004: 8). *Advancing the Inclusion* justifies the need for a public opinion survey on disability issues in advancing the disability agenda in these terms:

> Much evidence suggests that public attitudes may themselves be critical to either advancing or hindering the inclusion of people with disabilities in our society. What people believe about individuals with disabilities underlies the treatment of those individuals in all aspects of their lives. The cost of negative beliefs or inaccurate information is high, both for people with disabilities and for society as a whole. (Canada 2004: 12)

In an overview section on public attitudes toward disability, the report notes that most Canadians know someone with a disability, that most Canadians feel that despite progress on including people with disabilities in society over the past ten years that people with disabilities are not fully included, that discrimination is seen as the most significant obstacle to full inclusion, that most Canadians support the goal of inclusion and community-assisted living, and that most Canadians think governments play the lead role in supporting people with disabilities in a range of areas (Canada 2004: 13–14).

The rest of *Advancing the Inclusion* highlights select findings from the survey in what the report calls outcome areas of inclusion. In the area of skills development and learning, a box inset notes as barriers to fulfilling learning potential data from the survey that one in five Canadians with disabilities considers it 'very difficult' for Canadians with disabilities to get a good education, and that one in four Canadians with disabilities has personally faced at least some discrimination in getting a good education (Canada 2004: 29). In a chapter on employment among Canadians with disabilities, results from the survey are

reported that underscore the not infrequent experiences of discrimination and a widespread felt awareness of the stigma attached to disabilities in workplaces (Canada 2004: 45).

Being a random sample of the general population, the survey offers
findings that can corroborate, in certain aspects, findings from other
studies, quantitative and qualitative, based on smaller samples. Focus
group data are not noticeable in the report nor are survey results mentioned in chapters on disability supports, income, and health and well-
being, perhaps because other rich information sources are readily
available and since the survey on attitudes did not address all these
areas in equal detail. The absence of quotes from the focus groups,
however, limits the potential impact of real-life interpretations and
statements on these policy areas.

Among others (Frazee 2006), a coalition of fifty disability organizations, led by the Council of Canadians with Disabilities (CCD) and the
Canadian Association of Community Living (CACL), has employed
findings from the Environics survey in documents.[4] One such document calls for action by the federal government to combat poverty and
exclusion of Canadians with disabilities by investing in disability-
related supports, such as aids and devices, personal assistance, and
environmental accommodations (CCD and CACL 2005a). In that
paper, released just before the 2005 federal budget, the organizations
quote from the survey research (Environics 2004c: 26) that 'more than
eight in ten [Canadians] ... agree with the statement that persons with
even the most challenging disabilities should be supported by public
funds to live in the community rather than institutional settings ... By
a wide margin, Canadians believe governments have the primary role
for supporting persons with disabilities when it comes to providing
good health care, reliable transportation, specialized equipment, and
good education.' Citing that report along with others, the groups
argue that 'there is now an unprecedented consensus among the Canadian public, the disability community and experts about the need for
national action on disability, in particular to ensure access to needed
supports' (CCD and CACL 2005a: 1).

A second document with an open letter to federal/provincial/territo-
rial ministers of Social Services, CCD, CACL, and allied groups appealed
to governments to support a new strategic investment in disability-
related supports. Again, the coalition quotes the finding: 'By a wide
margin, Canadians believe governments have the primary role for supporting persons with disabilities when it comes to providing good health

care, reliable transportation, specialized equipment, and good education.' As disability organizations emphasize, their 'priority has been, and remains, an investment in disability-related supports that assist Canadians with disabilities to get an education, become employed, look after their families and enjoy the opportunities non-disabled Canadians expect as a right of citizenship' (CCD and CACL 2005b: 1).

That there is a compelling and urgent need to move forward on a national disability supports agenda invites little quarrel. Available research from various sources clearly documents the existence of extensive gaps in essential services and supports for children and adults with disabilities (Canadian Council on Social Development 2004). Then again, the ambivalent nature of the focus groups and survey data suggest a challenge to the disability community and sympathetic governments in advancing this agenda. Most Canadians have slight direct and concrete awareness of the met and unmet needs for supports of persons with disabilities or their families. Most are unsure if urban transportation services are adequate for people with disabilities and most have low awareness of issues of burnout among caregivers, some of whom have disabilities too. Many Canadians assume that people with disabilities are able to find the medical-related supports they require through provincial health care programs supplemented by the activities of non-profit agencies. Consequently, the general population has little appreciation of the everyday difficulties and heartfelt struggles of individuals and families in locating, accessing, and affording necessary aids, devices, and supports (Environics Research Group 2004b: 40–3).

Alongside the task of generating social data and evidence, an attitudinal challenge exists concerning social beliefs and value judgments in tackling the exclusion and poverty of people with disabilities. The 2006 edition of *Advancing the Inclusion of Persons with Disabilities* recognizes this challenge as follows: 'The obstacles that people with disabilities face are not always related to their impairment or health condition. Obstacles are often the product of the interplay between impairment or health problems and socio-economic and cultural environments, including attitudes. Research is therefore useful to identify the sources of stigma and negative attitudes and the means of addressing them' (Canada 2006: 56).

Such stigma and negative attitudes emphasize the ongoing cultural/symbolic exclusion of people with disabilities from Canadian society and state.

Conclusions

The prevailing sentiment in Canada on disability is one of ambivalence, with an odd mixture of positive and negative attitudes, beliefs,
perceptions, experiences, and behaviours. Such features are not unique
to disability issues, but rather are evident in other areas of social policy
today and in other periods of human history (Guest 2003; Söder 1990).
This points to constraints as well as opportunities in building an
understanding of, and mobilizing a strong consensus for, major reforms on disability issues by governments. The reality of ambivalent
attitudes among Canadians on disability and inclusion suggests there
is cultural work required in getting the public to see disabilities and
people with disabilities in more informed and positive ways than is
now the case (Rioux and Prince 2002; Titchkosky 2001). Value orienta-
tions and subjective perceptions of ordinary people on matters of
social policy, disability, inclusion, and citizenship often do not jive
with the views of advocates or academics or, for that matter, government administrators.

Whatever else, the absent citizen is socially constructed, created and
reproduced through cultural beliefs, material relations, political rules,
and everyday social practices. Devlin and Pothier contend that
'depending on what is valued (perhaps overvalued) at certain socio-
political junctures, specific personal characteristics are understood as
defects and, as a result, persons are *manufactured* as disabled' (2006: 5).
This production of disabled people as absent citizens occurs out of
public ignorance and lack of recognition; because of a lack of public
outcry and political pressure for essential supports to be provided;
through fear, pity and unjust treatment; and from people with disabilities living alone in a room or apartment and 'falling through the
cracks' of education, health, and social services. People with so-called
invisible disabilities, for instance, certain mental health conditions,
dwell in the shadows of prejudice and discrimination, less than full
members of Canadian society (Kirby 2006).

This state of affairs, although taken for granted by many people, is
not inevitable. 'Public attitudes are a key area to address, particularly
if in-roads are to be made with respect to public policy' (Burge, Ouellette-Kuntz, and Lysaght 2007: 36). In terms of recognition politics, the
project of enabling citizenship entails deconstructing the dominant
image of the 'disabled person' as someone with a visible, long-term
physical impairment; pluralizing the image with the realities of

diverse forms of disablements; and connecting the differences in relation to power relations and systems of inequalities. This kind of work has been occurring for some time by disability advocates and the disability rights movement (Cameron and Valentine 2001; Chivers 2008; Driedger 1989), and needs broadening to other groups and sectors of society.

Cultural work is quintessentially political work. It includes people with disabilities 'coming out' with their disabilities, giving a public identity and voice to their experiences; it also involves 'outing' cultural values on the 'normal body' as an ideology and celebrating human diversities as the ordinary state of humanity (Michalko 2002: 69–70). There is cultural work to do in teaching and learning curriculum for building awareness of disability issues, a process that also requires working with teacher federations to raise their understanding on issues of inclusive education from the perspective of the disability community (Ellis and Llewellyn 1997; Kirby 2006). In places of employment, there is work to do such as the orientation and training of supervisors and co-workers, a task that occurs both formally and informally, often by disabled employees as additional labour (Church, Frazee, Panitch, Luciani, and Bowman 2007). There is work also to do in raising the low level of recognition that presently exists of public programs, laws, and services, even among persons with disabilities. If left unaddressed, the risk is that public support for strengthening supports, employment opportunities, and the income security of individuals and families will remain mixed, unfocused, and thus politically feeble.

For disability organizations and their allies, the national survey is both a focusing event and a fact-finding exercise that concentrates attention and generates new information on public attitudes about disability and inclusion. National organizations in the disability community have taken the lead in using the survey results, in a strategic and timely fashion, as an analytical input to persuade governments to move forward on a federal/provincial/territorial disability support strategy and longer-term vision of reform. For advocates and activists, certain findings from the survey represent a strong indicator of agreement within the general population about the importance of the issues and needs, and about the legitimacy of the solutions for disability policy making. Conflicting and uncertain attitudes in the public opinion environment on disability, however, create political tensions and complexities that deter government decision makers and policy advisors from being involved in a sustained way. A recent study on Canadians living with spinal cord injury concludes:

> Almost 60 years after the first Canadian pioneers demonstrated that it was possible but difficult to live in the community using a wheelchair, legislation and policies to support a barrier-free environment have not been realized to any great extent in Canada. Good will on the part of some individuals has not led to the changes in political and social thought necessary to create legislation establishing accessible environments for all Canadians. Continuity in ideas and practices continues to weigh heavily upon the present, stalling significant changes. (Tremblay, Campbell, and Hudson 2005: 114)

If the Canadian public does not readily think about disability issues in terms of human rights, a serious test faces the disability community and allied social groups. The test is finding language that resonates with the general population, builds an understanding of disability in societal terms, and portrays inclusion as nothing less than full citizenship.

2 City Life and the Politics of Strangers

The Canadian nation is an urban nation. For most of us, our society is an urban-dominated society where organizational networks and institutional structures controlled in metropolitan centres significantly shape life for most people (Broadbent 2008; Greer 1989). It is surprising, then, that of Canada's three levels of public government, urban governance has received far less attention by academics than the federal government and provincial governments, though that appears to be changing in political science and public administration (Andrew, Graham, and Phillips 2002; Bradford 2004; Graham, Phillips, and Maslove 1998; Hiller 2005; Lorinc 2006; McAllister 2004). In the advocacy efforts of the disability community and the academic analyses in disability studies, urban politics remain relatively overlooked. With so much current consideration to global systems of capitalist structures, we should not lose sight of the role of local groups and urban elites in framing political choices, shaping policy decisions, and allocating community resources (Reichl 2005).

This chapter examines interconnections between urban settlement and disablement, and imagines the possibilities, within specific social contexts, for enhanced inclusion and citizenship in city spaces. I use Michael Ignatieff's (1984) work on the solidarity of strangers and Iris Marion Young's (1990) conception of city life as 'a being together of strangers' open to group differences to examine ideas about social differences, democratic politics, and inclusion in public realms of urban Canada. Of interest for disability scholars and activists are Ignatieff's and Young's arguments that the sphere of citizenship need not submerge social differences and must not insist on some homogeneous unity of the public good. Instead, if social justice, participatory democracy, and cooperation are to flourish, the civic public must acknowledge and support group differences in capacities, needs, and interests.

Aristotle, the ancient Greek philosopher, wrote that 'political society exists for the sake of noble actions, and not of mere companionship.' The twentieth-century poet and Nobel Prize winner T.S. Eliot wrote, 'When the Stranger says: What is the meaning of this city? Do you huddle close together because you love each other? What will you answer? "We all dwell together to make money from each other?" or "This is a community?"'[1] Aristotle and Eliot each suggest there are contending ways of thinking about cities. This chapter discusses four such viewpoints on city life, specifically, perspectives on the relations among urban society, the notion of strangers in cities, and social exclusion/inclusion, particularly as they relate to people with disabilities.[2]

Perspectives on Urbanism and City Life

Urban life has always had supporters and detractors. Differing perspectives to understanding cities derive from two analytical dimensions: one distinguishes between studies basically pessimistic toward the nature of urbanism and studies relatively positive about city life; the second dimension distinguishes between studies that chronologically and/or conceptually focus on modernist notions of urbanization and those that emphasize postmodernism and identity politics. The characteristics of these two dimensions, when joined, produce four general categories of viewpoints on cities as set out in table 2.1.

The first perspective I call 'lonely crowds' is the original view on urbanization first expressed in sociology and echoed in other fields that urban life inevitably results in alienation and social isolation. People with disabilities are commonly ignored in this approach. The second is called 'vibrant communities' and is a more positive look at the features of diverse neighbourhoods and urban villages located within large cities. While this perspective celebrates diversities in city life, again people with disabilities are largely overlooked. The third, 'excluded Others' is a postmodernist critique of urban society which emphasizes how many groups, including the disabled, are constructed as 'Others' who are then often segregated and subjected to coercive controls. The fourth perspective is 'diverse civic publics' and this, too, is a postmodernist view of urbanity, though one fairly optimistic at root about the potential for recognizing the needs and rights of social groups, including people with disabilities.[3]

Table 2.1
Four perspectives on city life, strangers, and social inclusion/exclusion

Viewpoints & Processes	Pessimistic	Optimistic
Modernism and Urbanization	(1) *Lonely Crowds* Strangers as the unfortunate outcome of mass cities, resulting in alienation and isolation	(2) *Vibrant Communities* Strangers as inevitable and desirable features of city life, urban villages, and neighbourhoods
	Exemplar authors: Simmel, Packard, Riesman, Wirth	Exemplar authors: Jacobs, Lofland
Post-Modernism and Identity Politics	(3) *Excluded Others* Strangers as constructed and subjected to controls and segregation	(4) *Diverse Civic Publics* Strangers as intrinsic to political life and communities
	Exemplar authors: Bauman, Foucault, Hughes, Imrie, Turner	Exemplar authors: Gleeson, Ignatieff, Leonard, Short, Wharf, Young

Perspectives 1 and 3, one rooted in modernity the other in post-modernism, both regard urbanization and cities as producing exclusions, enforcing numerous forms of social closure, and exacerbating social distances amongst different groups (Hughes 2002). By contrast, perspectives 2 and 4 present a positive recognition of diversities in urban communities and, on the whole, are optimistic about the possibility of including assorted groups within mainstream city life.

In relation to the history of theorizing on cities, perspective 1 (lonely crowds) is the oldest, with roots in urban sociology from at least the 1920s and perspective 2 (vibrant communities) emerging in the 1960s in large part in reaction to the first approach. Both share many core ideas and assumptions of twentieth-century modernism. In neither of these viewpoints do people with disabilities really figure. The first perspective on urbanism, however, would readily explain the institutionalization and segregation of many people with mental disabilities as the result of the weakening or breakdown of family supports and rural community networks, the rise of charitable organizations in cities, and the emergence of social and medical professions (Reaume 2000). In addition, modernist ideas and practices, as expressed in urban planning and design, resulted in 'disablist cities' with exclusionary spaces for people with disabilities (Imrie 1996). The second perspective, though celebratory of differences, conspicuously ignores persons with disabilities whether they be in asylums, other institutions, or living at home. This is common in modernist writing on cities and urbanism where attention to social differences typically concerns one or more of race/ethnicity, age, social class, and gender.

On the other hand, perspectives 3 and 4, that of excluded Others and diverse civic publics, are recent postmodernist approaches emergent since the 1980s, addressing the identities and experiences of people with disabilities more routinely and explicitly. Perspective 3, excluded Others, for example, includes works that examine the impact of urban industrialism in relegating people with disabilities to the fringes of the competitive economy and labour markets (Ross and Nelson 2005). The turn from modernism to postmodernism appears in the changing discourse in land-use planning and urban development policy in Canada and elsewhere. This shift is from a concern with imposing order on urban growth and basing decisions on the technical expertise of engineers and planners, to a concern with fostering environmental sustainability, encouraging cultural diversity, and promoting social harmony in urban centres (Graham, Phillips, and Maslove 1998).

Perspective 1, cities as lonely crowds, which goes back to the 1920s, is the classic approach to interpreting urban life, represented by the works of Simmel, Wirth, and others of the Chicago School of sociology, plus Packard and Riesman. A major focus of this approach is on the remoteness and unfamiliarity of urban centres and, therefore, the detachment of people in cities. Indeed, the Chicago writers developed the theory of 'social disorganization' which interprets urban life in terms of the breakdown of institutions that traditionally encouraged cooperation, resulting in individual isolation and an inability collectively to solve problems (Bulmer 1984). As Hughes (2002: 572–3) expresses this viewpoint: 'we are all strangers, separated from one another by the maelstrom of urban anonymity.' Wirth theorized the notion of urbanism as a way of life associated with large cities, a lifestyle of values and behaviours characterized by personal stress, aloofness, and indifference in social relationships.

In the 1950s, David Riesman coined the concept 'the lonely crowd' in reference to middle class people employed in white collar work living in American metropolitan centres. Riesman warned that people could be lonely in a crowd, even of one's associates, if they were not attentive to their own feelings and aspirations, and failed to pursue actively their individual autonomy. He said 'they can no more assuage their loneliness in a crowd of peers, than one can assuage one's thirst by drinking sea water' (Riesman 1955: 349). A generation later, the popular sociologist, Vance Packard warned that big-city life in North America was increasing anonymity and isolation, eroding old familiar neighbourhoods, and weakening stable communities within cities. He noted that much of 'the populace [is] living in high-rise apartments, multi-unit complexes, or subdivision tracts. All tend to make people more isolated as individuals. A mass society is created in which people are less likely to achieve any sense of community' (1974: 99). Similar to Riesman's lonely crowd, Packard's cities are 'places of strangers,' vast-throngs with 'distances between people' (1974: 2–3).

The work of Jane Jacobs (1961) typifies perspective 2 (vibrant communities), offering a much more positive viewpoint of actual and potential benefits of city life. In a critique of conventional modernist planning, Jacobs argued for city forms that incorporated and encouraged diversity, density, and democracy. Jacobs advocates for diverse and multi-functional neighbourhoods, with mixed-use development and variety in local facilities to ensure social cohesions, security, and economic development. She favours high urban density with short blocks; extensive park spaces, and vibrant public transit system, and an active role of citizen participation in planning processes and decisions. Jacobs also believes that most diversity in a city emerges outside of public policy and government structures through the interaction of countless individuals, groups, and private organizations and their divergent ideas.

Much of these interactions, though, take place in public spaces, a point Lyn Lofland stresses in her affirmative outlook of living amidst strangers. She writes: 'The locus of the city as a world of strangers resides in the city's public space. It is here, primarily, that the drama of strangers in the midst of strangers is played out' (Lofland 1973: x). Urban public spaces are 'those areas of a city [to] which, in the main, all persons have *legal access*' (Lofland 1973: 19). Implied in this analysis is the idea of accessible and inclusive spaces, an interpretation of city life with noteworthy implications for disability studies.

Perspectives 3 (excluded Others) and 4 (diverse civic publics), as postmodernist approaches, are both skeptical of contemporary urbanity, although perspective 3 is more a pessimistic critique of the past and present period, while perspective 4 gives more emphasis to possibilities of progressive change.[4] Both approaches critically question the idea of a universal experience of city living, deconstructing the notion of urbanism as 'a way of life' and rejecting it as a credible master narrative of cities. As well, both postmodernist approaches question the expert power of urban planners and the taken-for-granted beliefs of progress through economic growth. Strangers are culturally constructed and in urban contexts spatially contained (Imrie 2001; Mitchell 2003; Moss and Dyck 2002; Rahder and Milgrom 2004).

Behind today's rhetoric of celebrating multiculturalism and other differences, of recognizing fluidity in social categories, and of valuing plurality in belief systems, perspective 3 writers point to the persistence of inequalities and relations of domination in urban societies. Cities continue to be places of exploitation and exclusion for many women, the poor, ethnic minorities, sexual minorities, indigenous peoples, and persons with mental health conditions and physical disabilities. In this approach, persons with disabilities remain largely defined and governed by bio-medical and personal tragedy models, despite the rise of rights-talk. In the past twenty years, some changes have occurred, yet the world of policy and practice remains decidedly categorical, regulatory, and stigmatizing for Canadians with disabilities. Cultural practices based in notions of order, health, and normality still include tendencies of 'othering' people: to confine, invalidate, exclude, and fix individuals and groups of people seen as having differences and deficiencies (Hughes 2002; Kirby 2006). A main reason for this discouraging state of affairs is the negative impacts of neo-liberalism as revealed in welfare state rollbacks, social program cuts, and the offloading of responsibilities for public provision onto communities, private firms, voluntary agencies, and families (Isin 1992; Leonard 1997; Lorinc 2006).

The literature of perspective 3, excluded Others, (and that of perspective 4) draws attention to the rise of oppositional politics in resistance to the restructuring of state service, as well as to the legacies of modernity that remain rooted in exclusionary ideas and practices. Turner (2002), for example, is just one of many authors in this genre who points to the commercialization of downtown lands and the contraction of public places within cities motivated by the desire to boost development and generate revenues. Other writers, in a similar vein, discuss processes of the privatization of public spaces, the marketization of social relationships, and the production of 'bounded and barriered spaces' (Imrie 2000, 2001). From this standpoint, cities are multiple sites of segregation for persons with disabilities.

Admiring diverse civic publics, perspective 4 is the upbeat side of postmodernist critique, offering a progressive future direction for cities and urban life. While sharing many elements with the third perspective, notably the critical analysis, this approach is generally more optimistic about the capacity of local governments and community organizations to create cities 'where ordinary citizens can lead dignified and creative lives' (Short 1989: 1). It is also more hopeful and confident in the possibility of marginalized groups, such as persons with disabilities, to be included in the economic, political, and social mainstream of city life. The vision here of what is possible sees city life as 'the being together of strangers' open to group differences (Young 1990), a 'moral community' with 'solidarity among strangers' (Ignatieff 1984).

In a discussion of contemporary urban societies, Gerometta, Haussermann, and Longo (2005) note that cities are 'places of crisis' due to welfare state restraints, but go on to describe cities as 'multiplex places,' as 'arenas of social movements and other civil society social experiments.' For these authors, cities are webs of diverse groups and relationships where community groups promote issues of social justice, rights, and legal guarantees to public services. In the postmodern city, organizations in civil society, municipalities, and the social economy can engage in innovations in governance relations. Gleeson (1999) similarly argues for enabling urban environments that are inclusive, respect differences, and provide for the basic material needs of residents. For Scott Greer 'the city is a veritable hothouse of transplanted cultural complexes and traits. Hybridization and mutation are commonplace and often unnoticed.' Greer adds that the city is 'a crossroads where strangers meet and new structures are born' and, where integration develops across groups, city life 'humanizes strangers' (1989: 342–3, 346).

 Brian Wharf, a social work scholar, adopts what he calls 'an admittedly optimistic approach' in arguing that through their local organizations citizens can influence social services and community conditions, thereby better preparing them to influence even grand policy issues at the level of the nation state (Wharf 1992: 10). From case studies on municipal governments, voluntary organizations, social planning councils, neighbourhood-based associations, Aboriginal agencies and governments, urban interest groups, and social movements, Wharf sees myriad participatory opportunities for citizens to influence policy and decision making. Katherine Graham, Susan Phillips, and Alan Maslove picture Canada's urban areas as economically interdependent units that contain 'a variety of communities with different identities, but have a sense of cohesiveness' (1998: 35). These public administration scholars interpret urban politics as involving the provision of infrastructure and services, the planning and regulation of land use, addressing issues of differences and quality of life in culturally diverse social communities, and encouraging democratic participation and representation. These activities of urban governance contribute toward determining the nature of 'livable cities' (Graham, Phillips, and Maslove 1998: 35–7; see also Broadbent 2008).

Disability Studies and Urban Perspectives

Reviewing the four perspectives is helpful in revealing assumptions and beliefs in social science literature on urbanization, and the problems and prospects of cities. In disability studies, there is no single dominant conception of urbanism expressed; what we most often find is an implicit amalgam of ideas on what urbanism does or could mean for community inclusion, social cohesion, citizenship, and opportunities for self-development. For disability studies, the city past and present is a site of many contradictions: comforts and constraints, opportunities and oppressions.[5]

The disability studies literature is not nostalgic for an 'idyllic past' of pre-urban community living or city life expressed by perspective 1 (lonely crowds) and at times implied by perspective 2 (vibrant communities). This is the image of the closely knit community characterized by 'happy harmony.' The history of urbanization for people with disabilities involves a history of institutional segregation, sterilization, charitable responses to needs, stigma, and prejudice and the medicalization of conditions and identities. As a shift from agricultural to industrial labour, urbanization fundamentally altered the nature of paid work, family relationships, and social networks, producing new impairments associated with factory work, and, from the logic of capitalism, raising issues of the employability of people with handicaps (Barnes, Mercer, and Shakespeare 1999: 18–19). There are few regrets over the passing of these elements of past community life. Many features of 'the good old days' were far from good for many people with disabilities. Much of what cities and communities contained and offered in these good old days were out of bounds for many people with disabilities.

Disability studies writers approach the issue of *mobility* as both a policy principle and a social process that warrants critical scrutiny rather than simply understood as part of the definition of urbanization. Perspective 1, for example, takes for granted as a straightforward phenomenon the frequent geographical movement of people across living arrangements and locations in North America. According to this perspective, the easy and frequent mobility of people leads to uprooted-ness, a loss of community identity, and consequently social fragmentation (Packard 1974: 2–5). Disability writers, in comparison, question the ability to move about both within a city and across cities, even in the aftermath of deinstitutionalization initiatives. Mobility is a cherished value and policy goal eluding many people with disabilities. Disability activists understand mobility broadly, encompassing movement geographically across areas, programmatically across services, and developmentally across life stages and ages. And, *under supportive contexts*, these modes of mobility provide benefits of continuity, belonging, and a sense of social integration.

Present city living is not idealized either. Urban society still contains any number of what Michel Foucault called 'zones of darkness' and 'zones of disorder' – misconceptions, fears, silences, obstructions, and barriers to recognition, respect, and resources (1984). Moreover, Canadian disability writers note that many services are unavailable outside big urban areas (Stienstra and Wight-Felske 2003). The 'social model of disability' (Barnes, Mercer, and Shakespeare 1999; Barnes, Oliver, and Barton 2002) emphasizes how people with impairments are disabled by the failure of societal arrangements to accommodate their needs. This model readily sees cities as places of socially created and culturally imposed barriers that produce inequalities, disadvantages, and exclusions from full participation. The model's theoretical interest lends itself to a consideration of how built environments inhibit the ability of persons with a disability to get around a neighbourhood, to whether transport systems assist or prevent people with disabilities from getting around the city as regularly as they would like, and to whether community facilities, such as schools, libraries, parks, and community arenas, provide adequate assistance for participation by children, youth, and adults with disabilities (Crawford 2005a).

Though disability studies is critical of urban societies, past and present, the field is not so profoundly disaffected as to outright reject the existing system. Here, the field shares some of the optimism of perspective 3 (excluded Others) and certainly perspective 4 (diverse civic publics) of what might be possible – of what reforms and innovations might be achievable to obtain more accessible and inclusive cities and diverse urban environments. City life potentially offers a wide range of opportunities for participation in cultural, economic, political, and social activities and relationships. There is a faith perhaps in what city life should be and can be like. There is an expectation that public and private organizations tackle attitudinal, physical, and institutional barriers, and that existing public spaces are preserved and new spaces for social access and interaction created, serving to promote a sense of belonging and acceptance of differences (Beall 1997).

Another urban-related theme in disability studies is that a city of strangers is not necessarily a rootless place in which people are unconnected to other people. Cities contain all sorts of strangers, and this need not result in coldness in social interactions, anxieties in interpretations, or loss of self. Even the largest cities have countless networks of small-group life and social affiliations, what Neil Morgan calls 'communities of amiable strangers' – in which people are affable with their neighbours, even if avoiding close personal entanglement, offering assistance and displaying compassion in times of emergencies and special circumstances (cited in Packard 1974: 189). Social differences between groups of people need not create social distances if public institutions affirm such differences and cultural activities and symbols reflect those differences.

The Being Together of Strangers in Urban Communities

The idea of strangers appears in all four perspectives on urban life. In perspective 1, lonely crowds, strangers are the automatic result of the massing together of large numbers of people from different locales and backgrounds. Strangers are created and maintained by the modern lifestyle associated with urbanism: the new arrivals, the foreigners, the visitors and tourists, the outcasts. We all become and are strangers. In perspective 2, vibrant communities, the 'ideal street is [one] full of strangers passing through, of people of many different classes, ethnic groups, ages, beliefs and life-styles' (Berman 1982: 323). Lofland (1973) writes of the infrequent strangers as well as the constant strangers in city life. In the words of Jane Jacobs: 'The streets must not only defend the city against predatory strangers, they must protect the many, many peaceable and well-meaning strangers who use them, insuring their safety too as they pass through' (1961: 36). Perspective 3, excluded Others, sees strangers in relation to processes of 'othering' and systemic exclusion.

I consider perspective 4, diverse civic publics, in more detail through an examination of the ideas of Ignatieff and Young on city life and difference. As a form of social relationships, Young conceives of city life as 'the being together of strangers' and, at one point in her analysis, describes politics as 'a relationship of strangers' (1990: 256, 234). Urban affairs include vast networks of interactions among seen and unseen strangers in daily activities and encounters in public spaces. Young readily admits that contemporary American cities fall well short of the normative ideal of this perspective, in reality containing and reproducing many injustices, although she believes that the ideals of city life as the togetherness of strangers 'are realized incidentally and intermittently in some cities today' (1990: 241).

'In the city,' writes Young, 'persons and groups interact within spaces and institutions they all experience themselves as belonging to, but without those interactions dissolving into unity of commonness' (1990: 237). Several premises are contained in this statement. One is that people, as individuals and in groups, have the capacity and opportunity to participate and interact with other people. A second premise is that a sufficient supply of accessible public spaces exists throughout cities to enable being together. A democratic politics, Young stresses 'crucially depends on the existence of spaces and forums to which everyone has access' to participate – to speak, listen, and bear witness (240). A third is that such interactions generate common experiences of belonging, a basic component of citizenship according to most commentators on the topic. These public spaces require supports, services, and, likely, adaptations to enable all to speak, to listen, and to bear witness; this certainly, for people with disabilities and, in most cases, for all regardless of their abilities and capacities. A fourth premise is that individuals and groups participating in such public places and institutions are able, at the same time, to maintain a sense of their own distinctiveness, special status, or group identity. The perspective of diverse civic publics therefore contains, as do the other perspectives, a number of empirical prerequisites, behavioural expectations, and normative claims about the politics of representation, recognition, and redistribution.

In *The Needs of Strangers*, Michael Ignatieff emphasizes the silent relations among people with myriad combinations of needs, capacities, rights, and responsibilities, all 'mediated through a vast division of labour' in the welfare state, the market economy, and civil society. While we are 'a society of strangers,' Ignatieff sees the welfare state establishing 'moral relations between strangers' and, in turn, creating 'solidarity among strangers' (1984: 9, 17–18). While strangers in cities may be personally unknown to us and perhaps are different from our own reference group, in regard to the welfare state, we are 'moral strangers to each other' socially and politically connected through citizenship.

This ideal of city life envisions an urban environment that features social differentiation of groups without adverse exclusions. Individual and group differences are readily accepted and, following Jacobs, a diversity of activities and public spaces adequately supported. To promote social justice in the city, this politics of difference 'lays down institutional and ideological means for recognizing and affirming diverse social groups by giving political representation to these groups, and celebrating their distinctive characteristics' (Young 1990: 240). In the admittedly unrealized vision of this perspective, city life avoids objectifying and essentializing 'the other.'

This logic of inclusion values difference and variety over sameness. While recognizing in a positive way social group differences, Young does not romanticize such differences or ignore power relations among groups and issues of domination; nor does she reduce social groups to an essential unity, ignoring differences within a group or social category. Rejecting hard and fast dualisms, she conceptualizes differences 'as the relatedness of things with more or less similarity in a multiplicity of possible respects' (Young 1990: 98). Affirming group identities, this notion of differences avoids binary oppositions and the dangers of isolating and fragmenting human associations. Strangers in the city are more or less similar in many possible ways. For Young, the ideal city life includes the virtues of social differentiation without exclusion, variety in the use of spaces, the eroticism of novelty and excitement, and publicity in the sense of access to public spaces.

Ignatieff offers a similar vision of general inclusion realized through the acceptance of particular differences. In our urban societies of strangers, people 'feel common belonging and mutual responsibility to each other' based on human difference, not so much on abstract doctrines of the common identity of abstract subjects. As social beings, he suggests, 'our obligations to each other are always based on difference,' and it is difference which defines responsibilities and obligations in specific times and places. 'Only when difference has its home can our common identity begin to find its voice' (1984: 28, 131). The accessible and inclusive city then is one where difference has a home thus enabling the development of a sense of common belonging.

Building a city for all means 'creating inclusive urban spaces that welcome diversity and meet the contrasting needs of different social groups' (Beall 1997: 3). To a great extent, of course, creating inclusive cities concerns the built environment:

> The physical structure of the city is the product of conscious decision-making and social relations and therefore can never be neutral. What gets built, where, how and for whom, reflects relations of power and the often stereotypical assumptions of planners, architects and other urban decision-makers. Cities are literally concrete manifestations of ideas on how society was, is and should be. (3)

Among the values that constitute the inclusive city are accessibility, multi-functionality, equity, partiality, and universality. The following open letter to Canadian politicians at all levels of government underscores a number of jarring realities when these values are missing in city life:

I used to adore Toronto. As an able-bodied person, it was relatively simple to get around and I appreciated having access to all Toronto had to offer. I didn't pay attention to the lack of elevators, escalators and ramps. I am 30 years old and have multiple sclerosis now. I am no longer able-bodied but disabled. These days I use a cane or walker to aid my gait, making uncomplicated things more demanding. I now despise Toronto due to its lack of accessibility. I miss the things I once loved and want to enjoy them again but I cannot because establishments are inaccessible. Why am I being penalized for a disease that caused me to become disabled? Why is this kind of discrimination allowed?

I am appalled and frustrated at the lack of barrier free sites in this city, province and country.

The voters elected you into a privileged position to represent all people. You have a responsibility to disabled voters to address fundamental needs. We are being ignored, and I refuse to be treated as a 'second class citizen.' What will your course of action be? (Bernard and Bernard 2005: 5)

Among other issues raised, this letter vividly illustrates the 'disabling city' – the urban setting that restricts, ignores, and excludes people with disabilities from regular participation in everyday activities. The letter expresses elements of a social construction of disability, drawing attention to the importance of supports in the built environment, attitudes of city residents, and the actions and inactions of policy makers in shaping how much a person with a disability has difficulty in living, working, playing, studying, and generally moving about a city. As planners and geographers point out, realizing accessibilities in cities involve personal costs along with public sector and private sector investments in time, travel, finances, and other resources (Frug 2001).

We easily can read into this letter a social justice claim for inclusive policies and a view of politics as 'the art of representing the needs of strangers,' specifying essential human needs 'in a language of political and social rights' guided by commitments to 'a decent and humane society' (Ignatieff 1984: 12–13). What Young says of her own country, the United States, applies to a greater or lesser degree to Canada and other nations: 'Our society is only beginning to change the practice of keeping the physically and mentally disabled out of public view' (1990: 120). Inclusive urban spaces embrace human particularity, 'the plurality of moral subjects,' plus the ambiguity, variability, and specificity of people. The civic public, Young sees in terms of the subjectivity of bodily aspects of the human condition and the specificity of 'particular experiences and histories that constitute a situation' (1990: 100). This illustrates a growing body of literature that puts forth a model of social inclusion committed to an experiential perspective on issues. Such a stance, based on attachment, culture, and passion in contrast to 'objective' policy analysis and administration, fits with the interests of the disability movement and a social model of disability.

The inclusive home for this subjective difference rests on the foundational value of 'universality,' which refers to all persons being of equal moral worth, the participation of everyone in social life, and the needs, desires, and viewpoints of all groups recognized in encounters with others on equal terms and conditions of power (Young 1990: 105–6). Likewise, Ignatieff emphasizes 'the democratic requirement of informed consent,' while also acknowledging that another element of politics is 'the art of representing the needs of strangers' including, at times, 'the perilous business of speaking on behalf of needs which strangers have had no chance to articulate on their own' (Ignatieff 1984: 12). This formulation points to the importance of public attitudes, social relations, and authority structures, along with physical barriers, in creating inclusive communities. The vision of an inclusive city seeks the reduction and prevention of discrimination of people – when viewed through the dominant culture as having a spoiled identity, when institutional practices disenfranchise people in politics and policy making, or when environmental barriers constrain their daily living and active participation in society. Here, again, for the disability movement, we see aspects of an intertwined politics of recognition, redistribution, and representation.

Conclusions

Lonely crowds, vibrant communities, excluded Others, and diverse civic publics: this chapter examined these four perspectives on urban society. Variations of these perspectives on city living are more familiar to those in urban sociology, social geography, and political science than to thinkers and activists in the academic field of disability studies, with some notable exceptions (Gleeson 1999). Disability studies contains a mixture of ideas about urbanity. This field of inquiry is not nostalgic for some idyllic rural past; mobility is a concept and a process most likely with mixed consequences that deserves critical inquiry on a number of levels; and cities today remain inaccessible and exclusionary in many respects for people with physical and mental disabilities. As the social model of disability underlines, cities are full of structural and attitudinal barriers to participation by people with impairments. Nonetheless, there is another theme that there are possibilities for making cities more diverse, inclusive, and participatory places. Social differences among people and the presence of 'strangers in cities' are general and desirable realities of community living in urban societies.

Disability studies can greatly assist the 'sociology of the stranger' (Hughes 2002; Lofland 1973; Packard 1974; Vernon 2006) in thinking about the everyday context of exclusion/inclusion and normality/abnormality. The stranger is not a unitary or essential category: numerous kinds of strangers in cities and communities appear in this sociological literature, a multiplicity that unquestionably resonates with the diversities of impairments and disablement experiences of various social groups, families, and individuals (Bernard and Bernard 2005; Chouinard 1999; Driedger, Crooks, and Bennett 2004).

The sociology of strangers links to a political sociology of public policy restraints. To give one example, cutbacks to home care services correspond to cutbacks to social connections. Previously personalized relationships between providers and recipients decline, coupled with higher turnover in staff, producing new kinds of strangers. Elderly clients living with long-term disabilities or illnesses experience 'successions of strangers entering their personal worlds and requiring constant (and tiring) explanations of the particulars of their needs and the organization of their homes' (Aronson and Neysmith 2001: 157).

While social theorists of past generations warned of lonely crowds and current theorists frequently promote a vision of diverse civic publics, the reality still in urban centres is all too often of the excluded Others. To break through the patterns of absent citizens, practices of civic exclusion, such as not-in-my-backyard attitudes in local planning and development politics, need interrogating, whether those practices deal with panhandling, homelessness, group homes or the personal understandings and responses to people with particular disabilities. Potential contributions of disability studies to the study of city life are abundant. Much of the social science literature on inclusive and livable cities gives little consideration to people with disabilities, and so disability studies can advance understanding of urban politics in highlighting the significance for local citizenship, as well as for national issues of social policy, of land-use development (Turner 2002), access in the built environment (Imrie 2000), public transit, and other services (Broadbent 2008; Crawford 2005a; Wharf 1992). Exploring related concepts – for instance, 'the egalitarian city' (Boles 1986), 'urban citizenship' (Baubock 2003; Holston and Appadurai 1999), and 'the right to the city' (Mitchell 2003) – is worthwhile in encouraging cross-disciplinary exchanges; in that way, ensuring disability becomes a central social dimension alongside class, gender, race/ethnicity, and so forth, considered by geography, sociology, political science, and policy studies.

3 Social Stratification, the State, and Disability

In his classic work, *The Vertical Mosaic*, John Porter documented and assessed the structures of power and social class. The title refers to the popular image of Canada as a mosaic of many cultural and ethnic groups, joined with a macro-sociological analysis of the hierarchical relations between these groups across assorted institutional domains of society. With class and power as his major themes, Porter understandably relied on the concept of social stratification. 'Ranking of individuals or groups in an order of inferiority or superiority is a universal feature of social life,' Porter observed, adding that the term social stratification refers 'to this ubiquitous social ranking' (1965: 7). While all members in a liberal democracy may 'share a common legal status of citizenship' with certain rights and freedoms, a structure of inequality does exist in relation to education, employment, property ownership, and positions of power.

Numerous sociologists assert that these inequalities in benefits, prestige, and resources are not random or accidental, but structured in some manner, producing a systematic layering of groups, along with perpetuating 'an unequal distribution of economic rewards and power in society' (Schaefer and Smith 2005: 203). Social stratification links to a number of issues in disability politics and policy. What are the determinants of social status and the inequalities of condition, opportunities, and outcomes? What are the stratifying effects of social programs delivered by the provinces or the federal government? How does social stratification interact with social citizenship? What are the mechanisms or techniques used by governments in Canada that by establishing and enforcing status boundaries include some and exclude other groups of people? This chapter takes up these questions.

As a process of differentiation and evaluation, social stratification is of great consequence for social policy analysis and disability studies. It bears on matters of identity and differences, stigma, equity, segregation, and integration. Stratification is directly relevant to conceptions of community – of who belongs and who does not, and on what terms and conditions. This, in turn, shows how key stratification is to conflict theory where society includes struggles shaped by unequal relations of power among groups, as well as individuals.

For decades, research has reported persistent social inequalities across nations in the distribution of wealth, income, various life opportunities, as well as poverty and deprivation for some, and, for many others, marginal and precarious economic security. A Canadian political scientist remarks on 'the re-emergence of a political fault line that, while quite prominent in the politics of many societies, has generally assumed a rather muted form in Canada and the United States – class conflict and the politics of the distribution' (Brooks 2000: 19). Causes of this resurgence of conflict over the allocation of wealth, in low income and high income nations, reflect the adverse effects of economic globalization, increasing job insecurity, and widening income polarization, and a growing number of working poor (Martin and Torres 2004; Rice and Prince 2000; Turner 2001). These forms of inequality (which some commentators call domination and oppression) generate conflicts on many levels of interpersonal and social relationships, weaken community cohesion and public order, and, in terminology that emerged in policy circles in the 1990s, aggravate social exclusion and diminish social capital (Davies 2005).

Social analysts and political economists typically enumerate the following determinants of social status and life chances: age, class (often said to include the socio-economic dimensions of educational attainment, occupation, and income), ethnicity, family background and network, gender, race and ancestry, regional location, and sexual orientation. Through intentional and unconscious discrimination, life choices, and political struggles these multiple factors, interacting in countless ways, contribute to social inequalities. On socio-economic mobility and status achievement in Canada, a common observation is that 'gender, ethnicity, race, and family background continue to exert a tremendous downward pull on mobility,' restricting the ability of individuals to climb the so-called social ladder (Brooks 2000: 67). Other observers add the assertion that 'class is still demonstrably at the centre of most attempts to describe or explain social inequality in Canada today' (Allahar and Cote 1998: xi). Actions for addressing these social inequalities encompass claims for group recognition and enhanced political representation, along with socio-economic redistribution.

Though there are exceptions in the sociological literature in Canada (Anderson 1996; Michalko 2002; Titchkosky 2003a) disability is a dimension of social inequality and stratification usually overlooked by Canadian sociologists, or marginally mentioned in passing in relation to a discussion of illness, disease, and death (Carroll and White 2005; Curtis, Grabb, and Guppy 2004; Naiman 2004; Staggenborg 2008; Teevan and Hewitt 2005; Tepperman and Curtis 2002). Mostly, scholarship on citizenship, public policy, and social inequality tends to neglect disablement in the analysis of social stratification and the role of the welfare state (Duffy and Mandell 2001; Lightman 2003; Pupo 2001). We know, however, that disability is an important feature of Canadian society. Moreover, we know that disability-related barriers and exclusions are increasingly politicized, due to efforts by advocates, families, organizations, and the disability movement. One result of this mobilization is that disability issues are on governmental agendas in a way they were not a generation ago, even if the policy and program responses are not always prompt or adequate.

Social stratification has a symbolic dimension as well as the more widely emphasized material side of economic processes, class relations, and career structures (Allahar and Cote 1998; Esping-Andersen 1993; Naiman 2004).[1] Stratification attaches values and other cultural meanings to specific activities, roles, and resources. In social policy fields in Canada, Breton (1984) was among the first to give emphasis to the production and allocation of symbolic resources. This symbolic dimension to stratification is utterly significant to persons with disabilities and the wider disability movement, as it deals with public attitudes towards mental and physical impairments, beliefs about deservingness, in addition to assumptions and expectations about personal and family responsibilities as compared to community and governmental roles and duties.

Ableism captures many aspects of the cultural dimension of stratification – the process of being 'defined from the outside, positioned, and placed, by a network of dominant meanings' (Young 1990: 59). People with disabilities constitute one of the social groups 'culturally oppressed by being defined as the other, the different and the deviant,' thus rendering one's own experience, perspective, and aspirations marginal if not invisible (88). At a systemic or personal level, ableism can encompass silencing, segregation or exclusion, marginalization, denial, neglect, violence and abuse, and poverty based on one or more disability. Power, prestige, and privilege in society – all features central to social stratification, are distributed based on prevailing notions of ability and normalcy, thus downgrading the status of persons with disabilities. Not surprisingly, the modern disability movement engages in the politics of recognition, which 'questions certain everyday symbols, practices, and ways of speaking, making them the subject of public discussion, and explicitly matters of choice and decision' (86). Notice the shift in language over the past thirty years, in some jurisdictions, from mentally retarded, to mentally handicapped, to people with developmental disabilities.

Society and Stratification: Where Is the State?

Most academic writing on social stratification does not examine the role of the state, and specifically, its programs, as one of the features in society that generates social divisions (e.g., Macionis, Jansson, and Benoit 2005). As a major institutional domain, the state is rarely considered among the systems of society that stratifies people and maintains patterns of status hierarchy.[2] The welfare state is far less frequently considered than other institutions, such as the economy, the family, and the educational system (which, admittedly, can be regarded as a part of the welfare state if broadly conceived), as one of the axes of inequality.

Why is the state largely overlooked as an independent factor affecting a person's or group's life chances and social status? Perhaps it is because a traditional focus of this line of inquiry has been on social class and capitalism and their intersection with work, issues of poverty, and inequalities of income and wealth. Another reason the state is not routinely implicated in theorizing on social stratification might be because the welfare state is regarded in a positive light for the most part, as a progressive institution engaged in 'the issues of nation-building and social inequality' (Harrison and Friesen 2004: 125). Even in critical social policy studies, a tendency at times is to see patterns of advantages and disadvantages defined by class status and power 'out there' in civil society and the market economy, while the impact of welfare state social programs is examined in terms of effects on societal problems and (re)shaping structures of barriers and opportunities through services and controls (Spicker 1996: 26–33).

Contemporary texts on Canadian social policy do not use the term social stratification at all (Armitage 2003; Graham, Swift, and Delaney 2003; Guest 2003; Lightman 2003; Rice and Prince 2000; Westhues 2003; Wharf and McKenzie 2004). Indeed, a few do not profile inequality in their index or glossary, although they do address gender, class, and ethno-racial issues as regards a choice of social problems, including child poverty, disability, and homelessness (Graham, Swift, and Delaney 2003; Guest 2003; Westhues 2003). The emphasis is on diversity, questions of social exclusion and social inclusion and related issues of isolation, rejection, and non-involvement, as well as belonging and legitimacy, in short, the politics of recognition (Graham, Swift, and Delaney 2003). Other texts (Armitage 2003; Lightman 2003; Rice and Prince 2000; Wharf and McKenzie 2004) do discuss inequality and the values of equality and social justice, particularly in relation to income and wealth distribution, employment/unemployment, poverty, and mechanisms for the transfer of income, in short, the politics of redistribution. Cutbacks to public services and social programs over the past decade or more seriously aggravated social inequalities within the labour market and civil society. The shift to a neo-liberal ideology of governing severely constrains the potentially progressive redistributive role of the Canadian state in addressing human needs and tackling social problems.

The writing within three groups does emphasize the state's role as a relatively autonomous system in social stratification, some of it dating back to the early stages of the modern welfare state.[3] The three groups are the fields of social administration and the sociology of welfare in Britain (Marshall 1964, 1982; Room 1979; Titmuss 1958), feminist analyses of the state and social policy (Bashevkin 2002; Bryson 1992; Lister 1997; Little 2005; Sainsbury 1996; Williams 1989), and comparative studies in the political economy of welfare states (Bakker and Scott 1997; Esping-Andersen 1990; Naiman 2004; Panitch 1977). In each, explicit theoretical and empirical attention is given to how welfare state regimes structure social roles, identities, power relations, and life chances when the regime is taken as a whole, in particular fields of social provision (fiscal, occupational, social welfare), and by individual programs. Much of this work concentrates on economic dimensions of stratification of income, wealth, and labour market relationships, a focus challenged and accompanied in recent decades by feminist works looking at gender, patriarchy, family, and women's generally marginalized experiences apropos the market economy, the state, and official politics. A single chapter lacks the luxury of space to detail all the works that locate the state specifically in the processes of social stratification in societies. We can, however, survey a few studies that capture key ideas and findings.

In a book-length treatment, Graham Room (1979) examines several interrelations of social policy, social stratification, and political order, drawing primarily on the social policy literature and experience of the British welfare state. In summary, the major interrelationships he reports are that, first, 'private welfare schemes tend to reinforce and reproduce the prevailing map of inequality and the associated lines of social conflict'; second, some, although not all, public sector social programs 'involve distributional and/or relational modification in – if not radical challenge to – the stratification system'; third, selective means-tested programs 'create a negatively privileged status group of paupers'; fourth, universal programs 'may not ... challenge and reduce class gradients in deprivation, unless extended into positive discrimination' – that is to say, supplemented by programs of affirmative action and equity; while, fifth, at the same time, universal social programs have the potential of creating 'bonds of mutual obligation' along with 'new lines of interest identity and conflict ... aimed at redistribution' (250).

From this macro political viewpoint, social policy is 'the state's policy vis-à-vis social stratification, i.e., the wider distribution of power and advantage – whether this be a policy of reinforcing and upholding the prevailing distribution or actively challenging it' (Room 1979: 260).

Gösta Esping-Andersen (1990) is perhaps best known for his comparative work on the political economy of welfare states, *The Three Worlds of Welfare Capitalism*. In that book, he presented a typology of three welfare state regimes – conservative, liberal, and, socialist – and empirically illustrated the content of each regime type and, as a result, the robustness of his framework. The framework (with its core concepts of social citizenship and de-commodification and its comparative quantitative research methodology) has been widely cited in the literature, criticized – most notably by feminist and anti-racist scholars, and stimulated similar attempts at model development, testing, and refinement or reformulation. All this attention to the typology overshadowed an important element of his work; the idea that the welfare state is a system of stratification as well as a system of services and income benefits. 'The welfare state may provide services and income security but it is also, and always has been, a system of social stratification. Welfare states are key institutions in the structuring of class and the social order. The organizational features of the welfare state help determine the articulation of social solidarity, divisions of class, and status differentiation' (Esping-Andersen 1990: 55). Years before, T.H. Marshall (1964: 100) noted that 'citizenship operates as an instrument of social stratification,' owing to the divisions and hierarchies found in educational systems, wage structures, and occupational classifications. For his analysis, Esping-Andersen points to income maintenance programs and the organization of health and social services, along with education systems. For the three welfare regime types, he argues that embedded in each are distinctive logics of social stratification: 'welfare states may be equally large or comprehensive, but with entirely different effects on social structure. One may cultivate hierarchy and status, another dualisms [between the poor and the middle classes], and a third universalism. Each case will produce its own unique fabric of social solidarity' (1990: 58). The status differentiation he is particularly interested in pertains to differences among welfare state clients, and between welfare state clients and other groups participating in the labour market.

Canada is a strong example of a liberal-welfare state regime, the relevant measures for stratification being 'the relative salience of means-testing: in terms of the relative financial responsibility accorded to the individual insured; and in terms of relative weight of voluntary, private-sector welfare' (Esping-Andersen 1990: 69). The result: a modest set of social rights in public programs, a strong emphasis on individual self-reliance and attachment to the labour market to access certain benefits, and a general expectation that the private sector and voluntary sector both continue to play significant and valid roles in providing service and income assistance.

How the State Orders Social Relations

To explore how Canadian states structure social and economic roles this section examines technologies of stratification that governments and welfare bureaucracies generally use in policies. A brief case study of the Canada Pension Plan Disability Program is presented to illustrate more specifically the characteristics of stratification associated with the largest public disability insurance program in the country.

Technologies of Stratification

Beside personal and societal factors, social stratification also refers 'to how welfare states themselves order social relations through social policy and practice' (Bakker and Scott 1997: 288). But how exactly do government expenditure programs, public services, or tax policies create social hierarchies? In accessing and exercising rights of social citizenship, individuals and groups are subject to various organizations, measures, and controls: 'In "providing" rights, society and the state do not simply give them to citizens *gratis*; citizens must subject themselves to the procedures and institutions necessary to ensure that the state can continue to provide rights' (Gorham 1995: 29). As well as the procedures and institutions of the welfare state are the detailed design features of programs that emulate something of the struggles and inequalities of society.

The concept *technologies of stratification* relates to the methods, procedures, and discursive practices used by governments to establish and enforce status boundaries, to include some people and exclude others, and to rank and categorize individuals and groups for purposes of eligibility and the provision of social programs, in brief, constituting problems and governing citizens (Fraser 1989; Titchkosky 2003b). Technologies of stratification speak to the questions outlined in the introduction of this chapter of how exclusion is perpetuated, of why progress on advancing inclusion is slow, and what are the stratifying effects of social policies.

Technologies of stratification in policy and practice include the following mechanisms and effects. One involves the sequencing of policy responses: at any particular point in time, providing a program, service, benefit, or set of rules and rights for a particular group with needs, but not for other groups or individuals with comparable needs, workers' compensation, for instance (Jennissen, Prince, and Schwartz 2000). A second, related technique is categorizing groups by separate programs: over time, this technique involves 'legislating distinct programs for different ... groups, each with its own conspicuously unique set of rights and privileges' (Esping-Andersen 1990: 23). In recent decades, feminist scholars have identified and evaluated critically the formation and operation of dual or two-tiered tracks of programs in income security for men and women (Rice and Prince 2000; Sainsbury 1996).

Honouring certain groups is often seen as a politically acceptable form of status stratification in public policy. As an example, for veterans in general and in particular those with disabilities, relatively adequate and comprehensive provisions have been established in many nations, over the past eighty years or so, as 'a means of rewarding loyalty to the state and, in part, a way of demarcating this group's ... exalted social status' (Esping-Andersen 1990: 23) establishing veterans as warrior-citizens (Prince 2000; Turner 2001). Even within a group with the 'exalted status' of war veterans, are multiple social hierarchies. These include differences in benefits and services even for the same injuries or needs according to military rank, differences in the recognition of and treatment of physical versus psychological impairments, differences in subsequent dealings between Aboriginal and non-Aboriginal veterans after the Second World War, and differences in the status of veterans who volunteered compared to those conscripted or those who remained in Canada compared to those who went overseas. In other words, a process of privileging takes place even within a privileged social group.

Screening, monitoring, and investigating applicants are standard tools of social ranking in social policy. Establishing a general program for the population as a whole (or at least an array of status groups) through screening systems and surveillance practices in clinical encounters, investigation and enforcement procedures in program implementation, plus the inevitable discretion involved in human service provision, inadvertently or consciously stratifies by group attributes and shapes people's experiences (Crooks 2004; Frazee, Gilmour, and Mykitiuk 2006; Moss and Teghtsoonian 2008). Even if deemed to be part of a deserving group, in applying for and receiving benefits, people face risks of humiliations and administrative harassments for accessing social programs.

Making binary moral judgments is a classic technique in public relief and social assistance, among other program areas. This technique entails distinguishing between people in a twofold manner, such as between employable/unemployable, normal/abnormal, healthy/ill, or deserving/less-deserving individuals and groups. As Boychuk explains, 'it is impossible to separate the issue of employability from considerations of who is or is not deserving. To categorize mentally and physically handicapped recipients as unemployable is, in effect, to state that although the disability is not the primary cause for reliance on social assistance, the system will judge the disabled individuals less harshly because they are deserving recipients' (1998: 18). Such eligibility determinations are far from being technical matters and while persons with disabilities, relative to other groups, may be treated 'less harshly,' this does not mean Canadians with disabilities do not face incredible struggles with income assistance programs across the country; unfortunately, they do quite regularly (Chouinard and Crooks 2005). Reproducing existing status differences among people also occurs in income maintenance programs among people as a result of basing the value of benefits on earnings-related contributions, which is a standard feature of social insurance programs. It also occurs through the use of fees and charges to finance the delivery of programs and the use of tax credits, deductions, and exemptions to deliver benefits (Lightman 2003).

Another bundle of technologies reflects the impact of neo-liberalism on present age policies and practices. One of these concerns devolving public responsibility – locating accountability for policy design and program delivery to lower levels of government (at times called offloading or downloading), and therefore guaranteeing differences in scope, accessibility, adequacy, and quality of like programs across jurisdictions in the country. Another involves individualizing and objectifying people as cases – treating the needs and circumstances of people narrowly by ignoring applicants' and recipients' full social and economic location (age, ancestry, gender, language skills, educational qualifications, family status, strength of the local economy, and so on), and translating their life experiences and circumstances into administrative terms and program imperatives (Fraser 1989). Encouraging market solutions is still another technique of stratification. It involves giving room for private sector measures in health and social policy, and often promoting the market economy, through incentives, to supply more adequate benefits or services to those able to afford such measures. Closely related is the process of governments privatizing, commercializing, and divesting themselves of clients and services. A study of privatization measures in family and children's services in British Columbia catalogues several such measures. These are cancelling the provision of non-statutory services; reducing the provision of some statutory services through 'bureaucratic disentitlement,' a process of modifying internal practices that exclude certain clients or increase barriers to obtaining services;[4] contracting existing and new services to nonprofits and for-profit organizations; transferring services to other jurisdictions (First Nations, school boards, and municipalities); increasing user fees for services; and 'reframing the nature of family and children's problems so that their solution lies mainly outside of the government ministry responsible for social services or outside of government entirely' (Callahan and McNiven 1988).

These technologies do not exhaust the possibilities, but the point is made: governments have at their disposal numerous practices that structure social relations, the status of groups, and their life chances. In an assortment of ways and for a variety of reasons, political and bureaucratic officials engage in structuring relationships with citizens through welfare state activities, shaping identities in workplaces, families, and communities.

For groups already marginalized in society, people experience these techniques as exercises of disciplinary power, whether in the form of initial ineligibility, subsequent disentitlement, increased regulations, enhanced surveillance and enforcement measures, or in the physical design of social service offices (Callahan and McNiven 1988; Moffatt 1999). Assessment tools in health care or community supports define public and private responsibilities, producing new kinds of segregation and surveillance. One outcome can be a falling number and proportion of legally entitled recipients actually obtaining benefits. A related outcome can be a shift to more reliance on provincial social assistance than on national social insurance programs for sickness and disability income benefits. Both outcomes call into question the meaning of universal rights of social citizenship (Gorham 1995; Turner 1986). Differential programs result in constructing different rights, obligations, and benefit levels.

A BRIEF ILLUSTRATION:
THE CANADA PENSION PLAN DISABILITY PROGRAM

To illustrate the workings of stratification in a specific social program we can consider the Canada Pension Plan Disability Program (CPP-DP). Following Max Weber, social stratification has three dimensions: legal-political, economic market, and cultural relations. In each, human agency and social struggle interact yielding multiple hierarchies. Together, these dimensions offer a useful general framework for assessing the stratification effects of an individual social program, a given policy field, or the welfare state as an entity. As well, they correspond to the three dimensions of disability politics in our analytical framework – recognition, redistribution, and representation.

The CPP-DP exhibits aspects of all three dimensions of social differentiation. As a public program, based on a 1964 constitutional amendment to permit federal action on disability benefits, the CPP contains legal and political features of stratification dealing with rules of eligibility, rights of review and appeal, and relations to other agencies of government. An amending formula governs major changes to the program's benefits, entitlement criteria, and financing arrangements, with the requirement for consent by two-thirds of the provinces representing two-thirds of the Canadian population, plus the approval of Parliament (Guest 2003).

The CPP is a social insurance program, with employees and employers making compulsory contributions to the plan to both finance it and, for workers, to establish a basis for an earned right to disability, retirement, and other stipulated benefits. There is a 'work test' of a defined attachment to the paid labour force prior to making any claims, indicating that economic market features are key elements underpinning this program. Moreover, CPP disability benefits are, to some degree, earnings-related. Consequently, on average men receive higher disability benefits than women, as a result of the gendered differences in income, family responsibilities, and work trajectories (Prince 2002a, 2008b). Furthermore, the CPP is a 'first-payer' of benefits, which means private insurance companies and provincial program officials responsible for workers' compensation and social assistance insist that a person first apply for CPP-DP benefits before they can obtain any payments from another public or private plan to which they may be entitled. This feature generates considerable tension, confusion, and anger for people seeking to claim disability insurance benefits.

The CPP-DP is an important expression and embodiment of cultural relations and identities as they pertain to impairments, illnesses, and capacities. This program is not a universal or comprehensive national program for all Canadians with disabilities whatever the cause or type of disability. The program addresses a defined group of people considered as a category of risks: employed workers between the ages of eighteen and sixty-five that, in social insurance terms, are insured against the contingency of certain mental and physical disabilities. There are no partial benefits. To qualify, a person must be determined, through a process of medical assessment, to have a severe and prolonged disability that does not allow them to pursue gainful employment. In these terms and demarcations is a particular construction of disability, ability, and eligibility – a construction very much shaped by bio-medical knowledge and experts. Also, the determination process for eligibility generates a series of social dualisms. One is between those covered and those who are not. Like any other program, this one marks off some people as entitled, in principle, because of the severity and prolonged nature of their disability, from the many others who, because their disability is deemed to be mild or moderate and is more episodic in nature perhaps, are excluded in practice. Another dualism is between those workers with intermittent work force attachments, who would not meet the work test, and those workers with more traditional employment records who do meet this test. Such dualisms might pose political challenges in efforts to build solidarity among workers with disabilities as well as in forming coalitions with other disability groups in order to mobilize and advocate for policy reforms.

The CPP-DP is a major income maintenance program for persons with disabilities, allocating more than $3 billion each year to eligible individuals and family members. But the program is much more than just about dispensing cash benefits. It is clear, even from this brief analysis, that the Canadian state's involvement (or states' involvement, since the provinces share jurisdiction for the program) in disability income support has implications for structuring values, roles, and relations tied to the market economy, health professions, and general cultural practices (Prince 2008a).

The Welfare State, Social Inequalities, and Social Inclusion

What are the prospects for reducing inequalities and advancing inclusion? I identify five such perspectives on the role of the state, its relation to social inequalities, and the possibilities for reform. These are progressive intervention, retrenching public provision, reproducing exclusions, generating contradictory effects, and renewing an active state. Each contains beliefs and assumptions about our present age, past record, and about how the welfare state tends to act as a system of status differentiation and inclusion. Each viewpoint has different adherents and therefore variations and nuances on the basic ideas. The five perspectives are presented roughly in a chronological order of developments in social policy and social theory over the past half century or more.

Progressive Intervention. This is the most optimistic perspective, or naïve its critics would claim, about the possibilities for reducing barriers, tackling inequalities and inequities, and thus widening social participation. Underlying this point of view is a belief in progress, a faith in government intervention, and a commitment to equality of opportunity. The state is not seen as part of the stratification process, but more readily as part of the solution. In many respects, this is a traditional social policy outlook. The state offers universal and targeted public services, enacts human rights, develops fair tax measures, and provides income benefits all guided by goals to relieve poverty, redistribute some resources, insure against certain risks of life, and promote community ties. The welfare state represents the institutionalization of a level of social responsibility for certain inequalities in the distribution of resources. Adherents to this perspective claim that the welfare state has in the past, and continues today to be a major contributor to the declining importance of many barriers and to the shift toward more positive attitudes about disability, race, sexuality, and other aspects of human and social development.

Retrenching Public Provision. This is a gloomy and pessimistic outlook of the state's potential to achieve many of the social security and equity goals conventionally attributed to the welfare state, including full citizenship (Turner 2001). This perspective relates to the previous one, since the pessimism is a relative frame of mind, in reaction to what many saw as a golden age of progressive intervention, with governments of late, under the influence of neo-liberalism, retreating from those commitments (Guest 2003; Martin and Torres 2004). Lois Bryson (1992: 154) links this downturn in possibilities to 'a reassertion of the ideology of inequality as those in traditionally privileged positions claw back the gains made by less-privileged groups,' whether those gains were achieved in the 1960s and 1970s or, for some groups, including persons with disabilities, more recently in the 1980s and 1990s. The result, in the dramatic language of one policy analyst, is akin to 'waging war on the welfare state' (Campeau 2004).

'The direction of social policy in Canada over the past decade,' observe Richard Schaefer and Edith Smith (2005: 225), 'has been toward a leaner, more restrictive access to government subsidies for the poor' as well as for the unemployed. Groups disproportionately affected are visible minorities, especially recent immigrants, women, and persons with disabilities. Across North America, there has been a hostile political response against social welfare recipients, while services, expenditures, and tax benefits to affluent individuals and families, as well as to corporations are conveniently overlooked (Lightman 2003). With the privatization of certain state care programs, persons with disabilities 'are not seen as worthy of investment for future return' in market terms of profit margins (McDaniel 2002: 143). As the welfare state has shrunk, there appears to be a disturbing trend toward what Susan McDaniel calls the criminalization for not caring: 'Individual responsibility is stressed, with structural inequalities either not seen or denied. A struggling lone mother, for example, caring for a disabled child with dwindling supports from the state, may be charged with neglect despite the reality that she may be doing all she possibly can with limited or no supports' (144).

Reproducing Exclusions. In this standpoint, the welfare state is directly implicated in the stratification processes of society by virtue of maintaining and aggravating inequalities, and likely creating new disparities. As one analyst expresses this view: social welfare provision 'rarely alters the relative position of people in the social hierarchy;' basically, with some variations over time and across nations, when all the social services, tax breaks, employment-based and earnings-related benefits are taken into account, welfare systems 'entrench the current social hierarchy' (Bryson 1992: 131, 154). In *The Vertical Mosaic,* recall that Porter, writing in the 1960s, found that Canada's modest welfare state at the time altered little the class and power structures of the country. Another commentator on our more recent times, states that 'social policy does not affect or address inequalities,' because that is not the primary goal of most income benefits or health and social services, and that 'even if social policy makes a difference to inequality, it does not make very much,' because of the strength of deep-rooted interests, structural relations, and divisions (Spicker 1996: 33).

Observers coming from more critical stances, be it anti-racist, feminist, or political economy, argue that social programs do, in fact, contribute to social stratification by widening social divisions, by exacerbating inequalities, and by maintaining old forms of exclusion as well as creating new forms. Disability studies, notes that medicalizing illness and impairment led to the rise of the field of rehabilitation and to health professional dominance in treatment and diagnostics, encouraged and expanded the segregation of people with certain disabilities into institutions, and thus limited self-responsibility and restricted self-determination. 'This medicalization of disability represented the establishment of an "individual" model of disability that became the professional, policy and lay orthodoxy through the twentieth century' (Barnes, Mercer, and Shakespeare 1999: 20).

Generating Contradictory Effects. Whether at the level of a single program or the overall welfare state, for a specific person or an entire client group, social policy has contradictory effects for the status of people. A classic effect occurs with social security providing much needed income benefits to a person, but simultaneously administered in a way that divides, controls, and stigmatizes the client population (Graham, Swift, and Delaney 2003; Williams, 1989). By comparing a number of policy fields, Pupo (2001) sees the welfare state as having diverse and opposing consequences for the social structure. She describes the public education system as 'reproducing inequality' in relation to the labour market, the social welfare system as 'preserving social relations,' and other social and family policy as 'promoting equality.' In short, the design elements and actual effects of social programs can be exclusionary and enabling. Identifying and explaining the occurrence of contradictory effects is a particular focus of class analysis (Naiman 2004; Panitch 1977).

In a politically strategic sense, contradictory practices can offer spaces for human agency and social action: 'While we cannot view the state *per se* as a vehicle for social change or ignore its overriding function to facilitate capital accumulation and maintain the structure of class and power under capitalism, at the same time the state inadvertently provides an avenue for resistance' (Pupo 2001: 137). Given the reality of contradictory effects by social provisions, critical policy writers reject a 'simple binary opposition of inclusion/exclusion,' choosing an approach that considers 'the way various social relations interact to create particular circumstances and specific conditions for membership of the social' (Taylor 1996: 3), all embedded in welfare state regimes with distinct logics of social stratification (Esping-Andersen 1993).

Renewing an Active State. This perspective is about restoring public faith in the power of the state and reaffirming the importance of social justice. As expressed by Duffy and Mandell (2001), the roots of poverty are found in the unequal distribution of wealth, income and work, capitalism and its pattern of booms and busts, and in gender ideologies. They view in fairly positive terms, the poverty reduction record of federal and provincial governments. A wide range of government transfer payments, social services, and 'many other measures speak to the power of governmental responses to poverty and inequality. These actions have transformed the face of poverty in Canada and alleviated considerable social suffering' (102). They acknowledge that governments' attention in the 1990s to deficit reduction stalled progress, with cutbacks and restraint, and in some instances, eroded previous achievements in reducing inequalities. On the whole, however, they maintain an underlying belief in a progressive, humanistic capacity of public action and, with other commentators (Chappell 2006; McQuaig 1999; Saul 2005), reject arguments that the nation state is powerless in the face of economic globalization. Despite his critical findings of pervasive and deep-rooted social inequality in Canadian society, Porter held to a strong personal belief 'in the creative role of politics, and in the importance of political institutions as the means through the major goals of society can be achieved' (1965: xii). More recently, another social policy analyst, after reviewing the realities of income and wealth inequality in Canada, also sees a good deal of scope for progress within economic and social structures (Lightman 2003).

There are signs of policy innovation called 'directed incrementalism,' an approach that sets bold goals and works toward them step by step over the long term, informed by a relatively more activist welfare state than in the 1980s and 1990s (Prince 2002b). Two recent examples of apparent renewal and reform are noteworthy. One, at the federal level, is the Canadian Forces Members and Veterans Re-Establishment and Compensation Act, enacted in May 2005, with a new Veterans Charter of programs and services to assist Canadian Forces' veterans and their families. This new charter includes disability compensation, rehabilitation services, and health benefits – suggesting once again that military and war service remains an effective route to social entitlements (Prince 2000; Turner 2001). The second example, at the provincial level, is the Accessibility for Ontarians with Disabilities Act, passed by the legislature in May 2005. The goal of this legislation, which has been more than a decade in the making, is to enhance significantly the accessibility of public and private sector facilities, workplaces, and practices over the next twenty years. Sector-based consultative bodies are developing enforceable mandatory standards for removing and preventing barriers, supported by a public education component and an advisory council to the government.

At the very same time, however, the Ontario government launched an appeal of a May 2005 Superior Court decision that certified parents and their children with severe disabilities as a class in legal terms, thus enabling the families collectively to sue the province for failure to provide essential supports for their children (Matyas 2005: B3). This court case and appeal by the government underscores the devastating effect of another technology of stratification: essential services not provided or under-funded can drive parents to put their children in the custody of a children's aid society so that they can access services. This story also reminds us that even when there is success on one front, there are setbacks in other realms for Canadians with disabilities.

Conclusion: The Provision/Division Dynamic

Much social science scholarship and social movement activism focuses on diversity and difference, the challenges of social cohesion and inclusion, and the importance of social capital, notions linked in the Canadian context to the mosaic image of society. 'The study of social inequality,' one sociologist comments, 'has withdrawn to politically less risky and intellectually less contested terrain' (Baldus 2004: 578). Comparatively less attention is paid, it seems, to discrimination and oppression or to the necessity of social struggles for rights to participation and membership. Social stratification, in comparison to the vocabulary of social differentiation, denotes divisions, hierarchies, and economic, political, and cultural inequalities, hence, Porter's evocative phrase, the *vertical* mosaic, a metaphor that empirically captures significant status inequalities in Canadian society today along ethnic and racial lines (Lian and Matthews 1998).

The idea of social stratification, with its historic concerns with community, hierarchical divisions, and inequalities, has genuine analytical benefit for social policy and disability studies. The concept also has normative and political value in better understanding the potential of tackling inequalities and advancing inclusion of marginal groups in society, especially when we adopt the view that social programs and the welfare state are systems of stratification in their own right. Behind the term social stratification, is a way of thinking and looking.[5] It draws attention to the distribution of symbolic resources (Breton 1984) in addition to material resources; to the dynamics and interplay of political, economic market, and cultural relations; and, to the systemic and macro-level of a community or nation. Research on inequalities that concentrates on diversity, echoed by a governmental discourse that celebrates social, cultural, and regional differences, encourages a decentralization of thought and inquiry about inequality and thus threatens limiting the scope for understanding 'the organization of our society as a whole' (Baldus 2004: 578; see also Fraser 2000).

All too frequently, studies on stratification in contemporary societies overlook disability. We know however, that disablement features in today's struggles over full citizenship, individual dignity, group recognition, and social provisions. Impairment-related dimensions of inequality are considerable social forces deserving more critical and empirical analysis. From a disability perspective, the significance of stratification is that it alerts us to pay as much attention to social division, inequality, and mobility as policy makers appear to be giving to social capital, cohesion, and inclusion. We cannot understand the latter, or hope to move toward attaining them in any authentic way without addressing honestly the former issues of redistribution.

There is a necessary interplay between social programs and social stratification, a *provision/division* dynamic. Social provision and social division are interrelated in practice through discourse and everyday lived experience. Welfare state programs are not neutral about inequality and social status; depending on one's perspective on the role of the state in Canada, social policy can make important contributions to alleviating disadvantages and reducing barriers or reproducing and aggravating inequalities. What is not in dispute is that social policy is involved in ranking groups of people and allocating economic-material, political-legal, and symbolic-cultural resources. Along with the capitalist market economy and social class, the state's actions and inactions are significant determinants of stratification. Where there is social policy and program provision – be it in health, education, income support, housing, or community care – there always is social differentiation and division.

Governments employ a range of technologies of stratification that evaluate, rank, label, and monitor groups of people. The importance of any given technique depends on the particular context, historical period, and political setting, among other probable factors. With cutbacks and privatization in the 1980s and 1990s in many jurisdictions, and continued restraints today, a substantial shift in the actual and perceived mixture of technologies took place. Perhaps more recently, we are witnessing the return of some former techniques, with a shift back toward more general programs and less severe targeting with the reinvestment of funds and the investment of new resources into certain services and benefits. Nevertheless, all of these technologies, as Foucault might say, are dangerous even if they are not intrinsically bad: the lesson is to be socially vigilant and politically active in discerning the major threats and resisting (Tremain 2005).

Thinking of social policy as a stratification system is useful as long as there is proper attention to other structural forces of the larger capitalist economy, civil society, and international politics that surround the nation state and sub-national governments. Otherwise, undue weight will be placed on social programs, invariably making them the scapegoat for not solving homelessness, ending poverty, or preventing ableism. Certainly, the state has a key role to play in addressing all these problems, and countless others, but we must not divert our gaze from the fundamental power of other institutions, and the inequalities produced and contained within them.

PART TWO

Capacities, Engagements, and Inclusions

4 Mainstreaming Disabilities in Public Policies

Alongside citizenship, social inclusion is a flagship concept in disability politics, associated with the active participation of persons with disabilities in all life domains. Do we have the necessary societal indicators and information sets to track and assess performance in advancing inclusion for Canadians with disabilities? In comparison to feminist studies on gender mainstreaming strategies (Grace 1997; Hankivsky 2007; Squires 2007), little exists on the concept of mainstreaming in relation to disability issues and policies. A recent international report observes, 'There is currently no officially accepted definition of mainstreaming disability' (United Nations 2008: 3). This chapter therefore offers a preliminary account in the context of federal policy making, and considers lessons from Canadian and international experience with gender mainstreaming initiatives. I argue that disability mainstreaming is a meaningful addition to existing accountability frameworks. Macro-policy indicators enhance the capacity to assess the performance of the Government of Canada's disability-related programs and services. A disability lens offers new opportunities for some and new demands on others in this policy community. Relating a national social inclusion index to this vision of citizenship could guide the selection of variables measured and the values attached to them. Likewise, an inclusion index on disability that incorporates a qualitative element can provide insights into what persons with disabilities feel are the effect of different factors on their sense of inclusion in society.

Mainstreaming Disability

In disability policy and practice, the concept of mainstreaming arose in the 1960s and 1970s in the context of education for children and youth with significant physical disabilities and mental retardation, now referred to as developmental or intellectual disabilities. More recent decades have witnessed the drive for the deinstitutionalization of persons with disabilities and provision for their support within local communities. In the women's movement, ideas on gender main-streaming arose in the 1990s in relation to international agencies and transnational networks of women's organizations for advancing gender equality. In brief, gender mainstreaming refers to a set of tech-niques and processes for ensuring the systematic consideration of a gender perspective in policy making across the whole of government, including program evaluations, public consultations, and budgeting decisions. In this same way, I will speak of disability mainstreaming as a theory and set of practices only just emerging in Canada.

Conceptually, disability mainstreaming encompasses a mixture of techniques for instituting equality for persons with disabilities in Canadian society by inserting norms of access and inclusion in policy processes of governments and public sector agencies. Of course, other policy measures exist for advancing the equality of persons with dis-abilities. There are legal measures and affirmative action initiatives, most notably human rights legislation with anti-discrimination and reasonable accommodation provisions, the Charter of Rights and Free-doms, employment equity laws federally and provincially in Quebec and, more recently, accessibility laws in a few jurisdictions. There are, as well, various public services that ostensibly offer benefits and opportunities generally to the whole population, although access can be a problem for some groups and individuals.

But, the focus of this chapter is three techniques of disability main-streaming: a social inclusion index with disaggregated disability-related statistics, a disability policy lens, and disability oriented budget statements for reporting on expenditures and tax measures with a particular bearing on individuals and families living with dis-abilities. Each technique involves particular resources and each implies certain identities of people with disabilities. Table 4.1 provides an overview of these tools for disability mainstreaming.

While each is distinctive, all three tools focus on policy development work and potentially are government-wide in scope and effect. The immediate goal of disability mainstreaming is to routinely anticipate impacts on individuals with disabilities and their families, and to alle-viate problems such as the provision/division dynamic (as discussed in chapter 3). The ultimate goal is to advance the access and well-being

Table 4.1
Policy techniques for disability mainstreaming

Technique	Key characteristics	Images of persons with disabilities
Social inclusion indicators	Informative and monitoring	Demographic categories with socio-economic status
Disability policy lens	Inclusive and analytical	Social group with diverse experiences and inequalities
Budget statements	Accountable and committed	Program recipients, revenue contributors, economic actors such as consumers and workers

of Canadians with disabilities and to attain equality with Canadians living without disabilities. Can such strategies as an index of inclusion usefully contribute to establishing a national focal point for concerted action on disability issues? What are the merits, challenges, and limitations of producing a single overall index of inclusion, and how might it be constructed? What lessons come from other Canadian and international reporting frameworks, in particular gender issues and the literature on women's budgets, gender lens analysis, and gender equality indicators?

Social indicators and outcome measures developed for research and policy development have a number of possibilities. A fundamental one that pertains to agenda setting is attracting public attention, plus raising awareness and understanding of issues of disablement and impairments in Canada. A second possible benefit is involving the disability community, and other partners, in the planning, development, and review of indicators, policies, and programs. Prompting governmental action is a third benefit, the result of monitoring the progress or otherwise of state and societal initiatives for advancing the full participation of all Canadians. A fourth potential benefit is to encourage a horizontal cross-governmental approach to collaborative and coherent action on disability policies and programs, in turn, providing a basis for the design of measures that effectively remove real barriers and discriminatory practices facing persons with disabilities. Crucial in light of the analysis in chapter 1, a longer-term outcome would be attitudinal shifts among the general public and policy makers, so that persons with disabilities are respected as fellow citizens.

At the same time, there are challenges with constructing, using, and interpreting social indicators. Aside from important design and measurement issues, struggles can arise in disentangling the net contribution of public service programs from other factors in economic and social well-being, in attributing results to federal social programs and expenditures as compared to provincial or territorial efforts, and in engaging the general public or specific client groups in these processes (EKOS 1998). Despite these challenges, citizens are increasingly calling for publicly reported measures of progress on economic and social programs. There is also a renewed interest in and activity on social indicators among academics, civil society organizations, and governmental agencies.

Political Context

Certain trends in Canada's general political environment need to be understood to appreciate the context for and feasibility of strategic policy tools for social inclusion. One trend is the evolving thinking on disability policy in recent years (Bickenbach 1993; Lepofsky 2004; Rioux and Bach 1994; Titchkosky 2001). The contemporary emphasis on approaching disability issues in terms of citizenship, equality rights, and inclusion had clear and passionate expression by the Federal Task Force on Disability Issues report, *Equal Citizenship for Canadians with Disabilities: The Will to Act* (Canada 1996a). This report argued strongly for a renewed leadership role by the Government of Canada on disability issues.

A second trend is the enunciation of collaborative statements on a disability policy framework by federal, provincial, and territorial social service ministers and governments. In 1998, the federal government, in partnership with provinces and territories, published *In Unison: A Canadian Approach to Disability Issues* (Canada 1998), expressing a shared vision of promoting the full participation of persons with disabilities in all segments of Canadian life. In 1999, the federal government issued its own disability agenda, called *Future Directions*, and first ministers (except Quebec) signed the *Framework to Improve the Social Union for Canadians*. In 2001, a second edition of the shared intergovernmental vision on disability issues, *In Unison 2000*, was released (Canada 2001).

Increased expectations by the community for more open, accountable, and effective public services, is a third noteworthy trend. We can observe increased attention by governments to setting measurable goals, defining indicators and preferred outcomes, monitoring performance and progress, and then reporting results to the public on a regular basis (Jennissen, Prince, and Schwartz 2000; Orsini and Smith 2007a; Torjman 1999). A basic purpose of these sorts of evaluations is to produce evidence-based results, discern best practices, or at least determine what works and what does not work in regard to programs and service delivery mechanisms. At the level of a department or entire government, evaluations can involve drawing fundamental lessons about the role and capacity of the state in addressing social issues and community needs.

To be truly strategic, disability policy must be long term in outlook, comprehensive in perspective, and consultative in policy development. A strategic approach by the Canadian state requires a horizontal method to governing the disability agenda. This requires systematically addressing and coordinating the connections between programs and organizations within and across governments. This would be assisted by the use of an access or 'disability lens' by federal officials (Echenberg with Valentine 2001) in concert with representatives of community organizations. Reporting on and assessing the aggregates of taxing, spending, and legislating from the perspective of the government as a whole and the overall disability agenda is another element in a strategic framework. So, too, might be a discussion of the preferred relationships (and division of roles) among the federal government and Aboriginal, provincial, territorial, and urban governments. Timely, reliable information on program indicators linked to societal indicators would greatly facilitate future dialogues. Moreover, such information would help ensure that a social perspective on disability routinely informed public policy making (Barnes and Mercer 2003; Cameron and Valentine 2001; McColl et al. 2006).

A Canadian Index on Social Inclusion

In contemplating where federal reporting on disability issues is at, and what reforms might be added in future reports, one possibility is the construction of a summary index on social inclusion. A summary index combines a range of social or economic dimensions of a given phenomenon, measured by various indicators, into one single measure. As a macro or aggregate indicator, a summary index measures a major aspect of social well-being in society. Whereas micro indicators seek to monitor the effects of specific programs on particular groups or conditions, macro indicators seek 'to assess where we stand and are going with respect to our values and goals' (Noll 1996: 2). In the context of Canadian disability policy, an aggregate index would aim to measure the level and distribution of inclusion in society, with advancing the inclusion of persons with disabilities recognized as a central element in the larger process of realizing full citizenship.

Interest is growing about such macro social indices in Canada and elsewhere. Examples include the United Nations Development Programme's Human Development Index, published in an annual report since 1990 (United Nations 2002), Economic Gender Equality Indicators (Status of Women Canada 1997), Genuine Progress Index (Osberg and Sharpe 2003), the Index of Economic Well-Being (Osberg 2001), the Early Childhood Education and Care Community Indicators Project (Campaign 2000), and the Personal Security Index (Canadian Council on Social Development 2003).

A composite social index has desirable qualities and distinct shortcomings. Advantages are that a single index is a useful way to observe trends that can be easily communicated; it can compare trends across jurisdictions; and it could be disaggregated by age, sex, education, and income, among other possible dimensions. In turn, shortcomings include the lack of agreement on what variables should be included in the composite and on how the variables should be combined, that is, the relative weight of each; there is the problem of multiple interpretations of what does a rising or falling index mean for particular groups in society, except that overall social inclusion is up or down; and composite indexes are not usually based on a conceptual framework for policy making (Human Resources Development Canada 1997).

Despite these limitations, the development of an aggregate index on inclusion that compares a bundle of actual social conditions with authoritative goal statements fits with a pan-Canadian approach to policy issues and reinforces a citizenship perspective on disability (Canada 1996a; Council of Canadians with Disabilities 1999). The case for a summary index also rests on the empirical reality that human rights in all their facets – civil, cultural, economic, political, and social – are multidimensional and interdependent in practice, and unless monitored in a comprehensive way, the outcome for Canadians with disabilities will continue to be 'citizenship by instalments' (Prince 2001b). The United Nations Convention on the Rights of Persons with Disabilities, which came into effect as an international treaty in 2007, underscores this point. Furthermore, an index of social inclusion 'may help citizens to organize their perceptions of social and economic outcomes and thereby help them make better political and public policy decisions ... affecting public policy is the whole point of constructing an index of society's well-being' (Osberg and Sharpe 2003: 22).

Social indicators can be 'subjective' or 'objective' in the nature of information. Subjective social indicators rely on individual perceptions and personal evaluations of social conditions, commonly reported through surveys in terms of life satisfaction or job satisfaction. So-called objective social indicators rest on administrative statistics collected through public agencies, such as the unemployment rate, poverty rate, and mortality rate (Doern, Maslove, and Prince 1988; Noll 1996). In this context, if a single aggregate index on inclusion for persons with disabilities is worth considering, what mix of objective and subjective indicators might be included, if a mix at all? If the summary index were on well-being or quality of life, rather than social inclusion, then the emphasis would seem to be appropriately placed on subjective indicators to monitor and report on individual assessments of satisfaction. On the other hand, a social or environmental model of disability suggests that objective indicators – with their emphasis on living conditions, institutional processes, and opportunity structures – would be the preferred type of indicator to use. Inclusion and citizenship are not just in the eye of the beholder; they are relational phenomenon and behind the perception of individuals are cultural, political, and other external factors that present obstacles and possibilities to persons with disabilities.

Whatever specific measures are included in a national social inclusion index, to make the index meaningful to the public and policy makers, the measures must be linked to disability policy objectives enunciated by federal, provincial, and territorial governments. Lars Osberg explains:

> Any summary index of social progress must therefore specify a list of social issues and find a way of weighing the relative importance of improvement or deterioration in each potential social and economic outcome for all persons – that is, a method of aggregating outcomes over individuals and across types of outcomes. (2001: 24)

For the idea of social progress in Canada, for instance, Osberg proposes that the measure be the percentage of citizens who actually enjoy all their basic human rights as expressed in international and domestic constitutional, legislative, and legal systems. It would seem reasonable that a concept of inclusion for persons with disabilities would also contain economic and social dimensions (Barnes and Mercer 2003) to get at issues of cultural misrecognition and the mal-distribution of resources.

A single index of social inclusion, if deemed worth implementing, should be designed to apply to any and all groups within society. There are good reasons for adopting a general index on social inclusion, one that could include measures and disaggregated data that specifically addresses issues of disability. The case for a general index rests on the belief that most factors that impact social inclusion and cohesion are widespread across groups, communities, and society: disposable income, employment, health care, education, housing, other aspects of the physically built environment, and quality of life. Likewise, most outcomes that illustrate social inclusion – such as participation in social networks, voluntarism, the labour force, community affairs, and political activities – are general conditions (Beauvais and Jenson 2002; CCSD 2000). Indicators of these conditions can be monitored and disaggregated by disability status, for example, from the Survey on Labour and Income Dynamics. By tracking trends of social well-being, cohesion, or inclusion for the overall population, one can avoid segregating groups and issues into data silos. More positively, a composite index on inclusion for all Canadians affirms that inclusion concerns society as a whole. As well, a national index on inclusion, with the corresponding data set, could encourage a more preventative and integrated approach to policy rather than the traditional ameliorative and piecemeal approach.

For successfully constructing a macro-index there are certain prerequisites. No matter what indicators are used to add up, the number of indicators cannot be too many and the link of the indicators to the overall idea of inclusion must not be too imprecise or the information will not be user-friendly. As two political economists express it, '"Keep it Simple" is a useful slogan in index construction, and the constraint of use in the public debate means that it is crucial for an index of well-being to have an intuitive justification that can be easily communicated' (Osberg and Sharpe 2003: 22). Comprehensive statistical sources readily available on a timely manner, adequate resources available for conceptual and analytical work, and a healthy appreciation of the inherent difficulties and limitations of measurement are preconditions for building effective aggregate social indicators. Still another set of crucial prerequisites is that there be a solid basis of political consensus about the broad societal goals in which disability policy should strive, about what constitutes social inclusion for persons with disabilities, and about what criteria are relevant for tracking and understanding social inclusion in both its beneficial and detrimental dimensions (Noll 1996: 5).

If only economy-wide or society-wide aggregates are used, they are insensitive to trends in the living conditions and experiences of specific groups in the population. Whatever the eventual scope and content of an index (or indices) on social inclusion, 'the data should be sensitive to the need for disaggregating (e.g. by region, age, sex, minority status, socio-economic status, etc) and the data should be collected as relevant to different levels of analysis (e.g. groups, institutions, the national level)' (CCSD 2000: 6).

Perhaps an initial approach is to recognize that the conception of inclusion be based upon human rights, equality of opportunities, and full citizenship. The inclusion of persons with disabilities in Canadian society is a broad concept embracing opportunities for involvement in 'all aspects of social, economic, political and cultural life that impact on how persons with disabilities are valued,' as well as 'recognition of rights in the justice system and by governments' (Beatty 2003: 16, 2). A definition of social inclusion by the Canadian Council on Social Development adds additional aspects – 'active participation in society and broad equality of access to opportunities to develop individual talents, capacities and capabilities' (CCSD 2000: 5). Another critical aspect is the equal respect and positive recognition and acceptance of persons with disabilities. This last feature points out cultural recognition and the symbolic side of inclusion (Breton 1984; Taylor 1992). Undoubtedly, there is important additional conceptual and theoretical work called for in better understanding the social inclusion of persons with disabilities as a lived experience and as a policy goal.

Another lesson to keep in mind while addressing the issue is to appreciate that there will be measurement challenges: 'the real objective in the measurement of social and economic rights is reliable comparisons over time, or over jurisdictions, rather than absolute accuracy in estimating the level at a particular place or time' (Osberg 2001: 33). A final lesson concerns the merit of combining qualitative and quantitative data in any such reporting framework. In the words of a social policy think tank, 'Perceptions and values are clearly an important element of social cohesion, and these are not reducible to objective socio-economic conditions. Perceptions can be usefully compared to reported conditions and outcomes recognising that both are important' (CCSD 2000: 6).

A Disability Lens and Disability Budget Reports

A disability lens (also called an access and inclusion lens) and a disability budget (a disability-responsive expenditure and revenue budget) are two horizontal policy tools of relevance to advancing the inclusion of persons with disabilities. Both are tools to incorporate the views and experiences of persons with disabilities into policies, programs, and services, and to ensure that disability-related considerations are an integral part of the policy development and resource allocation processes of government.

A disability lens has been promised by federal administrations since the 1980s. In principle, an access and inclusion lens has various purposes. First, to ensure that persons with disabilities are included in policy and program planning and program implementation; second, to identify and clarify important issues affecting the well-being of persons with disabilities; third, to help increase awareness of disability issues among policy and program management officials in government; and, fourth, to assess in a consistent manner the likely impacts of all proposed measures submitted to cabinet and to Treasury Board to ensure that such initiatives are barrier-free and have no other negative effects on people with disabilities. A fifth purpose is to identify gaps in existing legislation, policy, program, and services; and, last, a disability lens is said to assist in creating initiatives reflective of the human rights and fundamental freedoms and the needs of persons with disabilities, thereby advancing a citizenship approach to disability.

'Ultimately, access and inclusion lenses require a change in the way initiatives are planned, formulated and put into effect. It requires recognition of the differing requirements of those who need, for example, additional supports or accommodation to benefit from programs or policy and that "mainstreaming" does not necessarily mean equal results' (Canada 2000b: 2).

In addition, two Canadian social policy analysts view a disability lens 'as a tool for a government to determine whether existing and new programs, policies and laws have any disproportionate negative implications for persons with disabilities' (Echenberg with Valentine 2001: 2). By making visible discriminatory practices against persons with disabilities and their families, a disability lens could also direct attention and action toward the social/environmental facets of disability and not simply those related to functional limitations. An access and inclusion lens can be one of several important parts in a government's disability strategy 'because it integrates the particular and unique concerns of persons with disabilities at the level of policy and program development and analysis – rather than, as an add-on to existing policy and program frameworks' (2).

Changes to federal state structures are necessary to accompany the successful implementation of mainstreaming disability considerations. Organizational reform ideas include the creation of a joint working group of disability community and government representatives, a national advisory council on disability issues with members recommended by the prime minister and appointed by Parliament, and a commissioner for Canadians with disabilities as a federal officer of Parliament. Reforms to governance arrangements are critical to enhancing accountabilities and results by governments for disability policies and programs (Prince 2001c, 2002c).

The rudiments of a disability budget, providing an overview of the Canadian government's major disability-related programs, have been published since 2002 in federal reports on disability. This budget statement lists about twenty-five initiatives, grouped under several outcome areas, with both direct spending programs and tax support measures included. With this disability-related budget statement, the government conveys three messages. One is that the total expenditures of several billion dollars for a given fiscal year represent a considerable commitment. A second is that this commitment of resources has been growing over the past several years, most notably through tax assistance measures. A third is that these substantial investments are made available by federal government in order to meet the needs of persons with disabilities.

These disability-related budget statements do not put individual costs or the total expenditures into a context of federal social spending in general or of the overall federal budget for that year. As a snapshot, no historical information is given in constant dollars, capturing any enhancements, freezes, and cutbacks that could give a sense of the real value of program benefits over time to Canadians with disabilities. No information is given on the number of beneficiaries by programs, although one does get a rough idea of the clientele (for example, seniors, veterans, students with disabilities, Aboriginal peoples, athletes with disabilities, persons with disabilities who are seeking work, and employees with short-term illnesses or with severe and prolonged disabilities). Disability groups and advocates complain that the spending figures tallied exaggerate the genuine level of federal investment, since it is employees and employers, through payroll contributions, who fully fund Employment Insurance (EI) sickness benefits and the Canada Pension Plan (CPP) disability benefits, with no funds from the general revenues of government. If we remove the CPP and EI expenditures from the budget statement, then total federal spending on disability-related benefits and services drops dramatically.

What is the purpose of a disability budget statement in the public accounts of governments? For several reasons, government budgets ought to display their disability-related activities and their consequences for persons living with disabilities. Government budgets and their associated economic, social, and fiscal policies are commonly presented, in an implicit fashion, as 'disability-neutral.' Major policy decisions, and most public services and benefits are not seen as specifically directed at either persons with disabilities or persons without disabilities, but rather intended for all eligible clients or citizens in general. Still, as economists, feminists, and political scientists have long argued, budgets symbolize and help shape in certain ways, and not others, significant roles and relationships in the economy and community (Budlender et al. 2002; Doern, Maslove, and Prince 1988; Elson 2006).

Given that public budgets are sites for power relations and social values, the allocation of resources and the provision of programs cannot be assumed to benefit equally all groups in society. A careful assessment of the allocation and impact of budget resources is essential if we are to properly understand their tangible and potential role in advancing social inclusion. Expressed another way, a disability-neutral or disability-silent budget may seem unbiased and even-handed, but might actually be unfair in the treatment of Canadians with different resources and responsibilities, along with different opportunities and obstacles. This is where information from statistical sources is crucial for inserting relevant data on the needs and capacities, and public and private support arrangements for Canadians with disabilities.

A related critique, expressed by Harry Beatty, is that 'the real problem with the "big number" [on federal disability-related benefits and programs] is that it confuses spending with finding solutions. If the goal is to understand disability policy better, it is much better to keep a consistent and clear focus on outcomes and indicators, rather than bringing [in] issues of overall government spending' (Beatty 2003: 33). Disability-related budget statements, to be useful and insightful, should contain information on the tax measures and expenditure programs that directly relate to persons with disabilities and/or to those persons caring for them. Information could report on the average amounts and ranges of benefits received by diverse groups of persons with disabilities, such as by age, gender, province, and income class. The consequences of recently conducted program reviews for diverse groups of persons with disabilities also should be included, along with forecasts of what program investments would look like with no changes in policy. As well, tools for disability-sensitive analyses of budgets should include analysis of macro-economic policies and the budget decision making processes themselves (Elson 2006).

Lessons from Gender Mainstreaming

Over recent decades, reforms in many countries have sought to make policy making, public administration, and services more gender-sensitive and responsive (Hankivsky 2007; Squires 2007). Collectively, these reforms represent gender mainstreaming, which is defined as follows:

> Mainstreaming a gender perspective is the process of assessing the implications for women and men of any planned action, including legislation, policies or programmes, in any area and at all levels. It is a strategy for making women as well as men's concerns and experiences an integral dimension in the design, implementation, monitoring and evaluation of policies and programmes in all political, economic, and societal spheres so that women and men benefit equally and inequality is not perpetuated. The ultimate goal is to achieve gender equity. (Budlender et al. 2002: 178)

Tools for gender mainstreaming include the formation of women's bureaus and advisory councils, the introduction of gender policy lenses, gender budget analyses, and gender impact assessments. These gender-sensitive approaches to public administration seek 'to draw attention precisely to the gendered structuring of people's lives and to emphasise the importance of taking this reality explicitly [and routinely] into account in developing and implementing policy' so as to noticeably improve the social and economic status of diverse groups of women (Teghtsoonian 2004: 268).

Across varied jurisdictions, assessments of gender mainstreaming efforts in practice suggest modest impacts at best. The Government of Canada introduced a policy requiring the use of gender-based analysis for the development of policies and legislation in the 1990s. In support of this government-wide initiative, the Status of Women produced a guide for policy makers in the federal public service (Canada 1996b; Grace 1997). In a review of the implementation of this policy, Sandra Burt and Sonya Hardman conclude:

> If the policy context includes economic restructuring, balanced budgets, tax cuts, and globalization, and if these approaches generally disadvantage women, the application of gender-based analysis to specific policy initiatives will have only a very limited impact. Indeed, gender-based analysis may add the veneer of legitimacy to measures that do not contribute to women's well-being. (2001: 210)

A study of liberal and social democratic administrations in North America and Britain reports evidence that 'disconfirms expectations that more gender-sensitive public policy would necessarily follow from the presence of an active, mobilized female electorate, and from growing numbers of female decision-makers.' Indeed, 'female political elites, including avowed feminists, appeared complicit in the making of what were on the surface "gender-neutral" policies, which turned out on closer inspection to be highly gendered or, at best, gender-denying' (Bashevkin 2002: 15).

Gender mainstreaming activities by the Ministry of Women's Affairs in Aotearoa/New Zealand used three strategies to incorporate gender analyses into the work of government departments:

1 a voluntary, ad hoc approach that relies on persuasion and exhortation;
2 a regulatory approach requiring that a gender analysis be included in papers submitted to cabinet; and
3 a management approach that articulates, through performance management frameworks of individual government departments,

explicit expectations, incentives and/or penalties designed to ensure the incorporation of gender analysis into routine policy work (Teghtsoonian 2004: 274–5).

The actual effectiveness of these approaches is sobering: while all three approaches have been pursued 'their impact across government has been neither deeply-rooted nor widespread' (Teghtsoonian 2004: 275). Whichever approach tried – the voluntary, the compulsory, or the structured approach embedded in administrative systems – none has produced a substantial and ongoing incorporation of gender analysis into conventional approaches to policy work by government.

Feminist writers identify a range of factors as contributing to the limited influence of gender mainstreaming initiatives. Certainly, one factor is the recent context of government restraint and downsizing, including the retrenchment of women's bureaus themselves. Another widely noted factor is economic globalization and restructuring in support of enhanced productivity and market competitiveness. Coupled with these factors is the 'new public management' ethos, introduced in the bureaucracies of many countries, that privileges efficiency and private sector values over equity and social justice. Each of these factors represents important aspects of neo-liberalism. Two additional factors reflect classical features of complex organizations and bureaucratic behaviour. One of these further constraining factors is the intrinsic tension between the reformist and challenging aims and techniques of gender changes and the established procedures of government executives and bureaucracies. Moreover, public service structures rooted in vertical portfolios of program activities and ministerial accountabilities consequently often frustrate the ability to promote an integrated and horizontal cross-departmental approach to gender mainstreaming (Burt and Hardman 2001; Grace 1997).

A final observation on the future of gender mainstreaming, made by Kathy Teghtsoonian, highlights the trade-off between having influence within government and holding true to the aspirations of a progressive social movement:

[T]here is a belief that gender analysis mainstreaming is more likely to succeed to the extent that it can be presented as congruent with, and supportive of, the norms and values underpinning existing practices within the public service. Where these norms privilege a value-neutral and depoliticised approach to policy analysis, gender analysis initiatives must move away from their feminist roots in order to emulate more closely established and accepted practices. In so doing, there is a risk that gender analysis will become a mere technical tool rather than an instrument for change. Thus in a political context in which the government's policy agenda is informed by neoliberal commitments, advocates and practitioners of gender analysis must walk a thin line between framing arguments in terms which can be 'heard' and ensuring that the wellbeing of diverse groups of women remains at the heart of gendered policy analysis and the tools and strategies designed to support it.

Given the enormous challenge that gender analysis, properly done, poses to the existing distribution of resources and power, and in light of the deep-seated resistance to such change that is apparent, sustained pressure exerted from outside government may be crucial in generating the political will that appears to be necessary if gender analysis mainstreaming is to be implemented successfully. (2004: 281)

On this last point, Olga Hankivsky identifies three elements for effective gender mainstreaming: institutionalized gender policy machinery in government with a clear mandate, an active women's movement with adequate capacity and effective linkages with governments, and, within academe, vigorous gender research and theorizing on intersecting social inequalities (Hankivsky 2007).

Drawing on these lessons from mainstreaming gender, basic principles of mainstreaming disability likely include the following:

- Responsibility for implementing the mainstreaming strategy is system-wide, and rests at the highest levels within agencies;
- Accountability mechanisms adequate for monitoring progress;
- Identification of issues and problems across all areas of activity are such that differences and disparities between persons with and without disabilities can be diagnosed;
- Allocation of adequate resources for mainstreaming (and the clear political will to do so) – including additional financial and human resources – for translation of the concept into practice;
- Participation of persons with disabilities at all levels of decision making that is broad and equitable;
- Continuation of targeted, disability-specific policies and programs and positive legislation – and the continuation of disability units and commissioners (United Nations 2008: 15);

- Engagement with the Canadian state at all levels of governance by a well supported disability community;
- Research, empirical and theoretical, in disability studies and related fields of inquiry on interactions among various markers of social division and impairments.

Gender mainstreaming initiatives offer several lessons for disability organizations, parliamentarians, disability issue offices, program analysts, and service providers. It also poses questions of the relative merits of pursuing a gender mainstreaming approach versus adopting a 'diversity mainstreaming' approach that includes an intersectional analysis of gender in relation to multiple social categories such as age, class, ethnicity, and sexuality (Hankivsky 2007; Squires 2007).

Mainstreaming Disability Reforms: A Preliminary Assessment

As a theoretical concept and set of actual practices, mainstreaming disability is underdeveloped in Canada. Take-up of these mainstreaming reforms by federal and provincial governments is slow and uneven. Nationally and in some provinces there have been considerable investments in building a knowledge base on disability issues through a number of population surveys (see chapter 1). The federal government produces reports that provide basic information across the public service on programs, although it is largely descriptive in nature with little evaluative material that would shed light on results and the trajectory of reforms. While governments announce disability plans and strategies, often missing from these are concrete measures for tracking policy outcomes (Torjman 1999; United Nations 2008). A related mainstreaming measure is the formation of disability offices in or attached to governments. These offices have facilitated consultations with disability activist leaders and research specialists but the diffusion of a disability-oriented access and inclusion perspective into general policy processes seems cursory and intermittent. In general, disability mainstreaming is not practised comprehensively and systematically in policy development processes of Canadian governments.

Certain factors limit the impact of disability governance reforms. Resource constraints within government and, far more seriously, within the disability community – in the form of finances, personnel, information, and time – restrict the ability to generate and examine the data required to support disability sensitive policy analyses and evaluations. Cautious tendencies of bureaucratic agencies and government officials lead to an emphasis of disability mainstreaming as a way to improve the effectiveness of existing programs and services, and to avoid, or certainly downplay, an approach that would highlight the stratifying processes and effects of social structures and public programs. As well, the mingled and mangled beliefs of Canadians toward issues of inclusion and persons with disabilities (Overboe 2007), weaken the level of clear political pressure and support for disability mainstreaming and related equality measures.

Still, impacts are detectable. One is the involvement of disability academics, researchers, and consultants in governmental processes around developing information systems, designing or amending survey instruments, and reviewing draft reports. This may represent what Judith Squires (2007: 143) calls the 'democratization of expertise' in relation to mainstreaming strategies, enabling actors from disability groups and networks to convey their ideas, perspectives, and knowledge into policy processes.

A second impact is that governments undertaking disability-related knowledge production are generating various forms of information guided by considerations of access and inclusion, surfacing disability as an issue and persons with disabilities as social and economic categories for analysis. Within general measures of social well-being, disaggregated statistics on disability are vital for comparing over time the social conditions of persons with disabilities to those without disabilities. Disaggregated statistics are important also for recognizing differences associated with disabilities, so that disability is not a single category of essential traits thus isolating disability from general standards of citizenship. This growing body of data is a strategic resource for policy entrepreneurs and social movement activists to marshal arguments and mobilize campaigns informed by empirical data. This sort of 'hard evidence' seems unavoidable and indispensable for influencing policy debates and program designs (McColl et al. 2006).

Over time, we might see a contribution of these mainstreaming mechanisms to shaping the dominant frame of policy thinking by government advisors and decision makers. Even dominant policy models, such as the medical model of disability, are not static or wholly internally consistent, allowing spaces for challenges and changes by appeals to equality and a socio-political orientation to disablement.

Disability mainstreaming techniques will not radically transform the role of the state. These tools are modest opportunities for some members of the disability community to inject an access and inclusion perspective to collecting data, scanning for societal trends and issues, and analysing policies and programs. Mainstreaming tools are supplements to, not substitutes for, other measures for advancing the inclusion of Canadians with disabilities. Disability mainstreaming is complementary to reasonable accommodation, employment equity, disability-related tax credits, and other positive measures for persons with disabilities. Guided by the values of equality and equity, a social inclusion agenda must comprise two policy tracks: generic initiatives and rights for all members of the political community, plus specific measures that tackle structural inequalities and ableist beliefs confronting people living with disabilities. This is one response, at least, to the question of disability mainstreaming versus diversity mainstreaming.

Conclusion

Mainstreaming disability aims at building commitment and awareness of decision makers on disability, addressing barriers facing persons with disabilities, prohibiting discrimination and avoiding other negative consequences, and thus promoting public access and community inclusion. A number of tools are available for systematically addressing these goals.

A national index of social inclusion, a disability lens, and disability budgets are helpful additions to public policy making and public accountabilities. Macro-level social indicators enhance both a government's and the disability community's capacity to track, assess, and report on the performance of the federal government's disability-related programs and services. To be effective, disability mainstreaming requires the undertaking of four steps: the production of relevant knowledge, consideration of policies and their effects on the circumstances and capacities of persons with disabilities, formation of policy options and recommendations for tackling barriers and providing the necessary resources for advancing inclusion, and the adoption and implementation of equality strategies. Government insiders and community activists stress different aspects of mainstreaming. Government officials give emphasis to the steps of data collection and some research analysis, whereas disability groups look to the promise of a government-wide access and inclusion perspective on all major policy areas and a national plan of action, a topic I return to in chapter 9.

Two visions of mainstreaming disability are at play here, one as social research, the other as social reform. To date, the modest implementation of mainstreaming disability means that the more significant elements of public policy agendas for advancing inclusion and access are federal and provincial human rights regimes, affirmative action measures around employment, and general programs in the areas of education, health, and social security. Understood as a strategy of social reform aimed at advancing equality for a disadvantaged group, it implies the mainstreaming of persons with disabilities into organizational positions and decision-making processes along with mainstreaming disability perspectives into governmental agendas. In short, mainstreaming disability means systematically taking into account the needs and ideas of people with disabilities in the design, delivery, and evaluation of all public policies and programs.

Future federal reports on disability need to present explicitly the logic model of immediate, intermediate, and ultimate goals that inform the policy agenda and connect those with the results measured. Along these lines, the Council of Canadians with Disabilities has recommended that federal reports on disability 'should adopt, after consultation with Canadians with disabilities and the organizations representing them, an explicit value statement relating to disability issues ... reflect[ing] fully the constitutional equality rights guarantee given to persons with disabilities' (Beatty 2003: 5).

The case for a composite index on social inclusion can be made on several grounds, among them the point that any single indicator is just a partial picture of social and economic conditions. A national social inclusion index would 'constantly remind us of the need to be collectively attentive to and aware of, any kind of discrimination, marginality or exclusion' (Council of Europe 2001: 5). It would be an integrative measure that supports a horizontal approach to thinking about and tackling issues across a range of policy and program areas. More ambitiously, we can envisage that such an index, over time, could contribute to the modernization of the social and economic policy architecture and development of Canada. A disability lens has several possible uses in policy development, program design, implementation, and review. Canadian federal government officials note: 'It is crucial that lenses be as simple and 'user-friendly' as possible for policy and program developers and analysts to use since the lenses will be applied frequently to a wide range of federal initiatives' (Canada 2000b: 3). Given disparities in power relations, our politics of misrepresentation, it is even more crucial that a disability lens be 'user-friendly' for self-advocates, families, local service agencies, and national advocacy organizations.

Budget making and the allocation of public resources deeply matter to the disability community. Persons with disabilities face considerable barriers, including higher risks of unemployment, violence, discrimination, and poverty, than do other Canadians. With their authoritative allocation of resources and values, government budgets are central to supporting the principles of equity, inclusion, and full citizenship for all. And people living with disabilities have concerns about specific budget items as disability and medical expense tax credits. A properly constructed and presented disability budget, with accompanying information, can be a tool for raising awareness of members of Parliament, federal bureaucrats, journalists, and other groups on what is happening in concrete financial terms to Canadians with disabilities. It can be a tool also for highlighting what issues and values are being supported, or not, and at what levels of public resources.

Differential impacts of budget decisions on Canadians with disabilities as compared to other Canadians must be a component in such impact assessments. This would widen public debates on disability issues by considering the implications of budget measures for individuals, families, other sectors, and community supports. Furthermore, linkages could be made between program investments and results to the objectives and principles expressed in such vision documents. For government budgets to be not only disability-responsive but also enabling, they should contain an inclusive process. Budget making and budget analysis, therefore, can be significant occasions for exercising democratic citizenship.

5 The Canadian Disability Community: Five Arenas of Social Action and Capacity

In the past thirty years, Canada's disability community has expanded organizationally becoming more differentiated in activities and in the range of issues and groups addressed (Cameron and Valentine 2001; Chivers 2008; Enns and Neufeldt 2003; Rioux and Prince 2002; Stienstra and Wight-Felske 2003). This expanded scope and elaborated nature renders a mapping expedition of the community all the more necessary. What is the makeup of the disability community in Canada? Who belongs? Within disability studies, a prominent view in the United Kingdom is that the disability movement includes only those organizations *of* disabled people. In Canada, a more common outlook is that the community also includes organizations run by non-disabled people for people with disabilities as well as other organizations, friends, and allies that affect the interests of people with disabilities (Lord and Hutchison 2007). The argument put forward in this chapter is that the Canadian disability community comprises five arenas of social action. The community is a diverse sector of service organizations, a policy community of interest groups and coalitions, a comparatively new social movement, a constitutional category of citizens under the Canadian Charter of Rights and Freedoms, and a knowledge production network.

As used here, an 'arena' is an interacting set of individuals, organizations, ideas, interests, and processes engaged in social actions that affect disability. The term arena equates with other concepts in the policy literature such as 'systems' and 'sub-sectors' (Pal 1997). Each arena captures important features of the community, offering particular perspectives on disability that warrant the designation for analytical purposes. In varying ways, each arena aggregates interests and interacts with the Canadian state. This chapter draws some observations about the organizational nature of the disability sector, while recognizing the existence of multiple discourses within the community. The chapter offers a conceptual framework for analysing the issue of capacity and considers how the community's five arenas interrelate with the political struggles by disability activists for recognition, redistribution, and representation.[1]

No single model of collective action or specific academic discipline adequately depicts the disability community today. As an example, standard classifications of interest groups in Canadian political science distinguish economic and non-economic groups, service agencies and advocacy groups, and transient issue-based groups and more established organizations. Applying these schemes, we might say that most disability organizations are social groups with a service provision mandate and, though established, struggle for sustainable resources. These are useful descriptions up to a point. In disability studies, additional classifications exist, indicating other critical features that include organizations for or of people with disabilities, single versus cross-disability groups, and groups that espouse medical, social, or other models of disability. Given the diverse nature of the community, it is necessary to draw from theoretical works in various disciplines on human service provision, interest groups, equality-seeking, and social movements.

Mapping the Disability Field in Canada

In Canada's voluntary sector, according to a recent inventory, there are over 5,000 disability-specific organizations (Canadian Abilities Foundation 2007). At the core of the disability community, these include a variety of self-help groups, service providers, and advocacy organizations. Beyond these, however, a host of questions arises. What of the informal social support networks of families, friends, and helpful neighbours? What of private for-profit sector organizations that provide supports to persons with disabilities or fundraising assistance to disability-related societies? What about professional, medical, research, and rehabilitation organizations? What about generic community service agencies or public policy think tanks that may serve persons with disabilities among others in their clientele? And are government officials and political institutions included or not? Boundaries of the disability community, then, are not always clear or agreed upon.

Nor do those boundaries remain fixed. The community has likely expanded a great deal over the last few decades and, recently, has struggled with the impact of public sector downsizing.

The literature rarely defines 'the disability community' in an explicit manner in relation to these questions. The tendency in documents is to (a) *exclude* government officials and agencies, legislatures, the courts, the professions, business firms, and the mass media; (b) *include* individuals and families, formal disability-specific organizations involved in self-help, service provision, and advocacy, and associations and coalitions representing these interests; and (c) *differentiate* this community from others within the voluntary sector in Canada, such as those for women, Aboriginal peoples, and seniors.

Consider, for example, the federal government's recent reports, *Advancing the Inclusion of Persons with Disabilities* (Canada 2002a, 2004, 2006). The report makes repeated reference to 'the disability community,' from which several features can be noted. One is that all 4.4 million Canadians with disabilities constitute the disability community. A second is that the community comprises 'a wide variety of disability organizations' in which persons with disabilities may be members. The report makes mention of provincial and national disability associations, veterans' organizations, and non-governmental organizations involved in international development. Aboriginal persons with disabilities and their representatives are referred to separately, raising the question, what is the relation of Aboriginal disability organizations to the larger disability community? The disability community is 'an important partner' with governments, organized labour, business, and others in working together and addressing disability issues. Overall, the image of this community is a system of organized interests and associations outside of the Canadian state, relatively segmented and specialized, although linked to certain other policy communities and social movements.

A Sector of Service Organizations

A diffuse and complex field, this arena is likely the largest in the community in terms of the sheer number of organizations and activities. The disability community entails far more than policy development and political advocacy. Indeed, most organizations in the community are concerned mainly with the provision of services and the acquisition of funds, staff, volunteers, and other resources for running their operations. Most, as well, are locally based non-profit agencies that receive funding and service contracts from governments (Canadian Abilities Foundation 2007; Bach 2002). Thus, the disability community – as distinguished from the disability policy community – includes individuals, groups, and organizations that are primarily or wholly engaged as caregivers, service providers or brokers, referral agents, consumers, and fundraisers. Their main orientation is to their members and clients. That being said some combine service delivery with public advocacy in their mandates, such as the Canadian Paraplegic Association.

Specific-impairment organizations remain an important feature on the disability community landscape in Canada. As a custom, they do not participate directly or regularly in public policy and political processes. This is not to suggest that these service organizations do not have political effects. For example, local service agencies stratify relationships, producing, intentionally or otherwise, a 'hierarchy of help' or pecking order among clients, front line service providers, program managers, and agency executives (Higgins 1992; Wharf and McKenzie 2004). Some traditional care and service agencies are undergoing deliberate changes to adopt new values and approaches, shifting from an ethic of benevolence and compassion towards a philosophy of self-determination and person-centred supports (Lord and Hutchison 2007)

Rather than policy instigators, most service organizations are policy takers, working on the edges of public policy processes. This seems the case especially for specific-disability service groups run on behalf of people with disabilities. Lobbying is usually not held to be a part of their mission. Any activism and social change is low-key and non-political, pursued through public education and role models (Boyce et al. 2001: 56).

In addition to mandate and mission, diversity in the disability community is apparent in many other ways. One profound difference, already implied, concerns the particular disability perspective embraced by specific organizations. An organization may be working in accordance with a perspective on disablement that gives more or less emphasis to biomedical factors, economic and labour market concerns, environmental barriers to integration, or a human rights and equality approach (Bickenbach 1993; Rioux and Valentine 2006). There are, of course, differences in philosophy and working styles.

Lord and Hutchison (2007) distinguish between service agencies with a traditional approach that emphasizes 'client hood' and 'victim hood' among families and individuals living with disabilities, and a new approach which promotes personal choice and self-determination. It is the latter approach, which is the emerging pathway to social inclusion, especially by 'user-led' and so-called 'consumer-driven' or controlled organizations, such as independent living resource centres, that has arisen in the non-profit sector since the 1970s (Driedger 1989; Hutchison et al. 2007a). Here is an instance of social liberalism – the idea that as consumer of services, people with disabilities ought to have the right to decide which service to access, a right to monitor the quality of service provision, and ultimately a right to change services if they so decide. Examples of national consumer-driven disability organizations controlled mainly by people with disabilities, are the Alliance for Equality of Blind Canadians, Council of Canadians with Disabilities, People First of Canada, National Network on Mental Health, and the Canadian Association of Independent Living Centres.

With respect to their capacity, disability organizations vary in the sources and amounts of their funding, numbers of paid staff, and reliance on volunteers. They differ in terms of the size, continuity, and nature of membership base – whether they are an organization of individuals with disabilities or of family members or of professionals or an organization of other organizations. Disability groups certainly vary with regard to their organizational history, general stability, and internal complexity (Canadian Centre on Disability Studies 2002).

In probably the most detailed mapping of the community anywhere in the country, Proulx, Dumais, and Vaillancourt (2006) surveyed 1,357 community-based organizations in Quebec connected with people with disabilities. They found that the main fields of activities of these organizations are psychosocial support; social activities, leisure, and culture; rights and law; and family support. In contrast, relatively minor activities included prevention, transportation, and communication. Proulx, Dumais, and Vaillancourt also found that 33 per cent of the organizations in their survey dealt exclusively with mental health, 23 per cent with physical disabilities, and 10 per cent with intellectual disabilities; while 13 per cent handled both physical and intellectual disability, 16 per cent dealt with all three domains of disability, and 5 per cent still other combinations of activities. This shows a significant level of differentiation within the community, with two-thirds of the organizations specialized in just one type of incapacity, raising a series of interesting questions about governance and capacity, a topic further explored in chapter 7. Examples nationally include the Canadian

National Institute for the Blind, the Canadian Paraplegic Association, and the Easter Seals/March of Dimes.

Encounters with these service agencies, and their public sector counterparts, provide a growing body of critical autobiography, oral history, and other narrative forms by people living with disabilities. This can involve a shared production of knowledge on disability between the editor/researcher and the narrator/storyteller (Church 1995; Crooks 2007; Krause 2005; Moss and Dyck 2002; Raoul et al. 2007; Tremblay et al. 2005). Such narratives connect the private and public domains of a person's life, and cast light on coping and the healing provided by community services as well as by peers and families. Disability service agencies can be 'on the leading edge of testing and demonstrating the worthiness of new ideas' such as community living options for people with intellectual disabilities (Enns and Neufeldt 2003: 4).

A Policy Community of Interest Groups and Coalitions

For some organizations in the disability community, their primary orientation is to the political and governmental systems, with the aim of shaping public policy and practice. All groups regularly active in these activities comprise the arena of interest groups, lobbyists, and advocacy coalitions. These groups represent, in a formal way, certain interests of their membership. They formulate and present their ideas and claims to one or more of governments, cabinet ministers, administrative officials, legislators, tribunals, and courts. Like interest groups in general, rather than actually exercise public authority, disability organizations seek to exercise influence over policy strategies, legislation, regulations, and budget decisions through consultation, mobilization, litigation, and deliberation. In the Canadian disability community, consumer-led organizations enable self-control and voice by persons with disabilities and by their families (Hutchison et al. 2007a; Panitch 2007).

Participation by some advocates and groups is episodic, triggered by a personal incident or a public issue. One meaning of building the capacity of the disability community, therefore, is to explore how to incorporate strategically more of these potential and peripheral participants into the core of the community. At times, political participation may seem like 'accidental activism' as in the case of mothers with disabled children getting involved in public campaigns, but become more established by forming local, provincial, and national organizations (Panitch 2007).

Countless associations populate the disability policy community. On behalf of a cluster of interest groups or service agencies, associations may represent a particular disability, a distinct client group, a specific provincial or regional area, or a functional activity such as legal advocacy. The community differentiates significantly by perspectives and structures. A number of umbrella associations – at national, provincial/territorial, and urban levels – represent the relevant interests of a constellation of groups. Illustrations are the Canadian Association of the Deaf, the Canadian Hard of Hearing Association, the Canadian Association for Community Living, the Canadian Association of Muslims with Disabilities, the Manitoba League of Persons with Disabilities, the Ethno-Racial People with Disabilities Coalition of Ontario, and the Action des femmes handicapées in Montreal.

As policy networks, associations serve as structural bridges between the disability community and the disability state. Canada's disability state encompasses legislative, executive, judicial, and administrative agencies with a direct involvement in disability issues and with the disability community. Along with specific organizations and particular officials, the disability state includes the macro-institutions of parliamentary government, federalism, the inherent right of Aboriginal self-government, and the Canadian Charter of Rights and Freedoms. Policy networks are specific organizational relations between (a) government and other state institutions and (b) community agencies and actors. These networks form around particular issue areas, reform processes, disabilities, jurisdictions, and policy instruments of importance to the community. School testing, inclusive childcare, disability income benefits, accessible transportation, and labour market programs are illustrations of particular policy networks.

The idea of community implies a level of shared norms or common understanding among most members most of the time. In the context of public policy, this shared understanding relates to the substance of policy (the proper role of governments, and the vision, principles, and goals) and the process (structures, tactics, and conduct) by which groups engage with governments over these substantive issues.

The deinstitutionalization movement in Canada, in play since the 1970s, demonstrates this idea of community. Groups led by parents and families, supported by progressive professionals and sympathetic bureaucrats and politicians, work on policies for desegregating large numbers of people with intellectual and psychiatric disabilities in big residential facilities. This advocacy entails developing alternative provincial social policies, obtaining official commitments to stop admitting new residents, downsizing facilities, and eventually closing them. It also entails supporting individuals in the transition into the community and families, with sustainable supports and services, individualized funding, and a range of housing options. Recently, there has been more advocacy for supported employment and workplace accommodations to promote inclusion in the regular labour force. Through the 1980s and 1990s, this coalition witnessed province-wide closures of all large institutions in Newfoundland and Labrador, New Brunswick, and British Columbia, and Ontario is pledged to close the remaining large institutions in that province by 2010.

The disability community also contains a multitude of organizations and associations with specialized spheres of responsibility. In principle, the benefits of differentiation for policy engagement are that it provides the organizational means for expressing a diversity of specific interests, and for providing specialized information on particular experiences across the country. By comparison, the disability community is not integrated with one or two macro associations that span the entire community, coordinating the diversity of groups and broadly representing all the key interests. A potential drawback to this high level of organizational differentiation is that, on its own, it limits the capacity of the community to interact, to formulate strategies for the whole community, or to plan the actions of members in public policy processes (Coleman and Skogstad 1990: 16–21).

At the same time that the community is highly differentiated, 'the state presents itself to the disabled citizen as a complex set of institutions' (Cameron and Valentine 2001: 23). At the federal level of government alone, over thirty agencies, departments, and commissions have disability-related programs and services (Canada 2006). Behind this complexity is an array of programs and diverse eligibility rules that raise concerns about equity, access, coordination, accountability, and portability. Thus, to be more effective in disability policy engagement, the community and the state need to place more emphasis on integrative structures both within their respective sectors and between them. The disability community and governments have only had a national and intergovernmental policy focus for a decade; and even so, it is a partial and contested vision. Both the community and the state contain various perspectives on disablement, some of which are in sharp tension with one another (Bickenbach 1993; Devlin and Pothier 2006; Titchkosky 2003a). Not surprisingly, the level of shared norms is still forming within this policy field.

A New Social Movement

Academic writings commonly identify the disability community as a new social movement (Chivers 2008; De Jong 1979; Driedger 1989; Fagan and Lee 1997; Smith 2008), although not always (Staggenborg 2008). As a form of collective action, new social movements (NSMs) organize around diversity to promote social identities that originated in the 1960s in a number of countries. They are 'new' in contrast to the 'older' social movements initiated by trade unions and working class groups, organized to resist or restructure capitalism. Moreover, the old social movements were, and still are in some respects, male-dominated and premised on the able-bodied worker. By comparison, the basis of identity and political struggle for NSMs are their experiences of marginalization and oppression, and their goals expressed in a discourse of community (Leonard 1997: 155). Beside people with disabilities, examples of NSMs are those representing women, indigenous peoples, and visible minorities.

Based in felt grievances of shared discrimination and exclusion, NSMs challenge traditional authority of professionals and the related language, roles, and images of their group. In turn, social movement organizations endeavour to assist disadvantaged individuals to express their own voices in order to create new forms of public interaction as peers. Disability social movements have arisen worldwide when a substantial group of people no longer looked at a social situation as a misfortune that deserved charity and relief, but when it was seen instead as an injustice that warranted public policy and human rights (Driedger 1989; Enns and Neufeldt 2003; Rioux and Samson 2006; Valentine and Vickers 1996). Within this arena of social action are the consumer movement for independent living, the architectural barrier movement, the community living and deinstitutionalization movement, the school inclusion movement for children with 'special needs,' the psychiatric survivors movement, and the 'mad movement' (Capponi 1992; De Jong 1979; Reaume 2000; Shimrat 1997; Tremblay et al. 2005).

In the Canadian context, the disability community shares a number of features with the feminist, Aboriginal, and anti-racists movements.

Andrew Armitage (2003: 206) identifies the following common characteristics: a defined constituency of marginalized people, a goal to recognize distinctive needs, resistance to public sector cutbacks, political
organization through networks of agencies and alliances, a literature
and discourse of their own, and a role in the development and delivery of social services, particularly at the local community level.

Commentators suggest disability politics 'constitutes a "new social
movement" that rejects traditional pressure group and political party
activities in favour of more radical aims and forms of struggle' (Barnes
and Mercer 2003: 132). Other characteristics attributed to disability
politics as a new social movement, include the self-organization of
people with disabilities, an emphasis on non-economic or post-materialist values of identity, and, alongside local and national concerns, an
international outlook. Canadian experience differs in some important
respects from British disability politics. Unlike in Britain, disability
movement organizations in Canada do adopt interest group tactics
and engage with political parties to advance disability policy objectives. Canada's disability community is state-focused in pursuing economic and social reforms, interacting with various state institutions
and employing conventional tools of research, consultations, lobbying,
and litigation. Comparatively few disability groups pursue non-con-
ventional politics of radical protests. Canada's disability community
favours such terms as obstacles, inclusion, equality rights, and citizenship, rather than oppression and domination, a language more
common in British disability politics or the language of minority group
and civil rights in American disability politics.

At the same time, Canadian disability movement politics share features with the movements in Britain and the United States. Self-organization as a feature of NSMs is a notable characteristic of the disability
community today, illustrated with the rise of the independent living
movement since the 1970s and represented by Independent Living
Canada (formerly the Canadian Association of Independent Living
Centres). Like other disability movements, the Canadian community
does emphasize post-materialist values of cultural meaning. Renee
Anspach (1979) describes this activism among disabled people as a
shift from stigma to identity politics. Anspach uses the term 'identity
politics' in reference to altering self- and societal-conceptions of people
with disabilities from passive, deviant, and powerless to positive, self-
created conceptions for themselves. He also distinguishes the mode of
movement organizations from other arenas in the community. In con-

trast to service organizations, such as charitable agencies and self-help groups, disability movement organizations are political in outlook not therapeutic, of the disabled rather than for the disabled, and adopt a more polemical tone in their activities. 'Identity politics,' Anspach concludes, 'is a sort of phenomenological warfare, a struggle over the social meanings attached to attributes rather than an attempt to assimilate these attributes to the dominant meaning structure' (773).

But struggles of the disability movement are not to the exclusion of material issues of employment, accessible education, and income security or of governmental issues of public participation in policy making. A politics of socio-economic redistribution is at the core of disability activism in Canada, complemented by a politics of recognition and a democratic politics of representation, the latter of which involves claims for more accessible, empowering, and accountable policy making structures and processes. This view of Canadian disability politics thus departs then from the notion that new social movements focus exclusively or even chiefly on identity and post-materialist values. Active in claiming a self-defined identity in place of that previously dominant in society, disability movement organizations question traditional state practices and professional controls. Challenging a purely bio-medical perspective on disability, activists are promoting a socio-political model with a focus on the interaction between individuals and the larger environment. The psychiatric survivors' movement calls for drug-free treatments and greater use of peer counselling, while the 'mad movement' is promoting dignity and self-respect around bipolar disorder and schizophrenia. The movement conveys strong interest in social reform and in public services and programs generally.

An international dimension is noticeable in the Canadian disability community, through work by activists and academics such as Jim Derksen, Henry Enns, Steve Estey, Olga Krassiokova-Enns, Aldred Neufeldt, Diane Richler, and Marcia Rioux. Groups, such as the Council of Canadians with Disabilities and Canadian Association of Community Living, play an important role internationally on disability issues and the pursuit of equal participation (Driedger 1989; Enns and Neufeldt 2003; Rioux and Samson 2006). As a new social movement attached to transnational groups and reforms, the Canadian disability community transcends local places and provincial and federal jurisdictions, performing a significant role in the drafting and approval of the UN Convention of the Rights of Persons with Disabilities.

A Constitutional Category of Citizens

Entrenching the Canadian Charter of Rights and Freedoms in 1982 offered a challenging yet also strategic process for organizations representing people with disabilities to obtain explicit inclusion and recognition in the Canadian constitution. Specifically, placing the words 'physical and mental disability' in section 15 of the Charter 'ensured that disablement and persons with disabilities are recognized politically' in regard to equality rights and the legitimacy of affirmative action provisions in Canadian public policy (Cameron and Valentine 2001: 35).

No mere symbolic victory, including disability in the Charter means people with disabilities are in the most fundamental law of the land as a protected class of persons with a guarantee of equality rights. Explicit constitutional reference to people with mental and physical disabilities is tribute to the tenacious and artful efforts of disability activists in the early 1980s, finally moving the Trudeau government to add disability to the list of protected groups. In the words of disability rights lawyer Yvonne Peters, 'the struggle to obtain Constitutional recognition was more than just another political manoeuvre for people with disabilities. Indeed, it was a watershed event that occurred at a time when people with disabilities were just beginning to construct a new vision and analysis of the disability experience' (Peters 2003: 122). That new vision involves a rights analysis of discrimination as a prime cause for the exclusion of Canadians with disabilities from general society.

By virtue of direct identification in the Charter, disability and persons with disabilities have constitutional status. Section 15 offers an officially authorized space for disability groups to legally defend and advance their material, procedural, and cultural concerns. To define and enforce these fundamental rights and freedoms, such as mobility and equality, litigation has become an important strategy of individuals with disabilities and organizations representing their interests. This has raised the profile of the Canadian judiciary in the disability field and the wider social policy domain (Chivers 2008; James 2006; Pothier and Devlin 2006; Roeher 1997). Over the past few decades, however, disability advocates, families, and community groups have learned that judicial victories are not necessarily a case of winner-take-all. A rights-based approach to seeking equality through litigation can be lengthy, financially expensive, and emotionally stressful for individuals involved, and risks fragmenting wider campaigns for obtaining services or supports for all groups. In addition to courts ruling against disability claims, even victories can result in further delays due to appeals, discretion of public agencies in interpreting decisions, and then the frustratingly gradual, partial implementation of changes.

Inclusion in the Charter has given weight to a Canada-wide vision on disability issues. Sherri Torjman (2001: 194) notes that 'since the heady days of Canada's new constitution and the introduction of a Charter of Rights and Freedoms which guaranteed the protection of disability rights, the disability community has regarded Ottawa as the champion of its issues.' The disability community is not indifferent to federalism, particularly this equality-seeking arena of the community that seeks 'inclusion and respect in an overarching Canadian citizenship' (James 2006: 4). Many disability organizations have a federated structure with provincial and territorial chapters as well as a national office. For nearly twenty-five years now, disability associations, as representing a Charter-recognized group, have spoken out on constitutional reform ideas. Disability community groups are constitutional stakeholders, some of which watch carefully whenever Canada's political elite entertain changes to the division of powers between the federal and provincial orders of government or to central institutions of governance (Boyce et al. 2001; Cairns 1995).

At the same time, as representatives of Charter Canadians, disability organizations direct attention to provincial and territorial governments (as well as urban and local governments) in removing barriers to participation to advance accessibility, equity, and inclusion. The rights-based identity of people with disabilities is prominently linked to the Charter but that identity is also substantially linked to the human rights codes and related laws of the federal government and, for so many areas of everyday life, of the provinces and territories. Even with the constitutional entrenchment of the Canadian Charter of Rights and Freedoms in the early 1980s, provincial codes remain uniquely significant with their wider scope of application, extending beyond governmental activity to include private activities such as advertising, accommodation, business generally, contracts, employment, family law, and transportation services. Thus, the Charter supplements but does not supplant provincial and the federal human rights laws for advancing the rights of persons with disabilities.

The Courts Challenges Program of Canada, in effect from the late 1970s to 1992, cancelled and then reinstated in 1994, and then cancelled again in 2006, sought to clarify constitutional rights and freedoms, and to enable minority language groups and equality-seeking groups and individuals (particularly those mentioned in section 15 of the Charter) to pursue their legal and constitutional rights through the courts. With respect to equality rights, the program funded only cases that involved a challenge to a federal law, policy, or practice that raised equality arguments and that were test cases dealing with a problem or raising an argument not already decided by the courts. Such test cases had the potential to end discrimination or improve the way the law works for disadvantaged Canadians. People with disabilities were eligible for funding, as individuals or as groups, as a *party* directly affected by a case or as an *intervener* wishing to raise constitutional arguments not raised by others in a case. Disability issues were a prominent feature of the equality rights applications and the case funding decisions, and the Harper government's termination of the Court Challenges Program shut down a vital judicial vehicle for attaining full citizenship.

A Research and Knowledge Production Network

Production of disability knowledge is a crucial though under-resourced activity. In part, this knowledge production is an input to the other facets of the community, knowledge that supports service provision and administration, litigation or tribunal hearings, government lobbying, and cultural politics. A considerable part of disability research is in clinical and pharmaceutical trials, bio-medical studies, engineering research and development, and rehabilitation treatments and protocols. As well, a growing segment of the research community is involved in the area of disability management – with links across business, government, organized labour, medicine, and the insurance industry – addressing issues of recruitment, retention, return to work, injury prevention, and workplace accommodations. Frequently, the view of disability here is in terms of health problems and impairments of the individual.

Disability studies programs in Canadian colleges and universities are another part of this arena, one of recent and growing significance. Disability studies scholars and students are producing, critiquing, and disseminating artistic, comparative, historical, and theoretical forms of knowledge on disability and normalcy. Academe evaluates policies and practices as well as assists in bringing to wider audiences the narratives of people and communities. When done in an emancipatory manner, such research not only enlightens but empowers. When done imaginatively, such work shifts the boundaries between private and public domains, making personal troubles into policy issues, drawing attention to the absolute importance of 'the family' in understanding inclusion/exclusion and citizenship. Disability studies also has an important role to play in ensuring the effective design and implementation of disability mainstreaming techniques, and their evaluation, in state institutions.

Policy-related disability research considers public policy development and program delivery; examines the effects of policies and programs the social environments, life transitions, and opportunity structures of persons with disabilities; and critically assesses conceptions of disability contained in laws and social practices. Intended to be usable by policy makers and practitioners, such research may serve any number of purposes: the definition and understanding of an issue; the more effective response to and management of a need or problem; the resolution or alleviation of a problem or need; the expression of voice by a group and the recognition of their experiences; the empowerment of a group through the research process; and the identification of additional lines of inquiry.

In Canada today, at the national and provincial levels, is a blend of general think tanks and specialized disability-oriented think tanks. As well, within the federal government and provincial and territorial governments, plus the university sector are departments, agencies, advisory councils, academic programs, and research groups involved in policy-related disability research. For example, disability bodies in provinces and territories include Premier's Council on the Status of Persons with Disabilities (Alberta), Office of Disability Issues (Saskatchewan), Office of Disability Issues (Manitoba), Office des personnes handicapées du Québec, Premier's Council on the Status of Disabled Persons (New Brunswick), Nova Scotia Disabled Persons Commission, Yukon Council on Disability, and the NWT Council of People with Disabilities.

Statistics Canada, since the late 1980s, has undertaken national surveys of people with disabilities, an initiative widely endorsed by Canadian disability organizations. These surveys yield invaluable information on the lives of children, youth, and adults with disabilities and, in comparing their circumstances to Canadians without disabilities, documents the depth of the their precarious citizenship. Other administrative data sets reside in provincial workers' compensation systems, corporate insurance schemes, and health care facilities, much of it inaccessible or rarely made available to the public. Written records in the archives and file boxes of disability organizations are another valuable source of knowledge that offers insights and histories (Tremblay et al. 2005).

Federal advisory bodies concerned with policy-related disability research take in the National Advisory Council on Aging (Health Canada), National Council of Welfare (HRSDC), the Accessibility Advisory Committee (Canadian Transportation Agency), Gerontological Advisory Council (Veterans Affairs) and the Canadian Biotechnology Advisory Committee (government as a whole). In some of these areas, there is a long history of research, while in others disability is an emergent issue for further inquiry. In addition to these permanent bodies, ad hoc advisory bodies are used occasionally for disability policy matters. Recent examples of these are the Expert Panel on Financial Security for Children with Severe Disabilities (Finance) and the Ad Hoc Advisory Group on Special Needs (Veterans Affairs).

Parliamentary committees serve several useful functions for disability policy research and analysis, as well as for the wider disability community: raising and debating issues, engaging with groups in public forums, gathering information, reviewing legislation and considering bills, scrutinizing government performance, and recommending policy developments and program or administrative reforms. House committees of interest include Human Resources, Social Development and the Status of Persons with Disabilities, Finance, National Defence and Veterans Affairs, Health, Justice and Human Rights, and Status of Women. Relevant Senate committees to disability policy issues include Social Affairs, Science and Technology; National Security and Defence; and Human Rights. In our imperfect system of citizen participation and public accountability, legislative committees are significant political institutions for disability groups and disability policy. A recent example is the Senate Committee on Social Affairs, Science and Technology report on mental health, mental illness, and addictions services (Kirby 2006) which has led to the formation of the Canadian Mental Health Commission. As one of its activities, the Commission is building a national knowledge exchange network for public access to current information and research on mental illnesses.

Divergent perspectives on disability circulate within Canada's policy research community. One perspective, a social model of disability (and variations on that model) appears in the work of the Council of Canadians with Disabilities, Canadian Centre on Disability Studies, Status of Women, Caledon Institute of Social Policy, and university programs such as the Ryerson RBC Institute for Disability Studies Research and Education. This orientation emphasizes the values of equality rights and full citizenship, and usually employs a critical analysis for studying social structures and public policies. Another perspective prominent in disability research deals with functional impairments, rehabilitation, and integration. Disability management and rehabilitation therapy programs at certain universities reflect this perspective. So, too, do particular research centres on children and health services. In this orientation, people with disabilities commonly appear as individuals with special needs, facing possible risks, with official identities as program clients and care recipients. Turning to the issue of capacity in the disability community, we find a similar pattern of multiple interests and perspectives.

Capacities of the Disability Community

The skill, legitimacy, and effectiveness of the disability community are issues of strategic importance and abiding challenge (Boyce et al. 2001; Canada 1996a, 2002, and 2004; Canadian Centre on Disability Studies 2002; Driedger 1989; Hutchison et al. 2007; Roeher 1997). The concept of the capacity of the community is one of the central elements of inclusion for persons with disabilities in Canadian society, and it embraces these issues. Indeed, a federal government report measures the practice of capacity in terms of three measures: human resources, financial resources, and structural and systems capacity, and concludes the evidence on these measures points to some progress but also significant difficulties in the disability community's capacity (Canada 2004).

Strengthening the community's capacity is a laudable objective of governments and disability groups, but what exactly does it mean? Do governments and groups agree on what capacity building is about? The fivefold classification of the community presented here provides a way of addressing these questions, recognizing significant differences within the community. Each perspective highlights particular meanings of capacity, indicating that, at root, it is a relational phenomenon with assorted contestable dimensions.

In thinking of the community as a sector of service organizations, capacity relates to the ability of agencies, charities, and service clubs to provide programs to different categories of people with mental and physical disabilities. Capacity concerns aspects of organizational performance, such as the effective management of funds, staff, and volunteers; the efficient and responsive delivery of programs; and a transparent and accountable system of governance. This entails an administrative politics of agency-client and agency-funding relations. An extended notion of capacity, from this perspective, and one increasingly proposed by advocates, is the ability and willingness of traditional service agencies to reach out and build partnerships with other groups in the community engaged in social action and community development (Lord and Hutchison 2007). In this sense, capacity includes reviewing and redesigning services and programs so that they more fully respond to and include people with disabilities and their families in decision making.

In thinking about the disability community as a network of interest groups and advocacy coalitions, capacity building is about contributing to policy discussions, and program developments and reviews in an opportune and effective manner. Capacity requires the wherewithal of staff, time, information, and support by members to participate in consultations, respond to public issues and governmental proposals, and initiate desired solutions. Too often, even in cases where there is a consensus among disability organizations on a given issue, the consensus may partly be by default because some groups are unable to develop their own position. The federal government provides funding to several national disability organizations and their affiliates to work on fostering capacity to participate in social policy processes. Likewise, provincial and territorial governments create consultative spaces for disability groups, a topic examined in more depth in chapter 7. A major concern of capacity building is the recruitment and preparation of a new generation of leaders for the disability community across Canada (Hutchison et al. 2006).

Enhancing the capacity of the disability community as a new social movement involves augmenting such activities as social critique, consciousness raising of people in the movement and wider society, celebrating and communicating in a positive manner the varied experiences and identities of persons with disabilities, and challenging the ableist attitudes and actions in society and striving to institute progressive changes that tackle exclusion, cultural prejudice, and discrimination. In an important sense, NSMs are cultural movements, concerned with politicizing prevailing systems of values and norms.

Along with this politics of recognition, the disability community as a NSM is engaged in the 'associational politics' of forging networks and coalitions across different groups and sectors of society (Young and Everitt 2004). Thus, in seeking social changes, the disability movement is a cultural and political movement.

Increasing the role of disability organizations in their status as Charter groups and constitutional stakeholders implies an expanded ability in several areas: to access legal resources for litigation, to inter- vene in court cases, and to challenge apparent discriminatory laws, regulations, decisions, and programs before tribunals, human rights commissions, and the courts. This approach involves a discourse of equality, human rights, and, frequently, adversarial and expensive legal processes. Although a critical tool for effecting social change and advancing inclusion, rights claims through Charter politics is not, by itself, sufficient. It is also important to note that neither the federal nor the provincial and territorial governments like this approach for addressing disability issues (Canada 1998). Unfortunately, at times dis- ability groups reluctantly resort to this form of legal politics out of frustration over the lack of progress through other channels.

Thinking of the disability community as a knowledge production network raises implications that ought to figure in decisions about future research directions and funded projects. One such consideration centres on attracting organizations into this research community that previously have not been involved, thereby adding new players to the network, such as groups that represent employers, professionals, seniors, or unions. A second is the possibility of using the research agenda for fostering partnerships among organizations in the commu- nity and/or with actors in a related policy realm. Another is leverag- ing resources from the foundation sector, which, in Canada, is not a major source of funding for policy institutes and think tanks.

A fourth consideration is to ensure that disability organizations of people with disabilities are adequately included in research agenda setting, resources, processes, and products of policy-related disability research. The ways of actually doing a disability knowledge strategy must involve empowering and inclusive social relations. This is absolutely crucial – otherwise, other efforts at expanding capacity could inadvertently result in crowding out and further marginalizing of disability organizations within the research community. Overall, the politics of capacity building is about recognizing the multiple aspects of the phenomenon, the differing actors, goals, and preferences at work.

Conclusion

For an adequate understanding, the disability community needs looking at in a broader fashion than is often the case. Accordingly, this chapter proposes a framework that portrays the disability community as an interacting set of five distinctive arenas of social action. At times, these differences present tensions in the form of awkward relations between charity-based and consumer-led disability groups, or between impairment-specific groups and cross-disability rights associations. Such differences remind us that historical decisions and arrangements often shape identities and capacities today. In this regard, a core issue is how to build upon institutionalized differences in the pursuit of collective action by the community. There is a way to go in developing a strong disposition to work and act together as a community at large, although there are promising signs of enhanced collaboration (discussed in the final chapter).

Combining the five arenas of social actions with recognition, redistribution, and representation – the three dimensions of politics presented in the introduction to this book – yields an overview of the Canadian disability community as presented in table 5.1. Each arena is profiled in relation to the three types of political struggle by disability groups; cultural recognition, socio-economic redistribution, and democratic representation. Of course, it does not adequately capture all the interactions or tensions in the disability community. It does show, however, that elements of all three dimensions of activism appear in each arena, although the relative presence and content of these dimensions varies across arenas and, over time, within arenas. The analysis in this chapter suggests that Canada's disability community involves an increasing interplay among these arenas of social action. Illustrations of this are service agencies becoming more active in advocacy at individual and social levels, interest groups using Charter-based claims in equality-seeking litigation, and university-based researchers working with disability advocates often in mutually respectful ways. A trend over the last thirty years underlying all five arenas is the increasing orientation toward the state for realizing social change.

This examination also suggests that comprehension of any specific arena or dimension of politics requires explicit consideration of multiple organizational practices, capacities, and constraints. As providers of services and supports, advocates and promoters of policy and practice reforms, holders and claimants of fundamental rights and

Table 5.1
Mapping the Canadian disability community: A synopsis of arenas and politics

Arenas-Politics	Service Agencies	Interest Groups	New Social Movement	Charter of Rights	Research Network
Recognition	Diversity of disablements, often impairment-specific organizations	Visibility and legitimacy of a group, their leadership, and demands to government	Deconstructing traditional images and promoting differences as positive identities	Constitutionally and politically based identity for people with mental and physical disabilities	Exploration, description, and investigation of experiences: impairment and environmental perspectives
Redistribution	Provision of goods, supports for basic needs, personal safety	Advocacy for influence over public policies, programs, and budgets	Materialist concerns and values and process issues	Amelioration of disadvantages	Clinical trials, disability management and service practices
Representation	Within non-profit sector, rise of user-led organizations since the 1970s	Group and association member's demands for influencing policy	Celebration of voice, lobbying through conventional means and politics	Groups as interveners in judicial reviews, parties to litigation, and legislative reforms	Issues of emancipatory and participatory research
	Issues of personal choice and self-determination	Issues of capacity, self-control, and voice			

freedoms, creators and brokers of knowledge, and as carriers of group values and a new vision – these are the many ways in which collective action is enacted by the disability community. Canada's disability community is inherently political not because it includes interest groups and advocacy coalitions or even court cases, but because groups of people, through various forms of social action, are raising issues of inequality, making decisions on service delivery, affirming differences of the human condition, and seeking to shape societal attitudes and practices.

6 From Barriers to Ballots: Participating in Electoral Systems

Electoral participation is foundational to liberal democracies and to our understanding and lived experiences of political rights of citizenship. Voting is about many things, participation in elections to be sure, but also choosing representatives through a legitimate process, connecting with parties and the wider political and governmental systems, exercising democratic rights, as well as learning about, and debating social issues and public policy choices.

If certain groups, because of economic and social barriers and disadvantages, do not participate in elections on a regular and visible basis, then needs central to their lives remain at the margins of our politics and policy making. Significant differences in opportunities to engage in and exercise influence on community affairs persist among individuals and groups. Electoral systems are institutions of social stratification helping determine the political order. The goal of establishing accessible and inclusive voting procedures is an ongoing responsibility in Canada and other established democracies (Courtney 2004; Gidengil, Blais, Nevitte, and Nadeau 2004).

The challenge then, and topic of this chapter, is how to ensure that electors with disabilities can participate fairly and fully in the mainstream of democratic politics. The analysis proceeds in five sections. In the first, information drawn from a number of sources is presented to shed light on the electoral participation of Canadians with disabilities. The second section surveys international experiences from the United Kingdom, Sweden, and the United States in enhancing the voter turnout of persons with disabilities. The third reviews the provision of assistance to electors with special needs under election laws and procedures of the federal, provincial, and territorial governments in

Canada. The fourth section identifies some knowledge gaps on this core aspect of democratic citizenship, including the significance of an informal electoral system, and identifies some research directions. Last, the fifth section offers a brief conclusion.

Voter Turnout

Election studies that adopt a sociological approach to voting carefully examine the role of several social dimensions: language, religion, social class, regionalism, ethnicity, and more recently age and gender (Blais, Massicotte, and Yoshinka 2001; Courtney 2004). National election studies confirm that illness and health issues are among the reasons for people not voting. Otherwise, disability as a social dimension or social group is not studied systematically even though approximately four million Canadians with disabilities are of voting age. The literature on the electoral participation of Canadians with disabilities comprises a few academic articles and a host of newspaper and newsletter articles. What emerge from this material are the roles of people with disabilities – as would-be voters facing various barriers, as community activists advocating for changes to electoral systems and mobilizing voter participation, and as candidates and elected representatives of municipal councils and legislatures.

Academic and research articles, the few that have been written, document developments of the past thirty years in election legislation and administration and in outreach elector activities for persons with disabilities at the federal level (Davidson and Lapp 2004), a case study of Quebec (Leclerc 2004), and an overview of improving access to the vote at the federal, provincial, and territorial levels (Prince 2004a). There is only one article that examines persons with disabilities as candidates and elected representatives (D'Aubin and Stienstra 2004).

On the evolution of federal voting rights for Canadians with disabilities, Diane Davidson and Miriam Lapp note that 'successive Chief Electoral Officers have adopted a number of administrative measures to increase the accessibility of the voting process, particularly access to polling stations and information for electors with disabilities' (2004: 15). They conclude that while much has changed in recent decades 'to make the federal electoral process more accessible, more can be done. While a good deal can be accomplished through administrative measures, further changes to the *Canada Elections Act* may be required' (Davidson and Lapp 2004: 20). Michel Leclerc (2004) offers a similar picture and reaches similar conclusions on advances to improved access and room for continued reforms.

For many Canadians with disabilities, voting is a relatively new opportunity and experience in democratic participation (Prince 2001b), with a guaranteed access to the electoral process not existing until the last decade or so. Indeed, we can suggest that there are two contrasting stories about the right to vote, as outlined in table 6.1. One story is the dominant narrative of the universal franchise, joined more recently with the emergence of a malaise toward voting. In contrast, the second story, about Canadians with disabilities, presents a very different picture of experiences with voting and expectations of the electoral process. Although no national data set exists, in all likelihood, recent voter turnout among electors with disabilities would show a trend to higher voter turnout, from a comparatively much lower base than other electors (Prince 2004a: 3).

A survey of federal, provincial, and territorial governments suggests there has been much progress over the past decade or so in reforming electoral laws and administrative practices to enhance access. Most jurisdictions, for example, have opted for the use of special or mail-in ballots, rather than proxy voting, as an option for electors unable to vote in person in advance or on election day. However, across the fourteen senior governments in Canada, 'the ability to vote and to have effective and equitable access to the electoral process remains very uneven for Canadians with disabilities' (Prince 2004a: 6). In a survey of 198 Canadian associations representing people with various kinds of physical, sensory, and developmental disabilities, about the 2000 federal election, 57 per cent of these associations agreed that polling stations were physically accessible and accommodating, while 13 per cent disagreed; on mobile polling stations being available to their members, 28 per cent agreed while 22 per cent disagreed; and on interpreters being available to assist at the polling stations, 21 per cent agreed and 23 per cent disagreed (Elections Canada 2001).

Newspaper stories detail experiences people with various disabilities have in trying to access polling stations, campaign offices, candidates' forums, or access political parties' platforms and positions on issues during election campaigns. For example, Tom Blackwell (1992) describes the frustrations wheelchair users had during the 1984 federal election with inadequate access at several polling stations in Manitoba, an issue Elections Canada addressed to a large degree for the 1988 federal election. The outreach service noted in this story is the use of

Table 6.1
Two perspectives on voting and the electoral process

	Electorate in general	Electors with disabilities
Model of citizen	Able-minded and able-bodied individuals	Individuals with limitations and different capacities
Voting in Canada	A long-standing political process and traditional form of citizen participation based on a progressively more universal franchise	For many citizens with disabilities, a relatively new opportunity and experience in democratic participation
Recent voter turnout	Disengagement: A trend to lower voter turnout in many recent elections at the two senior levels of government	Engagement: In all likelihood, a trend to higher voter turnout, from a comparatively much lower base
Contemporary context	Disenchantment: Declining voter turnout seen as a result of growing public apathy, cynicism about governments, distrust of politicians, and a sense of disempowerment in lacking involvement in public policy discussions and formation	Expectation: Growing desire and claims to participate in electoral processes and other political institutions stimulated by disability rights movement and the Canadian Charter of Rights and Freedoms
Reform focus	Political party financing rules; enhanced accessibility of voting process; civic education	Changes to federal, provincial and territorial election laws, practices, and administration: mobile polls, level access to polling stations, mail-in ballots (where they do not yet exist); electronic registration/voting
	Beyond the existing electoral process: consideration of alternative electoral systems to single member plurality voting; changes to governmental and legislative institutions	

advance polls held in accessible buildings to allow people with mobility limitations to vote there if their own polling station was not easily accessible. A person who is a wheelchair user discovered he could not enter the advance polling station without help from two scrutineers, and is quoted in the article, 'I got in to vote but I felt it was degrading' (Blackwell 1992: A4).

Kim Lunman (1993) reports on a provincial election in Alberta in which several people with disabilities who lived in a city housing complex were shocked and outraged to find there was no ramp at the school in which their polling station was located. What made this especially newsworthy was that the incident took place in the Premier's riding and that the election was taking place a week after National Access Awareness Week. Two outreach measures appear in this piece. One is that newspaper ads placed during the campaign advised people that where there were inaccessible polling stations they could vote at advance polls. The second measure was that in this incident, the returning officer apparently offered to have an election worker bring a ballot outside the polling station to vote or to the person's home. The article quotes a voter with a physical disability as saying: 'I don't feel I should have to vote in a parking lot. In this day and age, they should make sure all polling stations are accessible.' At the time, the province's election law did not require that all polling stations be accessible.

Before getting to the polling station or to exercising the vote whether in a mobile, advance, or postal polling method, there are other difficulties for people with disabilities in openness to the electoral process. Newspaper articles on the 2006 federal general election drew attention to the inaccessibility of campaign offices, candidates' meetings in virtually all 308 federal ridings, candidates' and parties' materials on issues, and even television advertisements by political parties. In Canada, political party campaigns are not governed by election legislation, but left to the whims and wishes of party officials. Campaign offices frequently have neither typewriter services nor sign language interpreters available, leaving hearing-impaired voters frustrated and perhaps excluded from the process. No doubt, such access barriers deny a basic democratic right and discourage civic engagement by many people with disabilities, be that in the form of asking questions and expressing opinions, volunteering to work on a campaign, advocating for one's beliefs or preferred candidate/party, and voting (Sadava 2006). To tackle these barriers, there were five 'fully accessible' candidates' meetings in selected Ontario ridings during the 2006 federal election. Held in physically accessible buildings, the meetings included provision of American Sign Language interpretation, real-time captioning of the proceedings on computer screens, listening devices, and attendant services (Henderson 2006; Keung 2006).

Advocacy and mobilization activities of persons with disabilities and their organizations aim at pressing for reforms to election laws and practices. They are asking disability-related policy questions of candidates and political parties during election campaigns, thus raising their awareness of how decisions affect people with disabilities, and encouraging people with disabilities to vote.

Here are some examples: The Canadian Paraplegic Association Manitoba branch launched a complaint to the Canadian Human Rights Commission that Elections Canada had discriminated against voters with disabilities during the 1984 federal election by failing to provide adequate access to wheelchair users at various polling stations. After a seven-year process, a Human Rights tribunal upheld the complaint, and ordered the federal agency to provide level access at polling stations across Canada (Blackwell 1992). The Canadian Disability Rights Council used the Charter of Rights and Freedoms to challenge the exclusion of people with mental disabilities living in psychiatric facilities and institutions from voting in federal elections. In 1988, the Federal Court of Canada ruled that the restriction was arbitrary and did in fact contravene the Charter of Rights. The major federal political parties of the day also supported the removal of the restriction. In 1993, the Canada Elections Act was amended to reflect the court decision (CBC 2005). The Alberta committee of Citizens with Disabilities mounted a 'Listen Up' campaign in 1993 to mobilize voters with disabilities for the federal election that autumn. According to unofficial estimates, only about 12 per cent of the 427,000 disabled people in Alberta vote (Gold 1993). The committee sent election kits to more than 500 community organizations across the province. Questionnaires sent to candidates asked for their positions on a range of issues. Though not endorsing any particular candidates nor focusing on specific issues, the group was encouraging people with disabilities to learn how the voting process works and to ask candidates questions.

After the 2001 municipal election in Edmonton, a complaint was lodged with the province's Human Rights Commission to provide persons who are blind or visually impaired (and those with learning disabilities and low literacy skills) the right to cast a secret ballot on their own. This issue affects an estimated 3,000 city residents (Kleiss 2004). In response, and in consultation with the Canadian Council of the Blind and the CNIB, the city of Edmonton rented 21 audio-electronic voting machines for use in the 2004 city elections. For the 2006 federal election, a coalition of disability groups (Accessibility Centre of Sault Ste. Marie, Canadian Hearing Society, CNIB, Canadian Paraplegic Association of Ontario, Disabled Persons Resource Centre, and the Ontario March of Dimes) organized fully accessible candidates' meetings in five ridings throughout the province of Ontario, 'to make the electoral process more inclusive' (Keung 2006: B5). Additional efforts on electoral equality by disability groups include appearing before parliamentary committees and Royal commissions, drafting legislative reforms, and providing advice and information to electoral agencies.

A modest literature exists on persons with disabilities as candidates for elected office and as elected representatives in Canada. In perhaps the only academic paper on the topic, April D'Aubin and Deborah Stienstra (2004: 8) observe: 'Among those who participate as candidates in municipal, provincial and federal elections, there continues to be a significant under-representation of people with disabilities, particularly people with disabilities that require accommodations such as sign language interpreters, alternative media and other types of supports.' To explain this low level of political participation in Canada, D'Aubin and Stienstra identify the importance of three factors: 'negative public attitudes about people with disabilities, lack of knowledge about the costs and contributions of disabled people, and lack of resources for candidates with disabilities, including appropriate disability supports, money, and access to political opportunities.' A complex mixture of inadequate access to disability supports plus attitudinal, informational, financial, and physical barriers 'prevent the full and equal participation of people with disabilities in Canadian politics' (2004: 8).

In Britain, disability scholars Colin Barnes and Geof Mercer observe that 'disabled people who are elected rarely identify with disability issues. This reflects a general lack of interest in disability politics' (2003: 113). In the Canadian context, this seems apparent in the relative lack of emphasis given to disability issues in political party platforms, in sporadic and outmoded forms of media attention to disability issues, and in the modest influence of disability advocacy organizations.

A handful of narratives by Canadians with disabilities shed light on what it is like for a candidate with multiple disabilities to run in the 1997 federal election (Feld 1997), for a wheelchair user to be elected to Edmonton City Council and then to the Alberta legislature (Wickman 1987), for a person who is blind to run unsuccessfully in municipal and provincial elections before getting elected as a school trustee in Winnipeg (Eadie 2000), and for a deaf activist to be elected to the Ontario legislature (Malkowski 1997). Reflecting on his election experiences, Ross Eadie (2000) notes other ways people with disabilities can get into politics and influence government without running for office. One is to become a member of a political party and attend conventions where policies are proposed, debated and adopted. A second method is 'to convince people to vote for a person or a party that will make the required changes' for improving the quality of life for people with disabilities (Eadie 2000: 6).

International Experiences

International literature on electoral participation by people with disabilities is of three kinds. There are surveys of electoral systems and the experiences of voters with a disability in recent elections. There is also an extensive literature on the voting rights and experiences of Americans with disabilities and a modest literature on voting and people with disabilities in other countries.

Surveys of electoral systems and the experiences of voters with a disability in recent elections come from academics, government agencies, and a national organization representing disabled people in Britain. André Blais, Louis Massicotte, and Antoine Yoshinaka (2001) analyse restrictions on the right to vote in sixty-three democracies. Of several possible restrictions, the authors find that only two have near consensus among these nations, namely, that the minimum voting age should be eighteen and that the right to vote of 'mentally deficient people' should be restricted. The only countries, among this sample, that do not disenfranchise persons with a mental health disability or with an intellectual disability are Canada, Ireland, Israel, Italy, and Sweden. In most countries then, adults with mental disabilities do not have a constitutional or legal right to vote.

In the United Kingdom, a national disability organization named Scope, whose focus is people with cerebral palsy, has conducted an access survey at each general election since 1992 called the Polls Apart campaign. 'There are approximately 10 million disabled adults in the UK, an average of 15,000 in every constituency. At a time when voter apathy and disengagement is a high political priority we must consider those voters who want to participate but are prevented from doing so' (Scope 2005: 7). The 2005 survey, which covered 81 per cent of the constituencies in the UK, found that only 60 per cent of polling stations had level access into the building, only 64 per cent of ramps were appropriately designed (with handrails and firmly fixed), 30 per cent of stations did not display a large print copy of the ballot paper, and 28 per cent of polling stations did not provide a tactile voting device to help visually impaired electors vote independently and in secret.

In the United States, the General Accounting Office (GAO) studied voting access for people with physical disabilities for all fifty states and the District of Columbia, including access to polling places and alternative voting methods. Briefly stated, their key findings are that all states have specific provisions pertaining to voting by people with disabilities. The nature and implementation of these provisions, however, varies greatly across the states, reflecting the broad discretion afforded states under electoral laws. For example, the GAO survey found that nine states do not have specific accessibility standards established. Moreover, 'all states offer one or more alternative voting methods or accommodations that may facilitate voting by people with disabilities whose assigned polling places are inaccessible' (United States 2001: 6). From a Canadian perspective, the array of alternative methods seems relatively limited both across and within states. In addition, in comparison to the mandate and activities of Elections Canada in Canadian elections, the role of the Federal Election Commission in the United States in overseeing federal elections is rather limited.

'In 2000,' according to Mary Otto (2004: C4), 'more than 16.4 million disabled Americans were estimated to have voted, a 41 percent turnout rate.' Another study reports that, controlling for socio-demographic factors, people with disabilities are about 15 percentage points less likely to vote than those without disabilities due, in part, to factors such as the accessibility to polling places (Kruse, Schriner, Schur, and Shields 1999). This team of researchers produced a series of useful analyses on people with disabilities in American electoral politics that highlights, among other variables, the significance of paid employment and general mobility for voter turnout (Schriner and Shields

1998; Schur 1998; Schur and Kruse 2000; Shields, Schriner, Schriner, and Ochs 2000). A handful of American studies on voting and mental illness, using various empirical methods (election simulations, questionnaire surveys, comparison of election results from institutional facilities with local congressional districts), find that voting patterns and preferences of patients in psychiatric hospitals are similar to those of electors in the general population (Armstrong 1976; Duckworth et al. 1994; Howard and Anthony 1977; Klein and Grossman 1971).

On the voting rights and experiences of Americans with disabilities, a wide-ranging literature exists. A prominent theme is that despite several federal laws supporting the right to vote for persons with disabilities – the Voting Rights Act of 1965, the Voting Accessibility for the Elderly and Handicapped Act of 1984, the Americans with Disabilities Act of 1990, and the Help America Vote Act of 2002 – serious concerns persist about barriers to access in voting opportunities. American studies address advocacy and mobilization (Hardina 2003; Otto 2004; Schriner, Ochs, and Shields 1997; Shields, Schriner, and Schriner 1998), the role of complaints and litigation to enforce rights and enhance access (*CQ Researcher* 2001), and the limits in practice of the legislative approach to reforms (United States 2001; Schriner and Batavia 2001). In sum, the message is that substantial barriers and formal exclusions remain across most U.S. states preventing many Americans with disabilities to exercise the vote.

A third type of international literature is the modest number of studies in other countries; Sweden and the United Kingdom are examples. A qualitative study by Anette Kjellberg (2002) of Swedish men and women with moderate to mild learning disabilities describes how they understand opportunities to vote in general elections, a right granted in 1989. 'In the Swedish election of 1994,' notes Kjellberg (188), '31 per cent of the persons with learning disabilities voted, compared to 86 per cent of the total Swedish population.' This study reveals the impact of significant others – mostly relatives and staff members in residential facilities – in influencing the decision of people with disabilities of whether to vote. In the European context, the term 'learning disabilities' often refers to what in the Canadian context means intellectual or developmental disabilities.

Similarly, a UK study (Bell, McKay, and Phillips 2001) examines the legal situation of people with a learning disability who wish to vote. Legislation in Britain in 2000 removed restrictions on mental hospitals as places of residences for the registration of patients as electors, fol-

Table 6.2
Summary of international findings: Electors with disabilities and voter turnout in elections

Study	Group of disabled electors	Election	Difference in turnout by general population
Schur and Kruse (2000)	People with spinal cord injuries	1992 U.S. presidential	10 per cent lower than otherwise similar population
Shields, Schriner, and Schriner (1998)	Unemployed working age persons with disabilities	1994 U.S.	20 per cent lower than among other unemployed persons
Kjeller (2002)	People with disabilities	1994 Sweden	55 per cent lower than general population
Schur, Shields, Kruse, and Schriner (1998)	Unemployed working age persons with disabilities	1998 U.S.	13 per cent lower than among other unemployed persons
Kruse, Schriner, Schur, and Shields (1998)	People with disabilities	1998 U.S.	15 per cent lower than general population
Otto (2004)	People with disabilities	2004 U.S.	8 per cent lower than general population

lowing a number of legal test cases and the deinstitutionalization of many people with mental disabilities into communities. This study, and others (Smith and Humphreys 1997), found that one of the barriers to voting by people with a learning disability or mental health condition is 'the attitudes, beliefs and understanding of the regulations held by carers and the public' (Bell, McKay, and Phillips 2001: 122). Michael Nash (2002), in another UK study, points to voting as a pragmatic means of civic participation for people with a mental health condition and therefore urges health professionals to take up users' voting rights as an effective means of social inclusion in society.

Table 6.2 summarizes findings from international studies, where reported, on the differences in voter turnout of electors with disabilities as compared to a general population.

Canadian Election Laws and Procedures

Contained in election laws, regulations, and administrative practices are assumptions, often partially formulated and implicitly expressed, about ability and normalcy as regards literacy skills, functional capacities, and living arrangements. For instance, restrictions on the right of persons with mental disabilities or with mental health conditions to vote in elections were mostly removed in Canadian jurisdictions over the past fifteen years or so. Only two jurisdictions continue to have disqualifications in their electoral laws pertaining to mental disability. In Quebec, persons under the guardianship of the public curator (a role elsewhere in Canada known as the public guardian or public trustee) are disqualified from voting in provincial elections. In Nunavut, persons subject to a regime to protect his or her property due to incapacity to understand the nature and consequences of their actions, and persons acquitted of a Criminal Code offence by reason of mental disorder, and persons voluntarily in a psychiatric or other institution, are also disqualified from voting in territorial elections (Elections Canada 2003).

The rationale behind outreach programs to electors with special needs is that while the extension of the franchise as a democratic right is essential to individual members of these groups, this formal equality, by itself, is insufficient in promoting electoral participation. Specific measures are required to address and alleviate, in part, disadvantages and barriers to participation faced by persons with disabilities and other groups such as homeless people and individuals with literacy challenges. Being members of these groups has consequences for how individuals are treated and regarded as citizens. Table 6.3 outlines the provision of seven types of special assistance to electors by the fourteen jurisdictions in Canada. These kinds of assistance relate directly to the needs of electors with various physical disabilities as well as to electors with low literacy skills.

Just two of these types of assistance are available by all fourteen Canadian jurisdictions – mail-in ballots, and the ability to have a person accompany the elector behind the voting screen to help them mark their ballot. Mail-in ballots is an option for many kinds of electors, but can be a particularly helpful measure for electors with special needs. Admittedly, a mail-in ballot may be too complicated for some electors, but it is an option even for the homeless in federal elections. With respect to having a person accompany the elector, most frequently the designated person is a friend, family member, or deputy returning officer. Two other near universally available services for special needs are ensuring level access at all polling stations and the provision of interpreter services. In situations where an elector's polling station does not have level access, four jurisdictions use transfer certificates that allow the elector to vote at another polling station.

Curiously, level access for advance polls is less widely ensured across Canadian jurisdictions, with three province and the three territories not requiring every advance poll to have level access for electors. In recent elections in these jurisdictions, this represented 486 advance polls in total that were not required to have level access (Elections Canada 2003: 105). All electors are eligible to vote at advance polls and in four jurisdictions (Quebec, Saskatchewan, Alberta, and BC) election policies specifically mention that advance polls are for electors with physical disabilities and other electors who would have difficulty voting on polling day.

On-site interpreter services are available to electors in nearly all jurisdictions. For federal elections, these services are used by electors who do not understand either official language and by persons who are deaf or hard of hearing. Interpreters must be requested at least a few days before polling day by contacting the returning officer. A template (a card with holes in it that is placed over the ballot so that it can be marked accurately) allows electors who are blind or have visual impairments to mark their ballot by themselves. This service is available nationally and in seven provinces, but not in three provinces or the three territories. During the 2004 federal election process, an advo-

Table 6.3
Assistance to electors with special needs: Provision of seven measures by Canadian jurisdictions

Assistance Provided	Yes	No
Level access at all polling stations	All jurisdictions but one.	SK
Level access at advance polls required	Fed., AB, MB, NB, NS, ON, PE, QC	BC, NL, NT, NU, SK, YT
Transfer certificates	Fed, ON, NB, NS	AB, BC, MB, NL, NT, NU, PE, QC, SK, YT
Interpreter service	All jurisdictions but two.	NL, PE
Template for ballot	Fed., AB, MB, NL, NS, ON, QC, SK	BC, NB, NT, NU, PE, YT
Person may accompany elector behind voting screen	All 14 jurisdictions.	
Mail-in ballots	All 14 jurisdictions.	

Source: Elections Canada. (2003). *Compendium of Election Administration in Canada 2003*. Prepared for the Conference of Canadian Election Officials

cacy group representing blind people raised the issue of outreach services for blind and visually impaired voters. A chapter of the National
Federation of the Blind: Advocates for Equality challenged the use of
templates as cumbersome, liable to produce mistaken voting choices,
and a form of unequal access to the electoral process (Seymour 2004).
Instead, the group wanted Elections Canada to provide Braille ballots,
to make voting easier, to minimize the possibility of errors, and so that
poll workers do not have to tell a blind or visually impaired voter the
order of the candidates' names on the ballot.

Shortly after the 2004 federal election, Canada's then Chief Electoral
Officer Jean Pierre Kingsley sent a letter to the editor of daily newspa-
pers in that area to address this issue. In that letter, he said:

> Providing ballots in Braille would be a major undertaking, requiring
> extensive planning and resources. I do not mean to suggest that it is
> impossible; rather, I suggest that our discussions so far with the CNIB
> have not led to any final conclusion about whether it would be the best
> course to follow, given the other options currently available for fair and
> equitable voting by blind and vision-challenged Canadians, including
> other technologies that are coming on the market. (Kingsley 2004)

The newspaper article on this issue notes that local members of the
CNIB have never expressed concerns over their ability to cast ballots,
and that the National Federation of the Blind 'takes a somewhat more
activist and adversarial role on behalf of the visually impaired'
(Seymour 2004). This observation reminds us that social categories of
people are not homogeneous. Any particular community can include
a range of organizations with differing perspectives and styles, presenting challenges to electoral agencies in finding consensus or in sat-
isfying all demands. This example illustrates the role that community
groups in Canada serve in reviewing election processes, in generating
critiques based on experiences, and in offering solutions to electoral
agencies guided by core values to eliminate barriers and to equalize
access to voting. The case also raises a key philosophical question of
who should pay for services like interpreters or intervenors, which
enable electors with special needs to exercise their democratic right to
vote. What is the obligation of government, charities, or individuals
and families in meeting these costs of access, privacy, and autonomy?

For the 2006 federal general election, the Council of Canadians with
Disabilities (CCD) issued a challenge to all political parties and candi-

dates to conduct a barrier-free campaign. CCD outlined an accessible campaign as including literature available in alternate media, sign language interpretation at public meetings, public meetings held in accessible venues, accessible campaign offices, TTY (Tele-Typewriter) info lines, plain language information, and captioning of political party television commercials (Council of Canadians with Disabilities 2005). Few candidates or campaigns have adopted more than a few of these principles of universal design for accessible elections.

Research Directions

For some people, the franchise and act of voting is a privilege or moral duty, for other people it is a pointless and hollow symbol, while for yet others, electoral participation (or not) is thought to be determined by a personal calculus of benefits and costs, and for others still, it is a prized democratic right and potentially strategic political resource. The needs of persons with disabilities as electors are more than something an individual cannot do or something needed because of personal limitations. Participation needs also have to do with restrictive features of the built environment (inaccessible buildings), institutional practices (rigidities in residency requirements), attitudinal barriers (assumptions about what is a 'normal' reading proficiency among adults), and socio-economic constraints (unemployment, poverty, poor health). Without recognition of these contextual factors, attempts to increase electoral participation for electors with disabilities are unlikely to succeed on their own.

Increasing the participation of Canadians with disabilities as electors is a goal now accepted by elections offices of all levels of government and pursued through various outreach measures. Many of these reforms benefit the electorate generally – ensuring level access to polling stations, making registration processes simpler and less-paper intensive for electors, having dedicated special ballot poll workers to take the poll to house-bound voters, widening the range of facilities for which advance and/or mobile polls may be held (treatment centres, nursing homes, special care homes, extended care facilities at hospitals), increasing flexibility in election laws across Canadian jurisdictions in who can provide assistance to electors requiring help in voting on polling day or at an advance poll, and more clarity and consistency in public education materials on who may make use of advance polls and mail-in or special ballots. Outreach measures to electors are intended to advance the political citizenship of persons with mental or physical disabilities. Of course, political citizenship both as a formal status and an actual practice does not take place in a vacuum. For these elector outreach measures and any further reforms to be effective, they must be complemented and reinforced by investments in the economic, cultural, and social components of citizenship.

There is further important work to do, then, in tackling barriers to participation and self-reliance through improved access to public services and supports for daily living, and enhanced awareness and respect for the diverse groups and needs in our communities. Five areas of research warrant consideration using a range of research designs and methods.

First, there is an absence of quantitative studies reporting on the actual voter turnout of electors with special needs. Only twenty years ago, election laws in Canada routinely expressed the view that persons with mental health conditions and intellectual disabilities had no place in electoral participation and thus no right to vote. Authorities further assumed that Canadian electors, largely, had the ability to easily read and understand materials on election rules and campaign materials. Persons with no fixed or permanent address could not register to vote in federal elections until 2000 and after that in provinces and territories. Given the recent origins of most reforms designed to promote access and participation of persons with disabilities, low literacy levels, and the homeless, it is opportune to establish baseline data on turnout rates at the national, provincial and municipal levels in Canada. Until this type of research takes place, we will not adequately know the impact of such reform efforts on voter behaviour among these social groups.

Are they enabling more adults with disabilities to participate in elections as voters? Are they bringing the interests of people with disabilities and the issues of disability organizations into election campaigns and political party platforms? As recently introduced reforms, it is too early to properly evaluate the impact of electoral outreach measures on the electoral engagement of Canadians with disabilities. We should be cautious in expecting too much of these measures by themselves in overcoming larger systemic barriers and inequalities and in directly influencing public policy making. We might reasonably assume, however, that outreach services, in removing specific electoral barriers and offering assistance, are tapping into latent desires and frustrated wishes to vote and thereby increasing this form of democratic participation by Canadians with disabilities. Employing an intersectional perspective, how do such outreach efforts relate to differences in types of impairments, age cohorts, gender, labour force status, or being a member of a majority or visible minority group?

Second, another line of inquiry still largely unexplored concerns the repercussion and implementation of leading judicial decisions and human rights rulings for election policies and administration. To cite one example: In 1997, the Supreme Court of Canada held that a provincial government's failure to fund sign language interpreters in hospitals, under the public health insurance system, discriminated against patients who are deaf on the basis of their physical disability, thus violating their equality rights under section 15 of the Canadian Charter of Rights and Freedoms.[1] What does this decision mean for electoral systems across the country in terms of assistance for voters?

Third, we lack qualitative research (for example, ethnographic or case studies) that cast light on the role of local neighbourhood groups, single-issue movements, ad hoc groups, or community-based helping agencies and workers in fostering the political citizenship of marginalized Canadians. Taken together, these groups and actors comprise what we may think of as the informal electoral system. This system encompasses relationships between electors (actual and potential) and family members, friends, neighbours, co-workers, local activists, caregivers, and others significant in their lives. We know anecdotally that friends, relatives, and community groups are a source of information about voting procedures (such as how to register, how to vote and where), issues, and candidates, but know very little about their significance for voter turnout or voter preferences.

Available studies suggest 'having a social network gives opportunities to meet people and discuss societal questions, which in turn lead to the development of the citizens' political knowledge' (Kjellberg 2002: 202). In such networks, who plays a role in matters of deciding to participate or not in an election? What personal bonds, activities, exchanges, resources, skills, and considerations are in play? Who do people trust in sharing information about elections, residency, and identity; in giving or receiving advice on candidates; or in offering assistance at polling stations? These are largely questions of political psychology dealing with conceptions of the self as a person and as a citizen. Another set of questions deal with political sociology: Do informal systems of electoral support vary by type of group with special needs? More generally, do these systems vary accordingly by socio-economic status? What about by level of governmental elections? By location? Informal systems link in some respects to official electoral systems, for example, in the form of drivers to polls, babysitters, interpreters, and personal assistance in voting.

In theory, both systems can facilitate or frustrate voter participation, but we know little empirically about how formal and informal systems interact. Some practices of informal systems are officially recognized in legislation, in fact are relied upon for the effective functioning of elections; other activities in informal systems are semi-official in that they are permitted under regulations and discretionary guidelines; and still other parts are unofficial but may well seem authoritative from the individual's perspective. So, what can electoral offices do, what should they do, in further cultivating relations with groups in these informal networks and perhaps even building their capacity? What policy and administrative conditions are likely to promote vigorous informal electoral networks of support? A combination of case studies and comparative analysis seem *de rigueur* to begin addressing these questions.

Fourth, beyond voting, political participation consists of individuals and groups interacting with various state authorities, negotiating with public service providers, and engaging in democratic actions of protest and support such as marches and demonstrations. We do not know, for example, how many people with various disabilities may not vote in elections but, far from being totally apathetic, may well participate in other political activities in their communities. For people historically on the margins of conventional politics, these other forms of engagement seem especially significant. It is possible that people with disabilities who do not vote are active in local affairs because such events are immediate and relevant to their daily lives, with rules, structures, and processes more familiar to them. They may hold opinions on, and speak about all sorts of political issues. Thus, even though many persons with disabilities may not vote in general elections at the city, provincial, or national levels, these potential electors are not necessarily apolitical actors.

Fifth, another area that warrants research concerns the observation that 'disabled people who are elected rarely identify with disability issues' (Barnes and Mercer 2003: 113). If this is true, and impressions suggest it has some validity in Canada, then what is happening here? One line of inquiry could explore how electoral representation is shaped by cultural recognition, by what it means to be a person with disability in Canadian society. An elected official with a disability, say a visible one, may treat this aspect of his or her identity as less significant than other qualities, and downplay the 'otherness,' wishing not to be pigeon-holed as a single issue politician or one-dimensional person. Is this, then, a politically rational calculation, bearing in mind the continued dominance of 'able-bodied normality' and ambivalent attitudes toward disabilities in Canada?

Conclusion

This chapter examined disability politics and policy making in the world between environmental barriers and electoral ballots. Contemporary struggles by people with disabilities in obtaining the right to vote is a useful reminder of the significance of voting to formal citizenship, plus its importance, for many people, to exercising individual capacity, self-expression, and a sense of civic belonging. Electoral systems are terrains of democratic struggle to participate as equals. For many citizens with disabilities, voting is a relatively new opportunity and experience in democratic participation of the last few decades. A survey of federal, provincial, and territorial governments suggests there has been much progress over the past decade or so in reforming electoral laws and administrative practices to enhance access. Across governments, however, the ability to vote and to have effective and equitable access to the electoral process remains uneven for Canadians with disabilities. Electoral systems are simultaneously sites of positive inclusion, incongruous marginalization, and outright exclusion.

People with various disabilities have difficulties in trying to access campaign offices, candidates' forums, and political parties' platforms and positions on issues during election campaigns. Moreover, people with disabilities are significantly under-represented among those who participate as candidates in municipal, provincial/territorial, and federal elections.[2] Empirical studies on disability and voter turnout find that electors with disabilities have a turnout that is consistently below the general population, ranging from about 10 to 20 percentage points lower than the overall electorate. When they vote, most people with disabilities, like most other voting Canadians, prefer to vote on election day at an ordinary poll or perhaps at an advance poll, part of the electoral mainstream. Voting of course is but one kind of political participation, as Lisa Young and Joanne Everitt note: 'Citizens have a multiplicity of political interests and identities, which they cannot be expected to express in the simple act of periodic voting' (2004: 17). In the next chapter I examine the role of community organizations in speaking on behalf of people with disabilities and representing their interests in state processes of policy development.

7 Engaging in Policy Development Processes

Intertwined with struggles for recognition and redistribution, Canada's disability movement takes up a politics of representation, pursuing an agenda for equality by actively engaging in liberal democratic processes. Disability self-advocates and organizations regularly confront issues of misrepresentation: the denial of legal and civil rights if deemed incompetent or lacking capacity to make decisions; the denial of democratic rights by policy processes and information technologies, including online consultations that lack inclusive features to enable all citizens to participate. Such misrepresentations result from underdeveloped systems of representative democracy and antiquated practices in systems of public administration and communications technologies, effectively refusing people with disabilities respect for their right to participation and self-determination as members of a political community.

To address various democratic deficits, most notably public apathy and alienation, a literature on citizen engagement has emerged that looks beyond the apparatus of representative liberal democracy, concentrating instead on 'deliberative democracy.' Based primarily in political science and public administration, this literature studies and promotes recent innovations in two-way dialogues between citizens and the state, often led by independent bodies or local citizens. Analyses of citizen engagement in Canadian politics focus on 'the ordinary citizen'; individuals non-aligned with any interest groups, voluntary associations, or social movements (Laforest and Phillips 2007; Phillips with Orsini 2002; Sheedy 2008). In comparison, in this chapter I examine the participation of Canadians with disabilities as members of formally organized groups and coalitions. These collective actions are advantageous in aggregating experiences and interests of groups, communicating positions on issues, and seeking to influence governments, legislatures, and judicial decisions. Is engagement always a good thing for a disability group to pursue? As I will suggest in this chapter, alongside benefits of exercising citizenship, civic engagement holds risks. Indeed, for the disability movement, a potential danger of deliberative democracy – with its atomistic focus on the independent citizen, detached from social interest structures – is to reproduce individualistic notions of disablement that rest on pitying or pathologizing persons with impairments. Engagement is about more than individuals or small groups seeking input into policy dialogues. It is also about constructing social and political structural linkages both within and across social movements, and between citizens and various state institutions. The first section reviews the concepts of citizen engagement and community engagement, while the second section considers several models of engagement of the disability community in policy processes at the federal, provincial/territorial, parliamentary, and intergovernmental arenas. The final section identifies issues and offers conclusions about engaging with the Canadian state.

Concepts of Citizen Engagement and Community Engagement

Citizen engagement signifies a new kind of participation by individuals in public affairs, and a new kind of partnership between citizens and governments. At this early stage in the history of the idea, citizen engagement is more a democratic vision, in Canada and other countries, than a regular and specific set of legal or administrative arrangements. Typically, public consultation means government control of the agenda and who is invited, a largely one-way flow of information, and public processes that are episodic and short-lived. If traditional forms of public participation and consultation are state-centred, then engagement aims to be citizen-centred. Katherine Graham and Susan Phillips (1997) suggest that citizen-centred government stands for three elements. First, government practices 'encourage on an ongoing basis the exercise of full citizenship and its attendant responsibilities' as well as rights. Second, there is 'mutual respect and attentiveness to the respective roles of government and its citizens' by cultivating working relationships between citizens and public officials. Third, governments give recognition to individuals as mattering in democratic politics and policy making. These are key features of this new paradigm of citizen engagement.

I wish here to consider another type of public involvement in policy and decision making – community engagement. It shares with citizen engagement the intention of two-way exchanges of information between civil society and the state, and with it a shift in the relative distribution of influence over policy making and program delivery. But, instead of a focal point on the participation of individuals as individuals, the focus of community engagement is on the participation of organizations representing individuals, groups, and networks of the disability movement – otherwise put, the five arenas of the disability sector described in chapter 5. Community engagement entails the involvement of constituencies as collectivities.

From the perspective of disability organizations, there are multiple purposes in connecting with legislators, bureaucrats, judges, and human rights commissioners. Each target audience helps to address a different combination of aims for disability groups. Overall, these aims are ambitious to realize, even for a well-resourced national association. Achieving just some of these goals takes considerable investment in time, research, and commitment toward generating relevant information, forming contacts, building relations of trust, and establishing a political/public policy profile. To assist in these tasks, disability organizations forge linkages with professional associations, consultants, members of the media, and other advocacy organizations. The overall objective in all these forms of engagement is to maximize the influence of persons with disabilities and their organizations on public thinking and action as well as on policy officials, processes, and decisions. Behind these purposes are intended results – the hoped for benefits of engagement.

Being aware of this anticipated distribution of benefits can clarify expectations of the different parties entering into a citizen engagement process. To the extent that clarification occurs, a shared understanding of what engagement can and cannot do for the participants, separately and jointly, is more likely to occur. A clearer appreciation of the distribution of benefits from engagement may help to recruit, retain, and motivate the next generation of leaders in disability organizations and associations. And, it may show governments the advantages for policy making, administration, and the democratic community.

Benefits to government (politicians and public servants) from citizen engagement processes are readily identified. There is the acquisition of policy-relevant information, ideas, and knowledge for understanding the environment, making decisions, and evaluating performance. Governments benefit through the dispelling of myths about an issue, policy, or program and through an improvement in the quality, responsiveness, and effectiveness of decisions and services. Benefits to government could also entail enhancing credibility and legitimacy of public organizations, policy decisions, and programs; strengthening public trust or confidence in government, legislatures, and other public institutions; complementing the limited resources and capacities of public sector agencies; expanding community resources and social capital; and supporting active citizenship and building a vital democratic society (Boyce et al. 2001; Canadian Centre on Disability Studies 2002; OECD, 2001).

For community organizations, engaging in policy processes can include the benefits of expanding the inclusion of people traditionally left out of political life and public policy and administrative processes; generating knowledge, experiences, ideas, and insights in the community and with other sectors in society; transforming existing stereotypes, labels, and outmoded ideas concerning people with disabilities; and advancing the policy reform agenda of improving access, removing barriers, and addressing needs for supports and adequate income. Other benefits of engagement for individuals and groups involve promoting greater public and political awareness of disability issues and the experiences of Canadians with disabilities; achieving an enhanced level of self-worth through greater voice into policy development and evaluation processes; fostering a fuller sense of citizenship of individuals with disabilities; building civic capacity of organizations, associations, and coalitions; and realizing greater transparency of planning, priority setting, and decision processes.

Engaging in meaningful policy development exercises help avoid costly corrections to policies and programs in later stages of implementation because of inadequate input at earlier stages by the community. Beyond that, civic engagement for both government and community holds the promise of addressing pressing social needs, advancing inclusion, and enhancing the effectiveness and accountability of programs. For the disability community this requires governments and other social structures observing the fundamental principle of 'nothing about us without us' (Charlton 1998). On any policy or practice issue that affects the community generally or one or more groups specifically, engagement is essential for promoting empowerment and avoiding exclusion.

Models of Engagement in the Disability Sector

Methods to engage in policy relations occur at three levels: within the disability community, between this community and other communities, and between the disability community and the Canadian state. The Canadian state is a diverse collection of branches (legislative, executive, judicial, and administrative) and levels of governance (federal, provincial/territorial, First Nations, and local) linked in various ways through a web of intergovernmental relations. Table 7.1 lists seven major avenues of policy engagement between disability organizations and Canadian state institutions. I discuss each in turn.

1 *Intra-community* engagement involves disability organizations working in partnerships and forming coalitions with other organizations in the disability movement. It consists of such efforts as meeting with affiliates and locals to share information, obtain input, and develop positions on policy issues and priorities; collaborating with other disability organizations and associations to apply for joint funding or to advocate for a certain reform; and forming or joining partnerships with organizations in the disability community.

Transaction costs are associated with this series of activities; there are costs in time, budgets, and staff in forging and managing such relations. For disability agencies with extremely limited resources and a mandate for service provision, these activities represent considerable opportunity costs. Resources devoted to engagement undertakings are at the expense of other programming and service delivery work, hence, the need for collaboration among groups in the disability community. At community roundtables held at a local, provincial, or national level disability organizations come together to share their perspectives on needs, positive policy trends, and challenges on a given topic or a bundle of issues. Such events can involve an environmental scan, in which the current context as well as the climate for policy development is surveyed across groups, issues, and jurisdictions, possibly with an identification of priority issues, desired outcomes, and themes for further work. These events may only last a day or so, but can be invaluable occasions for bringing together representatives of organizations that may interact infrequently, building the morale and knowledge base of individuals, specific agencies, and the overall community.

Another type of intra-community engagement is when groups come

Table 7.1
Models of engagement between disability community and Canadian state

Model	Description
1 Intra-community	Within the disability community
2 Cross-sector	Disability groups working with organizations or associations in other parts of the voluntary or private sector
3 Community–political executive connections	Disability groups working with cabinet ministers, city councillors/mayors, and their staffs
4 Community–legislative interactions	Disability groups connecting with legislative committees and individual members
5 Community–judiciary relations	Disability activists and groups interacting with courts, human rights commissions, and other tribunals
6 Community–public service engagement	Among disability representatives and public servants
7 Community–intergovernmental engagement	Structures and processes to create a collective policy vision

together to formulate a comprehensive vision and action plan. A case in point is *A National Strategy for Persons with Disabilities: The Community Definition* (Council of Canadians with Disabilities (CCD)1999), a document produced by a coalition of thirteen national disability-related organizations.[1] Despite the identification of disability issues as a priority by First Ministers in 1996 and the release of the *In Unison* vision paper by governments in 1998, the disability community felt governments still were approaching disability issues in a piecemeal fashion. The creating of *A National Strategy* was therefore to present 'a united voice' by the community to government decision makers.

The strategy's comprehensiveness is manifest in its inclusion of Aboriginal peoples with disabilities (First Nations, Métis, and Inuit communities), children with disabilities and their families, and seniors with disabilities, thus broadening the typical emphasis in policy papers on the working-age population. *A National Strategy* also touched on roles and responsibilities within the cabinet, the legislative branch, and the public service bureaucracy. In the paper, numerous recommendations were directed at various federal government departments and agencies, but intended also for the careful consideration of the provinces, territories, and local governments in consultation with persons with disabilities and their organizations. It was designed to prompt governments to not only take further action on disability issues, but also act in a far more coordinated manner, informed by an access and inclusion disability policy lens, and in close consultation with the disability community. A recent example of formulating a comprehensive plan amongst disability groups (discussed in chapter 9) is the 2007 national agenda of policy actions toward ending exclusion.

2 *Cross-sector* engagement involves disability organizations and associations working with organizations in the larger voluntary sector through coalitions. Three types of coalitions are identifiable: virtual, ad hoc, and permanent coalitions. Table 7.2 outlines their features and functions.

In a given policy sector, any combination of these types of coalition building might be present at a certain point or over a period of time. In the past, ad hoc coalitions tended to be the most common type; that is now complemented by web-based forms of coalitions and 'virtual activists' (Meekosha 2001) and by permanent alliances forged between the disability community and the human rights movement, for

Table 7.2
Coalition building by disability groups

Type	Features	Functions
Virtual	– Communication networks – Loose affiliation – No formal structure	– Exchange information and ideas on shared interests – Learn from others – Build contacts/alliances
Ad Hoc	– Specific issue or purpose – Time-limited – Loose structure – Either within the disability sector or across sectors	– Rally support – Increase numbers – Share information – Present a broad and united front – Gain political attention
Permanent	– Broad area of concerns and issues – Ongoing activities – Formal structure with some staff to co-ordinate activities of mutual interest	– Raise numbers and profile – Generate and exchange information and ideas – Establish legitimacy and authority with political system – Build solidarity across groups

Source: Based on William Boyce et al., *A Seat at the Table: Persons with Disabilities and Policy Making*. Montreal and Kingston: McGill-Queen's Univ. Press. (2001:135–6).

example. Based upon a mutuality of interest, the foundation of support for disability-related issues has broadened and become more formally structured (Roeher 1997).

Coalitions are important resources for policy engagement, especially for marginalized groups such as people with disabilities. As with other socially constructed groups, Canadians with disabilities have some interests in common while others conflict in regard to policy goals and preferred actions. Differences among persons with disabilities and their organizations reflect differences in impairments, language, age, ethnicity, and place, among other divisions. These inevitable diversities present challenges in developing common policy positions maintaining 'a politics of solidarity in difference' – the need to bridge differences between people with disabilities and incorporate cross-disability experiences (Lister 1997). In the case of the Canadian disability movement, what helps is that most groups share a broad ideological position, a core set of beliefs about state and society. Most disability groups look to the state for actions, and are willing to work within the confines of federalism and capitalism. Most groups also interpret the causes of inequality widely experienced among Canadians with disabilities as rooted in attitudinal and environmental barriers and discrimination.

Deprivations associated with the structural inequalities of social stratification (discussed in chapter 3) offer a powerful basis and conceptual space for building solidarity among people with diverse disabilities. An organized unity among those struggling for access and inclusion can arise from the universals of diversity and poverty. For Peter Leonard, the way to build solidarity in this age of recognition politics is by making connections between social identities and wider material inequalities, joined with 'a focus on the similarity of different forms of oppression as well as their particularity' (Leonard 1997: 157). The harsh realities of unmet needs of inclusive child care, education, employment, or adequate income forge a widespread centre of attention for groups. An example at the time of my writing this is the Saskatchewan Disability Income Support Coalition, dedicated to developing a distinct and adequate income support system for people with disabilities. Formed in 2006, the coalition comprises several impairment-specific societies and some cross-disability groups along with anti-poverty, First Nations, and Métis organizations. The coalition's vision asserts that 'the only way to move forward is as one voice and in a collaborative, full partnership with the Government of

Saskatchewan and the Department of Community Resources. We believe that a program designed without the collaboration of community experts will lack credibility and be unsatisfactory in meeting the income support needs of people with disabilities.'[2]

Coalitions are strategic practices for articulating political critiques and for imagining new ways forward together. They are pragmatic devices for pooling limited resources, sharing information, and broadening representation, thus raising symbolic visibility via the media and enhancing democratic legitimacy. Until the 1990s, however, there was little success in or inclination toward coalition building between disability groups and other social movements, such as Aboriginal or women's groups. This was partially because of a concern that such alliances might overshadow disability issues (Boyce et al. 2001: 62, 130). Other factors were at play. DisAbled Women's Network (DAWN) Canada, a national feminist cross-disability organization, arose 'in response to the frustration women with disabilities felt because of the inaccessibility of the women's movement, and the indifference to women's issues from the disability community' (Roeher 1997: 166). In building coalitions, disability group leaders and members must attend to differences in privilege and perspective that exist within the movement.

In cross-sector engagement, competing advocacy coalitions can exist in a given policy sector – two or more coalitions of actors and groups with contending beliefs and strategies about disability policy. An example is the clash between the Ad Hoc Coalition of Service Providers and the Ontario Advocacy Coalition over proposed provincial advocacy and guardianship legislation in the 1990s. These two coalitions differed in many ways: their goals, membership base, funding, organizational structures, tactics, and perspectives on disability (Boyce et al. 2001). This case demonstrates that coalition building may not mitigate political conflict, at least in the short run. Coalitions can be a competitive as well as a cooperative affair. Such competition happens when challenging prevailing views of experts and professionals. A larger issue, in this regard, is determining if, and when, to join a coalition-building process. It may not be the right time if the group is fairly new and still forming its own mandate or if a group is undergoing a major reorganization or is facing major internal challenges.

3 *Community–political executive connections* involve relations between one or more disability organizations and a particular government

leader, minister, city mayor, and their political staff. To be sure, this can be a strategy for building relationships with members of the governing elite. Four types of engagement with political executives are episodic activities, cyclic process, temporary advisory structures, and permanent public bodies. Episodic links between the disability community and cabinet ministers take place around specific reform processes, ranging from constitutional matters to legislation and regulations. These often represent classic lobbying or advocacy efforts, and perhaps consultation exercises (Young and Everitt 2004). These activities may not qualify as engagement under the definition presented in the literature, but they are important connections for any group that wishes to influence the shape and direction of public policy.

In some cyclical policy processes, the participation of disability organizations is both expected by the community and accepted by government. A notable example is the annual pre-budget consultation process held by the finance minister at the federal level. A common refrain in budget speeches is that such changes reflect a process of ongoing consultations with representatives of organizations for Canadians with disabilities. Following the 1996 report of Federal Task Force on Disability Issues, recommendations on tax reforms were introduced in the 1997 and 1998 federal budgets. Since then, several disability-related tax initiatives have appeared, most notably of late the Registered Disability Savings Plan in 2008.

An example of a temporary advisory body on disability issues connected to ministers is the Technical Advisory Committee on Tax Measures for Persons with Disabilities, announced in the February 2003 federal budget. This advisory group had eighteen months in which to advise the ministers of finance and revenue on the administrative and eligibility criteria for the Disability Tax Credit and other tax measures affecting Canadians with disabilities. Intended to be independent of the government, the Technical Advisory Committee had twelve members, including several members of disability organizations, some tax law specialists, medical practitioners, and social policy experts (Canada 2003b). The committee's report yielded a new personal income tax measure, the disability supports deduction, and increases to a number of existing disability-related tax benefits in the 2004 federal budget, as well as further changes in subsequent budgets (Canada 2006).

Ongoing formal linkages between the disability community and political executives in Canada exist with cabinet ministers responsible for disability issues and with advisory bodies on disability issues that are attached to the premier's office. Typically, in jurisdictions where a minister is designated responsible for disability – for example, Canada, Ontario, Manitoba, and Saskatchewan – there is an office for disability issues located within that particular minister's department or ministry. In Alberta, Saskatchewan, Quebec, New Brunswick, and Nova Scotia responsibility for disability issues is located in public bodies with a statutory foundation attached to the legislative assembly or the premier's office. This affords these bodies profile and stability in their role. Temporary advisory committees and permanent statutory councils sit outside the regular bureaucracy, and both types potentially serve several functions for governments and the disability community. These include representation of particular groups and expertise on the organization; consultation with the public by holding hearings; collection of information and conducting of research on an issue; evaluation of policies, programs, and administrative systems; and recommendations to a minister or cabinet committee.

4 *Community–legislative interactions* include relations between disability groups and parliamentary committees and with individual members of parliaments or members of provincial/territorial assemblies. At the level of the local state, legislative encounters are with municipal councillors, school trustees, transit commissioners, hospital board members, and other local government decision-making bodies.

Since the early 1980s, an important legislative space for disability groups has been parliamentary committees. In 1980–1, a special committee of the House of Commons on the constitution provided the first significant involvement of disability advocates and groups as parties to constitutional reform, providing the opportunity to alter the language in the Charter of Rights and Freedoms. In the same time period, the special parliamentary committee that produced the important *Obstacles* report (Canada 1981) hired a staff member of the Coalition of Provincial Organizations of the Handicapped (predecessor to the Council of Canadians with Disabilities (CCD)), to serve as a consultant to the committee. This enabled the consultant to gather information on the political landscape in Ottawa, and relay knowledge on key policy issues to the coalition.

Parliamentary committees have served as vehicles for involving and consulting with disability groups and, at times, are useful catalysts for policy change. Through their public hearings and reports, legislative bodies promote the equality of rights of persons with disabilities, highlight the costs of inaction, monitor and assess government initiatives, and recommend reviews and reforms to the tax system as it affects persons with disabilities. In all this, legislative bodies draw political and public attention to the needs of Canadians with disabilities and contribute to the expression of a new disability policy paradigm. The disability community values parliamentary committees as a place to voice their concerns and to fill a gap in access to other parts of the government and political system (Torjman 2001: 167).

A variant of community-legislature engagement was a federal task force on disability issues, appointed in June 1996 by the ministers of finance, human resources development, and revenue. Their mandate was to define and make recommendations regarding the appropriate role of the federal government vis-à-vis Canadians with disabilities. The task force included four members of parliament. The Office for Disability Issues within the federal public service provided support to the task force. Representatives of about twenty national disability organizations participated in numerous ways. The representatives formed a reference group that identified issues and refined research themes, and sent observers to all the public meetings of the task force. Specifically, three representatives from these organizations selected by their colleagues acted as observers of the task force meetings. Community representatives provided the task force a rich knowledge of and deep commitment to disability issues; they were with the task force in community meetings held across the country. Experts commissioned to do research collaborated with a working group of representatives of the national organizations. In fifteen forums the task force held across the country, some 2,000 people participated, most of whom were people with disabilities. They released their final report, *Equal Citizenship for Canadians with Disabilities: The Will to Act*, in October 1996.

E-consultation is another tool in engaging parliamentary bodies with the disability community. For example, the House of Commons Sub-committee on the Status of Persons with Disabilities (Canada 2003d) held an online consultation on the Canada Pension Plan Disability program, the first by a Canadian parliamentary committee. As this consultation concerned the review of an existing program, it illustrates online engagement at the evaluation stage of the policy process. Featuring a dedicated web site, this online engagement provided information on the issues of CPP disability, included a participatory issue poll, and invited feedback from all interested citizens. Over four months, there were more then 15,000 visitors to the web site and over 1,400 people completed a survey with their comments. This represents a significant level of public participation, most likely extending opportunities to people who otherwise would not have participated with a parliamentary committee (Sheedy 2008; Stienstra and Troschuk 2005).

This e-consultation complemented conventional techniques of public engagement used by the sub-committee of inviting briefs, hearing witnesses, and a roundtable with experts. A summary of the key points arising from that roundtable was later posted on the sub-committee's web site. This mixed approach has the benefit of joining newer information technologies with traditional consultative tools used by parliamentarians, thus supporting the role of elected representatives. The Senate Committee on Social Affairs that examined mental health and mental illness, heard witnesses between September 2003 and November 2005, also employed an online consultation along with hearings across the country that elicited more than 2,000 personal stories of Canadians living with mental illness, and their families (Kirby 2006). It would be both interesting and helpful if parliamentarians reviewed this exercise, and similar ones,[3] to ascertain lessons on promising practices. As an international organization points out in a recent policy report: 'Online citizen engagement in policy-making is new and examples of good practice are rare. Hence the imperative for building on the experience of others and the need for further comparative work on this emerging issue' (OECD 2003: 6).

5 *Community–judiciary relations* entail using the court system in advancing disability issues and rights. From the 1940s into the 1970s, provinces took the lead in developing human rights codes and commissions and by the 1980s, all codes listed disability as one of the prohibited grounds of discrimination. Thus, it is a mistake to call the judicial activism of the last two decades with the Canadian Charter of Rights and Freedoms an 'Americanization' of tactics used by the disability community; disability advocates and organizations have sought judicial solutions for a considerable period. Disability organizations resort to the courts and human rights tribunals in order to enforce reasonable accommodation in schools, transportation, and employment; to oblige governments to provide services and supports under existing public programs; and to end discrimination based on mental or physical disabilities (Cameron and Valentine 2001: 35).

For Canada's disability community, litigating against discrimination and for rights yield mixed results. In cases involving a diverse range of institutions including a local school board, the federal correctional services, and provincial health care services, the Supreme Court of Canada has held that employers have a duty, under section 15, to make reasonable accommodations to the needs of a person with a mental or physical disability. The accommodations, however, may often be narrowly interpreted and slowly implemented by governments (Hogg 2007).

6 *Community–public service engagement* entails disability groups and advocates engaging with public servants, such as offices for disability issues, advisory committees, program managers, and service providers. For example, Veterans Affairs Canada (VAC) works in partnership with the Royal Canadian Legion, as well as other veterans' organizations, on issues such as housing support for veterans with service-related disabilities. VAC also offers an advocacy service to departmental clients when they apply for benefits or are appealing unfavourable decisions about eligibility. Another example is Council on Access to Information for Print-disabled Canadians formed by the National Librarian of Canada in 2001. The Council has two core purposes. The first is to provide advice, identify funding requirements, monitor progress, and make recommendations to the National Librarian regarding the implementation of *Fulfilling the Promise: The Report of the Task Force on Access to Information for Print-Disabled Canadians*. The second purpose is to identify and recommend to the National Librarian opportunities for the Council (or its designated spokespersons) to connect, inform, and facilitate the work of the Federal Disability Agenda (Canada 2003c). The Council has twelve members, including a chair and eleven other members who come from alternate format producers, education institutions, public libraries, publishers, consumers, and consumer groups. Five policy advisors assist the Council, four of whom are from federal government departments, to forge links with the Federal Disability Agenda, and the other advisor is from the CNIB. The Council meets twice a year in person with other meetings by other formats if needed. A secretariat provided by the National Library supports the Council. Within provincial jurisdictions, consultations between government departments and organizations of and for persons with disabilities also take place on a fairly regular basis on various topics.

Federal and provincial/territorial instances of disability policy engagement reveal an assortment of practices and approaches. Some occurrences are relatively new, while others are longstanding; some are one-time and fairly specific, while others are more general and ongoing. A few are far more structured and officially mandated than many others; and they can focus on different stages of the policy process, from offering ideas and comments, to advising on evaluation designs through monitoring the progress of activities, to overseeing the actual delivery of services and programs on the ground.

7 *Community–intergovernmental engagement* promises broadening participation beyond ministers, senior bureaucrats, and program specialists to include organizations of and for people with disabilities, social policy consultants, and service provider agencies. It also entails establishing and strengthening lines of accountability to legislatures and other political stakeholders. Even so, most disability organizations feel 'they have little direct access' to federal-provincial-territorial (FPT) working groups and are concerned that they will be left out of these intergovernmental forums 'or at best consulted after the fact.' Moreover, they wonder 'how they can relate to, let alone influence, this process' (Torjman 2001: 163, 193). To illustrate the opportunities and challenges, two cases are briefly presented on disability community engagement with intergovernmental processes, both concern creating a collective policy vision.

Ministers responsible for social services agreed to embark upon the process of creating a federal-provincial-territorial vision of principles and objectives as part of an intergovernmental review of services affecting people with disabilities. This culminated in the *Pathway to Integration, Final Report* (Canada 1993). Called 'Mainstream '92,' the aim of this process was to develop a collective strategic framework, which explored the full integration of Canadians with disabilities into the mainstream of Canadian society. A related goal was to explore if governments and the disability community could agree upon a vision and statement of principles.

A consultation process ran for two years to explore creating such a shared strategic framework. The consultation considered current practices and possible strategic directions in the social services, employment programs, community independent living, income security, and disability related supports. Several techniques of engagement were used: holding focus groups across the country; receiving briefs from national associations and organizations that work with or represent people with disabilities; meetings between the organizing committee of the review and individuals with disabilities, policy experts, and representatives of advocacy and consumer organizations; and commissioning research studies on various disability issues. Mary Lee Alexander (2001: 29) neatly summarizes the interplay between governmental and community perspectives in this process:

> The development of a strategic framework required the creation of an agreed upon vision statement, a statement of principles and a series of strategic directions. The Mainstream 92 report points to the fact that from the outset there was disagreement between government and the participants from disability groups on the vision statement. The government came to the Mainstream 92 process with a vision statement that was based on the 'Open House' concept that emphasized the *'importance* of people with disabilities being able to participate fully in the mainstream of Canada.' Participants from disability groups brought with them a detailed *Equality and Citizenship Rights* paradigm that they had developed through the consultation process. Their vision was based on the belief 'that people with disabilities have the *right* to participate fully in their communities on equal terms as other Canadians.' Further it stressed that accommodation is required to ensure that people with disabilities have equity in relation to opportunities and outcomes. The Federal Government's statement was limited to stressing the importance of participation. While both vision statements were published in the Mainstream 92 report, the Federal Government's 'Open House' vision was adopted as the Mainstream 92 vision statement.

A similar process of parallel presentations of statements of principles took place, although the principles eventually agreed to and published in the Mainstream '92 report reflected more of a mix of the government and disability community perspectives (Alexander 2001: 30). The Mainstream '92 exercise was an essential effort at establishing relations and exploring ways of working together. A more consensual shared approach to disability issues, between the community and governments, would come with the Scott Task Force in 1996 (discussed earlier) and the *In Unison* document in 1998.

In 1998, federal, provincial, and territorial governments (except Quebec) agreed to a new approach to disability issues in Canada, expressed in the *In Unison* document (Canada 1998). The vision declares that persons with disabilities ought to participate as full citizens in all aspects of Canadian society. Actions are identified for three areas: disability supports, employment, and income security. In developing the *In Unison* policy vision, the nine provincial and two territorial ministers responsible for social services asked their officials to share the draft document with stakeholders from the disability community. Torjman (2001: 193), who served as a consultant to this exercise, describes the process and, based on her experience, raises the issues of when and how often to share intergovernmental discussions with a policy community:

> The federal-provincial working group on disability set up a reference group to keep consumers informed of the discussions and to receive their input on an ongoing basis. Questions arose around the *In Unison* document and the most appropriate stage for sharing the contents of this vision paper prior to its public release. Ideally, consultation should have taken place at a very early stage to test out the proposals before the document went to various governments for approval.
>
> However, officials on the federal-provincial working group were concerned that disability groups would be informed of the possible policy options in the vision paper before they had an opportunity to brief their ministers – let alone obtain agreement from them on the proposed directions. The consultations were eventually held, but at a relatively later stage in the process.

Contributions by the disability community stress the vital importance of personal supports for everyday living and participation, cooperative intergovernmental relations, and the necessity to establish jointly measurable and transparent indicators of results. Although episodic events in engagement, these intergovernmental processes have produced documents with agreed upon goals and a shared vocabulary shared for discussing policy reforms. More recently, two provincial governments, Quebec in 2002, and Newfoundland and Labrador in 2006, have introduced general anti-poverty strategies. Both strategies specifically include measures for people with disabilities, among other groups of people living in poverty, provide for structures and processes of consultation on a regular basis with civil society groups, and commit to reporting mechanisms to the legislature and public on the results from anti-poverty initiatives.

Conclusion

Canadians with disabilities are a social group that in large measure has not been well represented in mainstream political institutions. In recent decades, new disability organizations have formed and old organizations reformed, mobilizing to gain access to state structures and public policy making processes. Multiple approaches to engagement are necessary given a number of realities: the assorted needs and perspectives of social groups and service agencies, the widely varied capacities of disability organizations, the complexity and dispersed authority of the Canadian state, and the wide assortment of pressing issues facing people with disabilities. The potential of disability organizations to exercise influence rests on a bundle of resources. Canada's disability movement works in and through the core institutions of capitalism, cabinet-parliamentary government, federalism, and judicial authority. These multiple institutional sites for engagement offer an assortment of possibilities for participating in political affairs, yet at the same time pose risks of fragmenting disability movement politics and stretching the thin resources of most groups to engage with the state.

What are the requirements for an enhanced and more effective engagement between the disability community and governments? 'Community groups need to consult more amongst themselves more regularly, to build solidarity and establish common positions on issues. The administrative and policy capacity of groups need to be looked at more carefully by governments so that the opportunities for consultation and engagement are not burdensome to groups. Where they exist, legislative committees with responsibility for disability issues need to continue serving as a political space for this sector. Where they do not exist, they should be established' (Prince 2001d: 817).

A study on the Canadian disability community adds: 'Organizations require additional human and financial resources to effectively carry out their mandates and to undertake ongoing research to find solutions to issues raised by the disability community. Support is also needed to assist disability associations to form viable partnerships and to consult among themselves and with governments to advance the disability agenda within Canada' (Canadian Centre on Disability Studies 2002: 3). To improve the community's capacity for engagement, this study recommends that governments hire more people with disabilities in the public service, consult with the disability community on an ongoing basis before taking action, and increase the level of financing to groups and amend the form of funding from year-to-year to multi-year funding. In addition, knowledge is highly relevant to capacity, especially in relation to engagement. Knowledge capacity includes undertaking research; managing and disseminating complex information; knowing about the significant policy processes, structures, and actors; and conveying the community's experiences in language that politicians and government officials can understand and use.

When facing the state, disability organizations encounter openings for engagement mottled with significant barriers and challenges. At provincial levels, disability groups face a service sector with, in recent times, a considerable contracting out of public services to non-profit societies and for-profit enterprises. At all levels, disability groups face financial caution by cabinets, even with budget surpluses in many jurisdictions. Groups interact with government bureaucracies with policy and research capacities seriously diminished from levels in the 1980s and 1990s, due to cutbacks and a restrained role of governments in social policy reforms. Disability organizations labour to fund advocacy, policy research, and consultation work, infrequently getting funding for such activities from governments.

When facing the state, the disability movement sees episodic consultations, somewhat improved with online processes, but still feels pushed to litigation as a last resort tactic to achieve equality, though once again without support through a court challenges program. In our brave new world of online e-consultations for public policy making, Laforest and Phillips properly caution that 'the wiring may exist, but the power is not always on,' meaning it is not 'effectively plugged into decision making' (2007: 83). The movement sees relatively few people with disabilities in legislatures, cabinet roles, judicial appointments, or senior bureaucratic posts. Moreover, technically accessible information and communication technologies do not mean universally accessible to the circumstances of all persons with disabilities (Dale and Newman 2005; Stienstra and Troschuk 2005).

In jurisdictions across Canada with disability advisory bodies, and that is not the case in all, these bodies are often attached to a government rather than located within and throughout a governmental system. In British Columbia, there is a ministerial advisory council on employment issues for persons with disabilities; in Saskatchewan there is an office for disability issues housed in a department. A more extensive person with disabilities machinery exists in Alberta, with a Premier's Council on the Status of Persons with Disabilities, with a legislated mandate and chaired by an MLA, providing a link to the legislative assembly, and an office for disability issues in a social program department. Compared to the women's or senior's movements, the disability movement is not as well represented in the structures of government departments, central agencies, or legislatures.

In Canada, the traditional representative institutions of parliamentary cabinet government and their younger sisters, executive federalism and the Charter of Rights and Freedoms, prevail in most engagement relationships with the disability community. Public servants in program departments and in central agencies such as finance or treasury boards, and cabinet ministers determine when consultations will happen, under what terms and conditions, and timelines. At times, parliamentarians, the courts, or community groups play a decisive role. In many cases, public servants play the lead in gathering together and summing up community interests into policy recommendations and decisions. This is by no means a neutral or simple practical exercise. Always predisposed and partial, it is always political. It involves interpreting, filtering, and ranking suggestions within a pre-existing set of assumed constraints and opportunities, as perceived by state officials. At times, such constraints appear upfront in consultation processes; many other times, these dominant assumptions are blandly implied in bureaucratic euphemisms. Although the vague words framing a consultation may give little offence in the short term, because of their imprecision ultimately they are insulting to groups that feel misled and manipulated by tokenistic exercises in citizen participation.

In engaging with state institutions today, there is a serious risk in giving further legitimacy to neo-liberal values and practices that, for people with disabilities, mean environmental inequalities are basically unexamined and matters of socio-economic redistribution are largely contained. On the opportunities for equality-seeking social movements, a recent study concludes that we have in Canada today 'a national political life with a diminished array of voices and less space for materialist concerns' around economic security and social services (James 2006: 118). Spaces for disability community engagement in public policy processes are affected by this wider political context.

Indeed, opportunities for meaningful engagement in policy making by Canadian disability organizations seem less today than in the 1980s and 1990s.

A number of critical questions therefore arise whenever occasions for engagement are presented to the disability movement: How open and inclusive are such opportunities? Who has the ability to participate, when, where, and how? At what stages of public policy processes do groups have avenues for expressing their voices? What support is available to assist groups to engage? What accountability mechanisms are in place to monitor the process and report back on the actual results or decisions taken? How much is a given consultation a one-way or a two-way exchange of ideas and information?

Notwithstanding risks and limitations of engaging with state institutions, national and local disability organizations continue to participate, even if they are not enthusiastic about the prospects. They do so because that is their *raison d'être* and what their members expect of them as 'accountable representatives' (Laforest and Phillips 2007: 78). They do so because it is a means for building momentum and solidarity on issues within the movement and forging alliances with other social movements. They do so because such processes offer public spaces, however cramped or temporary, in which to draw notice to current inequalities and absences, to outline alternative approaches to disablement and community living, and to advance claims for social recognition and respect in the language of full citizenship.

PART THREE

Conclusions

8 Politicizing Citizenship:
Towards a Fuller Measure of Equality

In our current era of politics, citizenship goes well beyond legal and governmental conceptions to embrace economic and sociological notions of participation, reciprocity, and autonomy. Citizenship struggles connect people with disabilities to the courts, intergovernmental processes, educational institutions, labour markets, family members, and community agencies. In substantially improving the lives of Canadians with disabilities, the pace of change is uneven; the scope of reform is variable. Implementing the vision of citizenship – full membership in communities – carries on through a contingent series of instalments, not without contentions, setbacks, and disruptions. T.H. Marshall underscores the dynamics between citizenship and contingent change:

> Citizenship is a status bestowed on those who are full members of a community. All who possess the status are equal with respect to the rights and duties with which the status is bestowed. There is no universal principle that determines what those rights and duties shall be, but societies in which citizenship is a developing institution create an image of an ideal citizenship against which achievement can be measured and towards which aspirations can be directed. The urge forward along the path thus plotted is an urge towards a fuller measure of equality, an enrichment of the stuff of which the status is made and an increase in the number of those on whom the status is bestowed. (1964: 84)

How is citizenship, itself a concept rooted in public law and the polity, further politicized? It is through ongoing battles for membership and esteemed identities. 'The history of citizenship during the past two centuries can be viewed as a persistent struggle on the part of the "unfit," the disenfranchised, the marginalized, the dependent to be included in the ranks of "the citizen"' (Kivisto and Faist 2007: 18). In an essay on disability activism, Anspach refers to the politicization of life, 'a widening definition of politics to embrace all aspects of the person' (1979: 765). Instead of individual empathy, movement activists ask for institutional equality, for social justice. Canadian disability groups are politicizing citizenship by discussing the very idea of what being a citizen means in practice, contesting old assumptions about personhood and competency, litigating issues, and proposing new ways of delivering socially inclusive services (Lord and Hutchison 2007; Peters 2003; Pothier and Devlin 2006). The disability movement asks what rights people with disabilities should expect from the state at all levels of governance. The movement casts citizenship in a critical light, pointing out material, democratic, and symbolic gaps between citizenship and the lived experience of many persons with disabilities. With access and inclusion as core elements of citizenship, social realities of prejudice and segregation invariably draw attention to contradictions of official public discourse.

Just as significantly, the movement asks what responsibilities, as social actors in communities, people with disabilities have to themselves and to others. The politics of citizenship not only concerns demands for entitlements, but also obligations. Disability activists call for an expansion of the responsibilities associated with citizenship. This includes the duties of others toward people with disabilities to respect their rights in a formal and substantive manner, and the asserted duties of people with disabilities to have recognized and supported their legal capacity to make decisions for themselves, rather than by guardians, appointed trustees, lawyers, or family members through power of attorney. This call for citizenship obligations includes aspirations to attend regular classrooms in regular schools; to pay taxes as workers, consumers, and property owners; and to train for and accept real jobs for real wages, with associated duties of meeting schedules and performing tasks. Aspiring for concrete and personal obligations as active full persons is a feature in disability claims for full citizenship.

Full citizenship for Canadians with disabilities is still a developing institution, an ideal that appears in reports by governments, professional associations, and advocacy groups. Disability groups focus on social rights and they examine discursive, legal, political, and economic elements of citizenship. Progress to fuller inclusion in Canadian life along varying elements of citizenship is a variable and complex set of processes, yielding different achievements and disappointments. The status of rights and duties of citizenship for people with disabilities is differentiated, incomplete, and contested.

Public policy and the state are mixed blessings for people with disabilities. On the one hand, the state offers people with disabilities income benefits, tax measures, protective employment standards, and human rights laws. On the other, the state imposes controls, perpetuates stereotypes, and reinforces dependencies. Health professionals, educational personnel, or program administrators in the past and still today frequently impose disabled identities on people. They do so by suppressing differences, downplaying capacities, and fitting them into diagnostic categories. Despite some organizational reforms and consultative processes of democratic engagement, political systems remain ableist and exclusionary. People with disabilities are significantly under-represented at all levels of politics and governing. Even with these contradictions, the Canadian disability movement regards the state as the sector with the most potential for advancing equality rights and social inclusion of people with disabilities.

The rest of this chapter contains four substantive sections. In the first, I describe the national style of disability activism, and suggest that ideologically the characteristic Canadian approach is a form of social liberalism. In the second section, I relate the absences of action and inclusion of persons with disabilities to cultural and intellectual gaps discussed in part 1 and then offer the twin concepts of social intersectionalities and policy intersectionalities as tools for systematically linking disability with social stratification. In the third, I discuss broadening the definition of disability policy to a more social and political viewpoint, and note that disability reform takes place both as a dimension of numerous policy areas as well as a distinct policy domain itself. Finally, in the fourth section, I argue that disability issues are of growing importance as political matters and that the disability movement is caught up in the contradictions of politicizing citizenship.

Disability Activism as Social Liberalism

The disability movement in Canada with its associated discourse, politics, and policy making exhibits a characteristic style, as do the movements in other countries such as Australia, Britain, and the United States (Cameron and Valentine 2001; Chivers 2008; Stienstra and

Wight-Felske 2003). The distinctive approach of Canadian disability activism reflects the dominance of liberal values in Canadian society and political culture. Contributing to this style is the unique configuration of federalism, cabinet-focused parliamentary government, the Charter of Rights and Freedoms, and an increasingly multicultural society and urban nation (Broadbent 2008). Located well within a liberal-democratic tradition, the prominent philosophy in disability activism can be called social liberalism. Other terms for this form of ideology are developmental individualism, modified individualism, and moderate or welfare liberalism. This social liberalism embraces a number of beliefs about the economy, the nature of people, society, the state, and the necessity for change and political action.

On the economy, social liberalism accepts the existence and fundamental necessity of the capitalist economy and private market relations. The disability movement strives for greater participation of individuals with the full array of physical and mental impairments to participate in the mainstream labour market. The Canadian disability movement is neither anti-capitalist nor is it anti-globalization. Disability organizations believe significant changes for people with disabilities can happen within existing economic structures. A core element of the struggle for 'access' means access to paid labour. The economic dimension of full citizenship typically assumes gainful employment, rather than the alternatives of sheltered workshops or voluntary service masquerading as competitive and fair wage-based work. Disability activists recognize the importance of work incentives in social policy and condemn the work disincentives embedded in various income programs and public services. Moreover, the goal of community living rather than a segregated institutionalized existence also takes for granted the value of personal and private property.

Acceptance of the market economy is not unequivocal. Disability groups call for actions to shift workplace attitudes and practices about abilities; as well, they call for affirmative measures such as employment equity and reasonable accommodations to modify market values and forces. At the heart of liberalism is the primacy of the individual and enabling each person to develop and use their capacities to the fullest possible (Macpherson 1977). That every individual has innate capacities, dignity, and equal moral worth is a core belief that strongly resonates with contemporary disability movements. Liberalism with a social outlook relates to rights-based advocacy for equal treatment under the law. It also fits with social and environmental models of disability which, in essence, reject the atomized nature of humanity found in some expressions of rugged individualism, and in the personal tragedy and bio-medical models of impairment.

As an expression of social liberalism, disability activism in Canada places the individual within a larger societal context. Disability activists push hard against longstanding views of disability as a personal problem and private issue (Michalko 2002: 6). Alongside individuals, core elements of society are families, local communities, and other groupings. Disability groups often focus on individuals and their needs, but the general emphasis is not individualistic; individuals are interdependent and interconnected through myriad networks of roles, structures, and relationships, some of which are enabling, and many others, over the lifespan, disabling. We are all human, unique, and limited in known and unpredictable ways over the course of our lives. Human society has a moral value and material benefit linked with the status and practice of citizenship. Disability groups recognize that the possibility of people realizing their actual capacities relies in large measure on their membership, participation, and sense of belonging in a political society. Rights are for individuals as well as for groups. To advance substantive access and equality, it is necessary at times to treat people identically and at times to treat people differently. The disability movement asserts equality and equity, and individual and group rights as important values of justice.

A notable feature of Canadian disability politics is the state-oriented approach taken by most groups whether for services, agency funding, legislative reforms, policy consultations, or equality claims through litigation (McColl and Jongbloed 2006; Pothier and Devlin 2006). Reasons for a state-focus by disability activists are obvious. Many government programs related to disability have operated for many decades, some with profoundly harmful effects for which groups are seeking restitution of various kinds. Activists point out that the state has never been neutral regarding issues of disability, ability, normalcy, and deservingness. Other new social movements and long-standing interest groups in Canadian politics focus on the state, with varying degrees of success. Because of discrimination and disadvantages, people with disabilities as a group are more reliant on state services than people without disabilities. Instead of some mythical notion of neutrality, disability advocates argue for a state committed to social equity, as well as formal equality. State activities are pivotal in defining citizenship.

The state-focus of disability activism in Canada goes back to the early twentieth century and is an outstanding characteristic of contemporary activism. As the mass media and social sciences express general concerns about declining civic engagement in democracies, disabled people are striving to increase their voices and involvement in public affairs. The Canadian disability movement has a conception of 'the political' that includes not just governments, legislatures, and courts but also families and social networks, the voluntary sector, the economy, and cultural practices. As I have shown, the disability movement engages extensively with government bureaucracies, cabinet ministers, parliamentary committees, courts and tribunals, and political parties and elections. Conventional mainstream political activities are the route taken to mainstream disability concerns. Largely adopting a *reformist* view of politics, there is a commitment to pursuing societal change through democratic dialogue, where available, and to research on issues, and public awareness and education. The disability movement has some faith in the efficacy of public action for alleviating poverty, tackling inequalities, and promoting accessibility. Disability groups present issues to Canadian decision makers in terms of unfair obstacles, blocked access, unmet needs, and inadequate social inclusion; they engage in a liberal discourse of equality of opportunity and humanitarianism, compared to a more critical discourse of social oppression and economic exploitation.

Critics point out that policies motivated by social liberalism are surface actions rather than systemic transformations (Fraser 1989); that this reformist approach fails to tackle the deep structures in the economy and society that are disabling, structures that generate and reproduce divisions of advantages and disadvantages. That said, 'Citizenship rights are not simply empty civil rights which are utilized to reinforce existing inequalities' (Turner 1986: 136). As the mainstream constellation of values of Canadians, social liberalism does generate critiques of capitalist relationships and sets some limits on market practices. It is how most people make sense of their lives and the larger world. In other words, social liberalism is experientially close to the prevailing political culture of the general population and the political opportunity structures for change.[1]

As social liberalism, the political ideas of disability activism see a positive function for the state. There are active roles for the federal, provincial, and municipal governments in showing leadership, tackling obstacles, providing essential services and supports, and ensuring sustained efforts on reforms. Depending on program design and actual delivery, public services can have positive effects in alleviating social exclusion and improving economic security. Henry Enns and Aldred Neufeldt (2003) characterize the relationship between disability groups and government organizations as a positive one, with the two sectors performing different yet complementary roles in policy development and implementation. They draw attention to 'the mutuality of relationships between the "official" roles of government and the "unofficial" roles of disability organizations' (Enns and Neufeldt 2003: 4). There are two problematic aspects to this statement. One is that the terms 'official' and 'unofficial' create a hierarchy of legitimacy between state and civil sectors, and undermines notions of public accountability by governments to citizens.

Second, as disability activists and academics point out, roles between government and the community are not always complementary and certainly not symmetrical in terms of power resources. A naïve emphasis on 'the mutuality of relationships' can result in the imposition of official agendas, co-opting disability groups into uneven policy processes. David Kwavnick's assessment of interest group activities at the federal level in Canada still rings true:

> The most effective means of influencing government policy are activities which purport to mobilize public opinion, particularly broad representatives of inter-group activities such as national conferences. The most effective means of obtaining favours within the limits of government policy is the development of close day-to-day working relations with civil servants and ministers. Frantic pressure campaigns are rarely mounted and then only as a last resort. (1972: 222)

Since this observation on interest group politics, we have the Charter of Rights and Freedoms with the tools of litigation and an equality discourse. Overall, though, Kwavnick's comment emphasizes the importance of working on public attitudes and opinion, building coalitions with other groups, and holding national conferences to mobilize the movement and articulate an agenda for change.

As socio-political critique, liberalism has long aimed at 'freeing the individual from the outdated restraints of old fashioned institutions' (Macpherson 1977: 21). In this regard, disability groups are involved in challenging old beliefs and practices about the limits of impairments, the supposed unemployable status of many people with disabilities, and the assumed benefits of specialized institutions for persons with intellectual disabilities. Part of the cultural politics of this social movement involves disability groups and others challenging the paternalistic views that persons with disabilities are defective, helpless, dependent, and needy users of services, and instead, offering positive images of persons with disabilities as individuals with capacities, capable of diverse forms of self-development and social contributions, and as citizens entitled to the same expectations and opportunities, freedoms, rights, and responsibilities as other Canadians.

The community living movement continues to call for the closure of institutions in a number of Canadian jurisdictions that segregate people labelled as having an intellectual disability and as strictly limited in their ability to exercise control over their lives. Many within the movement are skeptical of the continued reliance on a charitable model for meeting needs and the worthy poor approach to disability issues (Hutchison et al. 2007a; Rioux and Prince 2002). They regard notions of charity and deserving poor as outdated perspectives that propagate a view of disability as an individual pathology, along with separate, disparate benefits and services that weaken both self dignity and social cohesion.

Of course, the disability community operates in a wider ideological context of Canadian society and political economy. As a broad collection of beliefs, liberalism contains different branches with different adherents and, in recent decades in many nations, neo-liberalism is the dominant perspective influencing the conduct of politics and policy (Bakker and Scott 1997; Orsini and Smith 2007a; Rice and Prince 2000; Touraine 2001). Core features of neo-liberalism are in tension with social liberalism. As a belief system, neo-liberalism accepts some forms of government action, yet seriously questions much of what contemporary welfare states do. With respect to citizenship, emphasis is on civil and political liberties and duties; much less priority is given to cultural, economic, and social rights. Neo-liberalism is skeptical about the efficiency, effectiveness, and basic necessity for many social services. Such programs and income benefits neo-liberals view as infringing on personal freedom, weakening self-reliance, and thus creating dependency. Championed by certain think tanks, economic interests, and political parties, neo-liberalism aggressively calls for retrenching the state and expanding responsibilities for social provision among the market economy, local community, and family. This translates into demands for less government, fewer· laws and entitlements, lower

taxes, smaller public services; this is coupled with a deep-seated preference for market solutions for many social problems and human
needs and complemented with greater responsibility by individuals
and families, with assistance from charitable and voluntary groups.

Neo-liberalism is a significant factor in Canadian politics and policy
today, as earlier chapters demonstrated. Chapter 1 showed relatively
few Canadians interpret disability as an economic issue of employment or as a matter of human rights. Neo-liberal thinking is apparent
in opinion survey findings that far more Canadians prefer to tackle
discrimination, exclusion, and stigma of persons with disabilities
through information campaigns than through public programs, legislation, and income benefits. This is a preference for what we might call
a 'soft' politics of recognition over a 'substantive' politics of redistribution. Chapter 2 suggested that some contemporary perspectives on
urban life emphasize the individualizing process of cities as places
with lonely crowds, excluded Others, and strangers, and chapter 3,
likewise, discussed the politics of retrenchment of welfare states. In
chapter 4, feminist studies indicate the considerable influence of neo-
liberalism, interpreted and implemented in different shades, on the
practice and form of public administration in numerous countries.
This line of research suggests that neo-liberalism constrains gender
mainstreaming reforms to policy making processes, although such
reforms and the alternative ideas behind them challenge neo-liberal
norms (Hankivsky 2007; Squires 2007; Teghtsoonian 2004).

Social absences and actions run through these competing belief
systems and with other ideologies of varying influence, such as social
democracy and nationalism. Through its activism, therefore, the Canadian disability community presses against ableist beliefs and practices,
as well as neo-liberal beliefs and practices, each with implications for
shaping conceptions of citizenship, policy, and politics. In recent times,
on most issues, it seems neo-liberalism has the upper hand in power
and governance in modern societies.[2]

Without doubt, neo-liberal ideas have made inroads in Canadian
social policies and practices. Marcia Rioux and Fraser Valentine (2006),
for example, argue that the dominance of neo-liberalism has resulted
in a conceptual and practical restructuring of disability, equality, and
citizenship. They suggest that in many public programs the idea of disability has slid back into a notion of 'individual pathology'; the notion
of equality has been replaced by that of fair opportunity rather than a
right to equal treatment or outcomes; and talk of citizenship gives

greater emphasis to domestic responsibilities and charitable giving. In a study on home support policies and services for people with disabilities, Kari Krogh and Jon Johnson (2006) found that neo-liberalism, in the form cost-cutting measures, meant 'fewer people being eligible for services, a reduction in the type of services available, and wider implementation of user fees.' The result was reduced expectations among people with disabilities for home supports, wider variations in services across provincial jurisdictions, and 'reduced life opportunities and options for people who rely on the service' (Krogh and Johnson 2006: 153). Aronson and Neysmith (2001) reach similar conclusions about the home care market in manufacturing social exclusion, as do Chouinard and Crooks (2005) on income and employment supports for disabled women.

We should not over generalize the depth or extent of these ideological and material encroachments. Neo-liberalism has not totally triumphed over social rights and citizenship in Canada (Armitage 2003; Bashevkin 2002; Boychuk 1998; McQuaig 1999; Wharf and McKenzie 2004). Across policy areas, client groups, and jurisdictions impacts are variable. Certainly, there is unmistakable contraction to major social programs such as Employment Insurance (Campeau 2004), greater stress on employability of income assistance recipients, and successive tax cuts. Over the same period, however, witness popular resistance to the privatization of public services, most notably health care, and the debate over extending coverage for palliative care and drug insurance, among other issues. Eligibility has expanded to some income programs and tax measures, and a number of new financial benefits have been introduced in recent years, including a universal benefit for all young children in Canada. Being indiscrete systems of ideas, neo-liberalism and social liberalism overlap, clash, and develop together. They will continue shaping both the context of Canadian politics and the content of public policies.

Ambivalences and Absences

That many Canadians with disabilities remain marginalized absent citizens is shaped in large part by the ambivalence of the general population and the competing perspectives on disability embedded in programs and structures. The general public's understanding of disability politics must include attitudes, values, and beliefs about inclusion/exclusion and disability. This understanding is influenced by the mass media, think tanks, and policy institutes.

Is there a consensus in Canadian public opinion about access and inclusion for persons with disabilities? Evidence reported in chapter 1 suggests that ideals of inclusion and full membership are issues subject to differing points of view, beliefs, and even fears. For the disabled, a hierarchy of recognition and esteem is operative along several markers of identity. 'In Canadian society,' Parin Dossa (2005: 2528) notes, 'disabled men have a greater status compared with their female counterparts; white women with disabilities have greater status and power compared with racialized [non-western] women.' Moreover, there are systematic differences in public attitudes towards people with physical disabilities, people with intellectual disabilities, and people with mental health issues. The ambivalence of Canadians on disability rights and opportunities is still not that well understood. Public hesitance on actively advancing an agenda of full participation of disabled citizens may derive from powerful underlying images of normality in everyday culture. Stories of people with disabilities, when not consigned to anonymity but told on a large public scale, often celebrate heroic triumphs of overcoming personal adversity and tragedy. Public hesitancy may also come from seeing the disability movement as a minority interest, and that advancing the rights of the disabled comes at the cost of others in society. This last point indicates the connection between social stratification and social reform, a connection that deserves far greater attention in policy analyses and political advocacy work.

A way forward is to consider systematically the issue of *social intersectionalities*. This can have at least three meanings. One is the consideration that initiatives to advance the rights of people with disabilities are inclusive of all types of impairments and conditions. A second meaning is that any policy initiatives take account of diverse populations, whether disabled or not; and a third is that initiatives specifically directed at the needs say, of youth or women or ethnic communities, take disability into account as well. In each case, an intersectional approach helps avoid essentializing disability. In each, as well, intersectional analysis acknowledges the phenomenon of social stratification with disability as a factor implicated in the stratification order of human societies (Jenkins 1991).

Politically, consideration of intersecting social inequalities facilitates building alliances among social groups and encouraging innovative approaches to services or governance. People with disabilities experience stigma and oppression, for example, based not only on incapacities, but ethnicity, gender, age, sexual orientation, indigenous ancestry, geographic location, or economic status (Dossa 2005, 2008; Ellis and Llewellyn 1997; Hankivsky 2007). These markers of identity, some more fluid and open to change than others, variously interact and shape a person's citizenship as formal status and lived practice. Disability studies and more established social science disciplines are still grappling with intersections of social divisions and their meaning for life chances. To be relevant, policy research must explore engagement/alienation and inclusion/exclusion as they play out in people's lives at multiple intersections of disability with other social markers and practices (Titchkosky 2003a). This kind of intersectional analysis familiar in social work, feminist studies, and race studies requires a sense of diverse and contested histories, context, and disaggregated data. Examples include anthologies of first-person narratives of living with various kinds of disease and disability across social class, culture, gender, sexuality, and space (Krause 2005; Moss and Dyck 2002; Raoul et al. 2007). Considerable theoretical and empirical work lies ahead in better understanding and applying intersecting inequalities in disability studies (Dossa 2005).

A second kind of intersectional analysis involves *policy intersectionalities*. This type of research examines the relationships among various policies and policy-related structures and contextual factors. William Boyce, Kari Krogh, and Emily Boyce (2006), for example, investigate linkages among income support policy changes, shifts in federal funding and programming to community organizations, and their combined impacts for people with disabilities at the individual level, as well as at the level of community-based organizations. Mary Ann McColl (2006b) explores the interplay between four types of policy-related barriers (physical, attitudinal, expertise, and systemic) to access to public health care by Canadians with disabilities; while Marcia Rioux and Rita Samson (2006) outline interconnections between ideas and organizations at national and international levels for advancing human rights for people with disabilities. To be policy-related research, the focus of analysis and knowledge development must be on one or more of the causes and origins of policy; the structures and processes of policy; the content of legislation, programs, and services; or the consequences, intended and unintended, of public policies for people with disabilities.

Professional associations and experts in health and social services are central to modern disability politics in shaping the meaning of disability. They create and administer an array of techniques for service provision, personal support, and social control. In the everyday world of living with disabilities, the personal and the professional intertwine; and both are political. Individuals and families struggle to gain official recognition of personal needs, to navigate the complexity of public, voluntary, and private agencies to secure essential services. They work to retain those services as a person passes from one life stage or age category to another; they lobby for improvements to supports, and perhaps, to resist cutbacks to programs. For many people with disabilities, politicizing citizenship centres on contested relationships with medical systems of knowledge and power (Charlton 1998; Moss and Teghtsoonian 2008). It may involve an individual or group grappling with and at times resisting an 'illness label' given to them that jars with their own understanding. Conversely, it can entail struggling for medical recognition of a condition as a legitimate one. Contesting care involves locating the cause of or experience with an illness to outside forces and broader ideas of equity and injustice. People with particular health conditions, such as hepatitis C, join together for support and solidarity, as well as activism, forming collective identities. Personal and collective action can challenge medical science and may result in changes to diagnostic protocols and treatment practices.

Just as the state has multiple governments and society is composed of multiple sectors, the disability community has multiple organizations, perspectives, experiences, and issues. But while we should not adopt an essentialist view that reduces disability to intrinsic nature, we also should not stress differences among disabilities so much that no common ground is apparent for mutual support and coalition building. Tackling social obstacles, removing economic barriers, gaining a voice in policy processes, and encouraging inclusion in schools and other public services – these are concerns widely shared among people with disabilities and community organizations. Such shared concerns represent solidarity, which Catherine Frazee describes as 'deliberate acts of coming together, across our differences, because what we share is more important than how we differ ... As disabled people advance toward a place of robust citizenship, solidarity demands that we leave no one behind' (2006: 2).

Broadening Ideas of Disability Policy

Disability policy has traditionally been *a dimension* of the health care, education, social services, and income security fields. In the past few decades, however, disability policy is *a distinct domain* and overarching policy file. Strategies link together programs with guiding principles and shared objectives at the level of intergovernmental relations, as well as for certain governments, national disability organizations, and Aboriginal communities.

Several sets of ideas are connected with Canadian disability politics. Expressed in different ways and in different policy areas, these include (i) individual liberty, and related concepts of self-development, competence, and self-determination; (ii) accessibility, inclusion, membership, and participation; (iii) continuity in social relations, including stability and portability in income and services through life transitions; (iv) equality rights as citizens in a range of life domains; and (v) equity and fairness in recognizing barriers and in addressing additional costs of living with disabilities. Dealing with material (education, health care, income security), cultural (attitudes, beliefs, identities), and structural (autonomy, participation, collective voice) dimensions of community, these ideas indicate the extensive scope of disability politics today. In regard to possibilities in urban settings the disability movement is inclined to building not just accessible cities but urban spaces that celebrate diverse civic publics. In regard to perspectives on the welfare state surveyed, the Canadian movement defended programs against cutbacks in recent decades, fully aware of the limitations and contradictory effects of many of these programs while, more recently, has worked alone and with other social movements, in renewing an active state in economic and social affairs. These are defining features of disability activism in Canada.

The ideas or models of disability that are adopted shape the meaning of disability policy. Just as notions of ability and disability are cultural conceptions, so too disability programs are historical constructs, their meanings varying over time and within a given period and given political context. Elements of this policy field are comparatively old, pre-dating the modern welfare state, while other parts are fairly recent (Armitage 2003; Finkel 2004; Guest 2003; Puttee 2002). Accordingly, the personal tragedy and deserving charity models of disability influence policy design in particular ways that differ from a model of disablement based on medical rehabilitation or a model based on equality rights.

Canadian disability policy making includes the governmental and related state machinery of the public sector, together with the structures and practices of the voluntary sector, families, and their informal support networks, plus the domain of Aboriginal governments and communities. Policies and programs nest in multiple environments – an assortment of policy fields, institutional sectors, and government jurisdictions and organizations – which interact in diverse and changing ways. In addition to the federally-based citizenship regime and territorially- and provincially-based citizenship regimes, other forms of collective membership are reviving or re-emerging in Canada, notably various indigenous citizenships through treaty settlements and land claims; and, in our urban political communities, city-based memberships combine the ancient idea of the city-state with modernist notions of belonging to urban settlements. This multi-level, multi-sector focus reflects Canadian federalism and our increasingly pluralistic society and welfare provision (Cairns 1995; Bradford 2004; Rice and Prince 2000). Policies and practices operate at the local, provincial-territorial, and national levels of government, across public and private sectors, Aboriginal communities, and family systems. The result is a country with complex political ideas and constitutional rules on shared-rule and self-rule in multiple communities, in which claims for citizenship must navigate.

Caught Up in Citizenship

Furthering the citizenship of Canadians with disabilities depends upon a complex interplay of factors. Active engagement of disability groups in the political system, representation in policy processes, solidarity amongst different groups within the movement, and alliances with other social movements are all significant factors, but insufficient by themselves. Essential too are positive outcomes from litigation and human rights investigations and the widespread availability of appropriate and affordable personal supports and other essential services. Also essential are shifts in community attitudes toward obstacles in public and private spheres of life for people with disabilities.

'Disability issues' is a short phrase full with diverse ideas and Canadian activists are expanding public thinking on what it constitutes.

Traditionally, and still today at times, disability issues are narrowly conceived as special concerns related to a particular group of individuals with a particular impairment or disease. Common misconceptions of disability issues are that they entail a narrow set of concerns, for instance, rehabilitation or ramps, and that they do not involve people without disabilities. Such misconceptions risk the further marginalization of people with disabilities, limiting the political profile of issues and thus narrowing policy responses. Often underlying this outlook is a bio-medical and individual pathology approach. A wider view is that disability issues are those issues that disability organizations and their political allies identify and develop as policy positions. A still broader perspective is that disability issues are any issue that affects the values, interests, resources, and identities of persons with disabilities, whether in a positive or negative manner, and whether in a material, symbolic, or structural fashion. The idea of mainstreaming disability asserts that disability issues are not a narrow and separate field of activity, but instead a perspective that relates to all agendas, policies and processes of the state.

In this context, disability politics embrace a dynamic matrix of issues relevant to full participation with myriad concerns bearing on people with disabilities, and without disabilities, and their social milieu. These include barriers and inequalities in resources, opportunities, and power. Disability issues include calls for equal access, full inclusion, and economic opportunity. They include claims for citizenship rights and responsibilities. They extend to calls for personal voice, self-determination, and individual choice. Popular beliefs about the societal meaning of ability, competence, impairment, and normalcy likewise are fundamental to disability politics and policy making. The medical model of disability emphasizes impairments of the person, while the social model puts emphasis on how the environment supports and constrains people with disabilities.

Relations between people with disabilities, fellow citizens, governments, and other sectors of society are political questions of growing importance. The significance of these questions comes from Canada's aging population; pressures on smaller sized families and aged parents to provide care and income support; public expectations for more flexible service provision, citizen voice in policy development, and stronger accountabilities of governments; further deinstitutionalization of persons with disabilities into communities; and projected labour market shortages for well educated and skilled people. Each trend presents social challenges, but also strategic opportunities for the disability movement to raise awareness of current conditions of exclusion and poverty, and to advance claims for accessibility and participation as peers.

Advocates, groups, and coalitions in Canada are caught up in a politicization of citizenship. The disability community understands that developing rights and responsibilities involves creating new choices, engaging in debates, building consensus, and changing policies. Disability activism expresses a multi-dimensional discourse on citizenship, addressing civil, legal, political, economic, and social elements in a broad agenda for policy action. At both individual and collective levels, persons with disabilities, and their allies, are often skeptical toward the authority claims of complex organizations. Canadian disability groups are challenging the established 'expert' and 'rational' beliefs that are presented as disinterested and uniformly fair. Instead, disability groups say these beliefs are limited to ways of knowing held by professionals and bureaucrats (Boyce et al. 2001; Stienstra and Wight-Felske 2003).

Employing notions of human rights and independent living, disability groups advocate for greater choice and control over decisions about assessing and addressing their needs. In so doing, they are challenging traditional ways of governments, charities, and various experts in organizing services and allocating resources to individuals and families. Decision-making powers, forms of service provision, and the structure of working conditions are issues all under scrutiny, whether the area is segregated classrooms, reforms to tax laws, community supports, or sheltered workshops versus supported regular employment. Disability politics, as previous chapters illustrate, is about opening up state processes, creating new public spaces in city life, and reporting on results of inclusion through social indicators.

In contemporary politics, people with disabilities are evoking the language of citizenship and making claims for substantive rights and responsibilities in areas of education, community and city living, justice, paid employment, and political affairs. Politicizing citizenship means challenging existing public assumptions, such as rigid notions of ability and disability or employability and unemployable. It means questioning conventional professional practices and conventional knowledge beliefs of health practitioners that conditions such as depression, environmental illness, or fibromyalgia are real and legitimate conditions. It means evoking classic ideals associated with citizenship, such as equality and dignity while, at the same time, modernizing the content of citizenship. Disability organizations are projecting a diverse mix of private and public images of persons with disabilities: roles as learners and teachers, workers and managers, family members, caregivers, as well as care recipients, taxpayers and consumers, voters and political candidates, athletes and artists, and so forth. This deepens our conceptions of membership in society. This modernization is toward an enabling and more inclusive status, refashioning citizenship as rights and participation for the diverse lived experiences of persons with disabilities in towns or cities, indigenous communities, or metropolitan centres.

Like all great social institutions, citizenship contains paradoxes. One such paradox is that 'citizenship is both an inclusionary process involving some re-allocation of resources and an exclusionary process of building identities on the basis of a common or imagined solidarity' (Turner 2001: 192). Of course, efforts at politicizing citizenship for Canadians with disabilities take place in relation to the growth imperatives of a market economy, the divided jurisdictions of a federal state, and the social individualism of a mass culture (Chouinard and Crooks 2005). A second paradox or contradiction is that 'Citizenship in capitalist societies constitutes a mode of identity that offers the promise of being equal in an unequal world' (Kivisto and Faist 2007: 71). This relates to a third inconsistency of citizenship, between symbolism and substance – there is always a gap between the formal status and the actual experiences of citizenship, intensely so for people with marginal resources and standing in society.

Citizenship is a strategic tool tied to the Charter and equality rights and a cohesive social union in the country. However, connections among social rights, social programs, and the social model of disability are not straightforward or without problems. Social citizenship often involves, not a system of equality, but differential access to services, supports, rights, and duties. Social policy, citizenship, and the welfare state are sites for stratification: simultaneously and in conjunction with one another, they are a tangle of inclusion and exclusion, of equity and injustice, of opportunities and barriers. Living with stratification invariably means living with contradictions. The challenge here, one not peculiar to disability politics but associated with many forms of social reform, is to pursue equal treatment and equitable treatment at the same time.

This is why disability politics is *caught up* in a politicization of citizenship. While actively engaged in advancing citizenship claims, structural forces of economic interests, complex and closed intergovernmental relations, and equivocal public support on disability reforms slow down the momentum of the disability community. In addition, in garnering public attention and political support for policy reforms, some activists wonder if the disability movement is over-involved in emphasizing a discourse of rights, instead of alternative discourses such as needs. Caught up in struggles for citizenship also entails seeking balances in political messages and social policy measures between equality and equity, diversity and universality across various types of disability, and in various branches of the state. In both the first instance and final analysis, disability issues are political matters that continue to be a pressing topic of citizenship.

Conclusion

The Canadian disability movement's main political outlook is a brand of social liberalism. It is liberal because the movement champions the autonomy and self-development of individuals, values of toleration and respect, and takes for granted market relations, the rule of law, and representative democratic government. It is social because the movement celebrates groups and group rights, while emphasizing the importance of active government. The movement works with the state, addressing issues of material needs of distribution (income, employment, housing, transit, and so on), cultural recognition (public attitudes, social values and beliefs), and democratic voice (constitutional, electoral, and legislative protections). Most of the disability movement's activism is squarely within conventional political practices and governmental structures, such as parliamentary committees, advisory councils, and election campaigns. As a form of social liberalism, disability activism is a wavering mixture of criticism and collaboration with governments, and of visionary ideals and incremental reforms. As earlier noted, the social liberalism of disability politics often clashes with the neo-liberalism of state retrenchment, charity, and privatization. Yet, in this ideological nexus, opportunities arise for at least some disabled people and disability groups, to advance greater self-control and acquire community resources.

If we are moving toward a 'post-welfare state' (Bakker and Scott 1997; McDaniel 2002; Wharf and McKenzie 2004), then thoughtful analysis of state-society relations must take account of the disability community as a political and cultural movement. Activism by disability organizations is having an influence on Canadian politics as well as on the image of people with disabilities (Cameron and Valentine 2001; Enns and Neufeldt 2003; Roeher 1997; Stienstra and Wight-Felske 2003). Through advocacy work on issues such as attendant care, personal supports, and home adaptations, disability groups are spanning the traditional divide between the private and public realms of life, making the personal a political topic (Chivers 2008).

Resembling many social movements, public cultures are under critique, with disability activists testing customary social practices along with established professional and administrative practices. Disability organizations are contributing to policy debates, challenging certain beliefs, shaping the knowledge base of decision making and service provision. Their most important contributions, however, are more than additions to existing ways of thinking; they are inserting previously ignored life experiences into valid knowledge about persons with disabilities, their families, and the effects of policies and programs on people. Effective instances are the 1981 *Obstacles* report, the 1996 Scott task force report, Canadian Senate reports in 2006 on mental health, and the End Exclusion events of 2006 and 2007.

Canadian disability politics is eroding old notions of the disabled as defective, sick, tragic figures lurking in the margins of communities. Through various kinds of engagement, disability groups are *representing* people with disabilities in two senses of the word: speaking on behalf of their membership, and depicting people with disabilities as persons with innate dignity and worth, as social actors with identities and capabilities, rights and responsibilities.

9 The Policy Record and Reform Agenda

Using political analysis, the overall purpose of this book is to understand the precarious status of citizenship for persons with mental and physical disabilities. A handful of questions guide this book: How does the public understand diṣability? What are the attitudes of Canadians toward the adequacy of social programs and the distribution of responsibilities for meeting needs and advancing the inclusion of citizens with disabilities? How does existing theory and social science research treat disability as a dimension in Canadian urban society? What kinds of politics do people with disabilities and organizations of the disability community practise? What are the consequences for citizenship of neo-liberalism and its chief alternative, social liberalism?

As it stands, students reading standard social policy and sociology texts do not encounter disability as part of the human condition, nor people with disabilities as a social group. They learn little about the inequalities and stratification associated with impairments and handicaps. In effect, most academic works reproduce the silences and reflect the marginal status of people with disabilities in societies. Issues of 'normal identity' and impairment, however, are becoming more explicit features of Canadian politics. Along these lines, this book contributes a political analysis and theoretical sensitivity to the academic field of disability studies. Together, chapters provide a series of concepts and frameworks for exploring disability politics and policies. Concepts were explored, theories reviewed, and community engagement and political participation examined to appreciate the circumstances of people with disabilities.

This final chapter addresses two general questions: What is the Canadian record on disability policy reform? How does the disability community envisage possible actions for advancing citizenship? The first section of the chapter recaps main points and themes presented in this book. The second section then assesses the disability reform record over the last decade, and the third section reviews two leading reform proposals, a federal disability act for Canada and a national action plan on disability issues.

Exploring Disability Politics

Conventional texts on public policy, the welfare state, and social inequality cast an incomplete gaze, ignoring persons with disabilities, their personal struggles and political activities. This book has sought to broaden this focus directing attention to how disablement is built into social structures and social programs, and how Canadians with disabilities are political actors at individual and collective levels of engagement. Chapters have considered the participation of people with disabilities in a range of public spheres: public opinion and attitudes; social programs and other state provisions; civic spaces in urban Canada; government policy techniques and processes for mainstreaming disability issues; multiple arenas of action in the disability community; electoral systems and voting; and state structures at various levels and branches.

Encounters between Canadians with disabilities and the Canadian state are numerous, complex, and often contested (Boyce, Krogh, and Boyce 2006; Cameron and Valentine 2001; Hutchison et al. 2007a, 2007b; Moss and Teghtsoonian 2008; Pothier and Devlin 2006). People with disabilities and disability organizations participate politically as clients and consumers of programs; as a social group or community; as strangers in cities; as experts advising on policy developments, budgets, or program evaluations; as voters or candidates in municipal, provincial, and federal elections; and as activists, litigants, rights-bearers, and equality seekers. These manners of participation differ by level of public prominence and legitimacy and, therefore, also by acceptability or controversy by state and social interests.

In the introduction, I argued the need to examine disability, citizenship, and public policy in relation to three modes of activism: a politics of cultural recognition, a politics of socio-economic redistribution, and a politics of democratic representation. Conceptualizing disability struggles for equality in this manner, I made use of the theoretical ideas of Nancy Fraser (1989, 2000, 2005), Bryan Turner (1986, 1988,

2001), and Iris Young (1990, 1997). Disability politics is a dynamic process in which absences and actions interact and change, both inside and between state and societal institutions. Accordingly, the organization of this book emphasizes examining struggles for citizenship in relation to obstacles and gaps confronting people with disabilities, and the range of measures and policy reform options available to social and political institutions.

Under the banner of full citizenship, struggling against absences of recognition, voice, and support are key features of Canadian disability politics. Discriminatory attitudes and behaviours by others produce wounding absences of connections and hope (Enns 1999; Kirby 2006). Another part of disability politics is the debate over what actions to take, when, how, and for whom. Actions encompass potential and actual measures of public persuasion, knowledge transfer, direct expenditures, general taxation, tax relief measures, service provision, and laws and regulatory activities by state and/or societal organizations. Thus, absences and actions are sites for political struggles. Linked in critical ways, absences and actions both take place within structural contexts of power relationships, resource choices, and constraints. The gaps between measures implemented compared against the actual needs of people is a seemingly constant issue in most public policy fields, and is a further characteristic of disability politics.

The introduction discussed varied meanings of disability, indicating that a central feature of Canadian disability politics is an ongoing dispute over the conceptualization and implementation of disability and related ideas that include reasonable accommodation, civic engagement, and self-determination. Empirically, disability is increasing in importance as a basis for social divisions for a number of reasons: the aging of the population and increasing life expectancy; the continuance of medical advances to enhance the survival of people with various injuries and illnesses, posing ethical benefits and challenges; a growing social acceptability, perhaps, of reporting certain disabilities in social surveys and social settings; and the concurrent deinstitutionalization and institutionalization of people with mental health issues as policy responses. In 2006, the latest data available, showed an estimated 4.4 million Canadians reported having a disability (Statistics Canada 2007). For understanding Canadian society and politics, disability is certainly a social phenomenon of growing importance.

The analysis in part 1 revealed a number of embedded barriers, rooted in attitudes, social structures, and the built environment of cities that constrain the positive recognition of and participation by people with disabilities. Chapter 1 showed that ableism – discriminatory assumptions and actions toward individuals or groups based on their disabilities – persists in Canadians' opinions. Often, people with mental illnesses are feared; people with learning disabilities are misunderstood; people with developmental disabilities are assumed to be incompetent.

Canada's mosaic remains vertical. It is full of social inequalities related to impairments, that is to say, disability stratification. A society characterized by persistent divisions and inequalities presents serious limitations to pursuing inclusion. Some years ago, a British sociologist urged that 'disability must be considered as a factor contributing to the production and distribution of stratification in its own right' (Jenkins 1991: 557). More recently, two disability scholars remarked how surprising it is that so few social scientists systematically examine disability as a social identity and division. Consequently, 'there remains very little research evidence on other key divisions such as social class and sexuality, or the effects of interaction between these categories' or, indeed, on the 'multiple layers of social division among the disabled population' (Barnes and Mercer 2003: 64, 76). There are exceptions (Anderson 1996; Michalko 2002), but in ignoring disability as a central feature of structural inequalities in Canada, the social sciences risk naturalizing disability-based inequities as biologically determined rather than socially and politically constructed.

Everything the state does has implications for structuring patterns of relations. As chapter 2 noted, instead of being seen as external or separate, the state is integral to the dominant processes of stratification. The disability community, as are other social movements, is challenged to pursue a dual strategy of advancing inclusion into a mainstream while simultaneously attacking systemic inequalities in that mainstream. The federal and provincial governments are a central focus of the disability movement, understandably so, given the distribution of public powers in Canada and the movement's discourse on citizenship. Through the analysis presented in this book, I argue for greater theoretical and practical attention to local governments. The interplay between ableism and urbanism has been lacking in Canadian academic discussions, and chapter 3 endeavoured to connect, at the level of theory at least, citizenship and disability to a conception of city life that acknowledges differences in status and identities among social groups.

In part 2, chapters examined disability activism and political citizenship in relation to formal state structures and policy processes, civil society institutions, and electoral systems. Experience at the federal level in implementing disability mainstreaming techniques has included the participation of independent disability consultants and experts associated with national organizations, think tanks, and universities. The techniques examined in chapter 4 represent an administrative approach to advancing social inclusion and inserting disability perspective into policy processes. Chapter 5 described the Canadian disability community as five arenas: a sector of service agencies, a new social movement, a constitutional category of citizens with rights-based identities, a policy field of interest groups and advocacy coalitions, and a research and knowledge production network. In each arena is a distinctive type of politics that corresponds with particular structures and functions. Thus, for the disability community, political capacity and engagement is a composite of relationships with particular components of the community. On that theme, chapter 6 discussed the political participation of persons with disabilities in electoral processes as voters, campaign workers, and candidates, and recent outreach reforms to encourage voting. Chapter 7 gave further attention to questions of collective action and civic engagement with state structures and policy processes.

In part 3, chapter 8 indicated the need for intersectional analysis of social differences as well as social policies. It also noted that disability policy is both a distinct domain and a dimension of other policy fields. This same chapter showed that the furtherance of access and inclusion by people with disabilities relies upon a dynamic interplay of state and society.

Assessing the Recent Disability Policy Record

If the meaning of citizenship and disability are in flux, as discussed in chapter 8, to what extent is the overall field of disability policy changing. In 1998, federal, provincial, and territorial ministers responsible for social services endorsed a vision of full citizenship for persons with disabilities. Reiterated in 2000, with express general support by the disability community, this approach continues to provide the intergovernmental framework and vocabulary for addressing disability policy issues (Canada 1998, 2001). The desired new approach to disability issues, outlined in the introduction, can be summarized as follows: Rather than identify clients as recipients who are dependent and labelled 'unemployable,' public programs should relate to clients as individual people, as participants with identifiable skills who desire independence and often work; and, in addition to providing necessary income support, have active measures to promote training and skills development, employment, and volunteer opportunities, and thereby enhance autonomy, participation, and well-being. The shared vision proposes a shift from disability issues as a government responsibility with multiple access requirements to an approach in which there is a shared responsibility for disability matters and access requirements integrated and buttressed with portability of benefits and services.

This intergovernmental vision provides a benchmark against which to consider the nature and degree of changes (and continuities) in policy and practice. To attempt this is to engage in interpretation and conjecture, partly because the state of measures and data sets are in early stages of development or analysis, partly because gains in one program area may be offset by practices in another, and partly because some planned changes, such as from government responsibility to shared responsibility, are debatable claims as to the actual provision of resources and distribution of burdens. Admittedly a politically crafted statement, this policy framework has become part of the vocabulary of officials in federal, provincial, and territorial government departments, in addition to activists in the disability movement (Michalko 2002: 146–8; Titchkosky 2007: 46–78; Torjman 2001: 188–92).

The specifics of reform no doubt vary by jurisdiction. In a federalized political state it is more useful to think of a multiplicity of policy records. Ideally, then, to answer the question of the Canadian record of progress on this disability vision, we would need a series of case studies that cast light on results spanning an array of government jurisdictions, local communities, types of disabilities, services, and other instruments of public policy. Moreover, the time frame to assess changes in approaching disability issues, and the expectations for major changes, likely vary among interests in Canadian disability politics. Behind this vision, officially expressed in the late 1990s, is a twenty-year period of developments in contemporary disability politics and policy.

Boundaries of the disability policy field can and do fluctuate. In some respects, policy has maintained the broad focus articulated by the Canadian disability movement and parliamentary committees in the 1980s, aided by constitutional reform and the entrenchment of the

Charter of Rights and Freedoms (Peters 2003). In other respects, policy focus has narrowed, as measured by inconsistent political attention, low priorities, and few substantive actions on major concerns. In a similar manner, policy discourse on disability has shifted over recent decades to a rights language of citizenship and equality, yet it is unclear that this discourse – preferred by many movement activists, used by public officials, and adopted in governmental statements – has widespread public acceptance or basic adoption in public policy making processes. If there is a shift in disability policy discourse it deals with employability as the dominant normative emphasis.

Positive developments over the last few decades in advancing access and inclusion for Canadians with disabilities include:

- New tax benefits recognizing additional needs and costs of persons living with prolonged or severe disabilities, and their families. Examples include the Child Disability Benefit, Disability Supports Deduction, and the Registered Disability Savings Plan.
- Public education and social awareness campaigns by governments, employers, and broadcasters that contributed, along with other factors, to a shift in discourse from a personal tragedy to a public participation viewpoint.
- Closure of several segregated institutions in a number of provinces that housed thousands of people with intellectual disabilities and a move to community-based residential services.
- Changes to federal, provincial, and some municipal election laws and procedures, including outreach measures to improve the accessibility of voting for citizens with disabilities. From a survey of almost 200 associations representing people with disabilities, about the 2000 federal election, 89 per cent reported a positive impression of Election Canada's role in federal elections, 75 per cent were satisfied with services to Canadians with disabilities during recent elections, and 72 per cent were aware of these access services.
- Technological advances in communication that include captioning of all national programming by Canadian television stations and some local programming, TTY (teletypewriter) access through telephones, video relay services, and, most recently, wireless pagers and messaging services.
- Legal developments regarding disability (Pothier and Devlin 2006) and political victories, such as the right to sign language inter-

preters in health care services; Quebec legislation in 2004 to further secure handicapped persons their rights to achieving social, school, and workplace integration; and passage in 2005 of the Accessibility for Ontarians with Disabilities Act.[1]

- A concerted effort by Statistics Canada since the 1980s to conduct surveys on Canadians with disabilities in order to identify their lived experiences, the barriers they face, and trends over time. Other federal departments and think tanks also have greatly assisted in the development, interpretation, and dissemination of much disability information.

- Establishment in 2007 of the Mental Health Commission of Canada by the federal government. The Commission's role is to support and facilitate 'a national approach to mental health issues; work to diminish the stigma and discrimination faced by Canadians living with mental illness; and, disseminate evidence based information on all aspects of mental health and mental illness to governments, stakeholders and the public.'[2] A wait and see approach seems in order, however, as the Commission has been criticized from within the community of people it purports to act for, as being unrepresentative on its board of people who have lived with psychiatric disabilities and being predominantly medical in its orientation.

- Adoption by the United Nations General Assembly, in 2006, of the UN Convention on the Rights of Persons with Disabilities.[3] The Canadian government in 2007 signed the Convention, with full ratification still to come, following consultations with provinces and territories. The Convention covers civil, political, cultural, economic, and social rights – the multi-dimensional conception of citizenship discussed in this book – supported by a monitoring body to encourage the compliance of states to their obligations.

As discussed in chapters 4 through 8, Canada's disability movement has expanded over time, becoming more structurally elaborate, operating in no less than five arenas of social action, forging various kinds of coalitions with other groups, and engaging with state structures. Since the 1970s, Canadian political scientists Young and Everitt observe that 'the disabled, among others, have gone from being almost entirely absent from political decision making to being taken seriously as significant players, at least in some sectors. This would not have been possible without group mobilization' (2004: 142–3). Activists long involved in disability politics observe a sea change in public awareness and support for removing obstacles, with the national and international work of the early 1980s being a pivotal turning point. Canadians are probably shifting in how they think and feel about disability and people living with disabilities. As compared to a generation ago, Canadians are not as apt to automatically equate impairments with inability to work, to learn, or to participate in the full fabric of life.

The disability movement has advanced through self-education, enhanced consumer involvement, and solutions developed through alliances across disability and coalitions with other social groups. Notable features of the disability movement today are, first, a solidarity expressed by honouring histories, leaving no one behind, and coming together around shared reform priorities; and, second, a belief in civic engagement as a crucial way for breathing life into the vision of access and inclusion. Some observers suggest the community's record is impressive. On the impact of disability organizations on the political process, Laura Bonnett notes: 'Not only have they influenced legislation in various parts of the country, they have also empowered and enabled many people with disabilities to re-envision what full citizenship looks like' (2003: 156). Another commentator remarks that 'the Canadian disability movement has made ... meaningful progress by working both against and within state systems to achieve recognition of disabled people's human rights' (Chivers 2008: 307).

Outstanding Issues and Concerns

And so there have been many achievements in Canadian disability policy and practice in recent decades, but they have been uneven and incomplete achievements. There have also been setbacks. In the mid-1990s, the federal government withdrew from cost sharing with the provinces the provision of core social services and social assistance across the country. In the late 1990s, the federal and most provincial governments approved reductions to CPP Disability benefits. Federal expenditures on employment services for persons with disabilities remain modest and, more significantly, stagnant in real terms over the last decade. As grounds of discrimination, disability is by far the most common type of complaint brought to the Canada Human Rights Commission. Since rights-based processes rely on complaints and decisions made on a case-by-case basis, the Court Challenges Program was introduced many years ago to facilitate more systemic reforms through litigation on strategic cases dealing with the Charter of Rights.

Regrettably, that program was cancelled by the Stephen Harper government. For these reasons, plus others, which could be referenced, current circumstances are decidedly of mixed signals.

Mainstreaming is occurring in education and recreation in some jurisdictions, although many of these and other services remain specialized or segregated from regular programs. A move to self-managed care is taking place, again in selected areas and selected program fields. Likewise, individualized funding to individuals with disabilities and their families remains a patchwork and often as pilot projects. A major shift in policy over the last generation is deinstitutionalization, the move to community-based delivery and group homes for people with intellectual disabilities. The shift in policy has not always been accompanied by a shift in practice, with adequate resources invested in communities to provide the requisite social supports. As well, some large residential institutions still operate and, on some provincial agendas, there are plans to establish new institutions or refurbish old facilities. Serious gaps persist in access to affordable, quality disability-related supports for a considerable number of Canadians with disabilities. The default is informal family care and charitable services, where possible, and, where not, isolation and unmet needs. In addition, for people with intellectual disabilities, guardianship laws predominate in provinces and territories rather than supported decision making models that recognize legal capacity and respect the right to self-determination.

In the words of a coalition of national, provincial, and local disability groups:

> Canadians with disabilities are almost twice as likely to live in poverty compared to other Canadians. Over two million Canadian adults with disabilities lack one or more of the ... supports they need to participate fully in their communities. Over 55 per cent of working-age adults with disabilities are currently unemployed or out of the labour market. For women with disabilities the rate is almost 75 per cent. More than 10,000 persons with intellectual disabilities remain warehoused in institutions across the country. Slightly more than half of Canadian children with disabilities do not have access to needed aids and devices. Rates of violence and abuse against people with disabilities, in particular women with disabilities, are among the highest for any group in Canadian society. For Aboriginal Canadians with disabilities, these rates are even higher. (End Exclusion 2007: 1–2)

Large numbers of people with disabilities are not receiving the essential services they require because of cost, lack of availability, and inaccessible environments. Entry to some supports are still tied to receipt of income benefits, most notably social assistance, which adds a barrier to gaining access to needed services (Crawford 2005a). Canadians with disabilities most likely to experience unmet needs for supports and service are people with severe impairments and with low incomes (Fawcett et al. 2004). Studies show that individuals and their families bear a disproportionate share of the costs, work, and responsibilities associated with addressing the everyday needs of living with disabilities. A recent Canadian study calculates that non-reimbursed costs to individuals and families in purchasing disability-specific supports are more than $4 billion a year (Crawford 2005b). As a consequence, individuals with disabilities and their families experience undue hardship and are restricted from full and active participation in economic, educational, and social life.

Institutionalization of people with intellectual disabilities separated them from their families and segregated them in facilities, 'in the vast grey space of state confinement' resulting in absent citizens, where basic needs were perhaps maintained but social capacities wasted away (Ignatieff 1984: 50–1). Deinstitutionalization may mean people with disabilities are no longer absent from the community, however, without sufficient social supports and public services they are marginalized as members of society.

At the core of the new approach to disability issues are employment and work skills. At the macro level of intergovernmental relations, labour market agreements between the federal government and the provinces and territories give greater emphasis to the employability of persons with disabilities than, say, twenty years ago. This promotion of employment and volunteer opportunities is apparent also in recent changes to the Canada Pension Plan Disability Benefit program (Prince 2008a). However, the general picture in Canada on employment for people with disabilities continues to be one of relatively high rates of unemployment and underemployment, with barriers to training and placement services, and workers with disabilities often concealing from colleagues and superiors their conditions (Church et al. 2007; Crooks 2007; Kirby 2006; Wilton 2006). Progress under federal employment equity legislation for people with disabilities has also stalled over recent years. In fact, of the four designated equity groups in the legislation (the other groups are women, members of visible minorities, and Aboriginal persons), persons with disabilities have benefited the least in advancing their representation in the private sector that is federally regulated.

Due to inadequate supports, attitudinal barriers, and insufficient employment opportunities, plus sustained provincial government efforts at moving able bodied people off welfare, people with disabilities now represent between 40 to 70 per cent of those on income assistance, the so-called social 'safety net.' This program of last resort has become the program of first resort for thousands of people with disabilities across the country – a program distinguished for minimal rights, complex rules, and the sting of stigma (Crooks 2004). More generally, too, the administration of services and benefits remain hierarchical, expert-based, often secretive, and loosely coordinated with related agencies and programs. Most policies still regard disability as specific impairments, diseases, and disorders; programs are categorical rather than a continuum of services, with sharp distinctions and abrupt changes when a person experiences a life transition. Living with a disability in Canada remains a strong predictor of welfare dependence and poverty for individuals, families, and many of the agencies struggling to assist them.

Additionally discouraging about this mixed record of results, is that the context of policy making and reform over the past decade is one in which economic trends have been largely favourable, as measured by sustained growth, low unemployment rates, and little inflation; the financial position of the federal government and most provincial governments has been strong, marked by a series of budget surpluses; and, after years of restraint of social provisions in Canada, there are selective reinvestments in health, education, and social services, as well as new initiatives in child and family benefits. Some disability policy reforms have taken place, at times appended to other reform initiatives and at times launched as specific measures. At the federal government level a favoured form of disability reform over the past decade is through the income tax system in the form of tax credits and deductions.

Disability Knowledge Production: Developments and Gaps

The vibrant presence of dedicated disability research centres associated with universities is a notable development in recent times. There is the Canadian Centre on Disability Studies allied with the University of Manitoba and University of Winnipeg, the Centre for Interdisciplinary Research in Rehabilitation and Social Integration at Laval, the Centre for Interdisciplinary Research on Rehabilitation in Montreal, and the Ryerson-RBC Foundation Institute for Disability Research and Education. The work of these centres, and think tanks such as the Caledon Institute of Social Policy, is amassing information, analysis, and insights into living with disabilities, and tracking the nature of policy responses from governments. This research is also generating interesting conceptual developments. For example, what are the roles and responsibilities of four sectors (public, private, social economy, and family and friends) in a given community; how the social economy plays a role in the workplace reintegration of people with mental health conditions; and the elaboration of the notion of *le double empowerment*, the inclusion and engagement of both service users and front line workers in the disability domain.

On knowledge gaps, there is little comparative research on disability policies, programs, or services across jurisdictions. Most survey data analysis reports on a national level. Little data are disaggregated to the level of provinces/territories or urban centres that would enable organizations in the wider disability research community to explore data sets and examine issues specific to their needs and interests. This would encourage the generation of research and transfer of knowledge to municipalities, school boards, hospital authorities, and other public bodies. In terms of types of disabilities, most research examines and assumes disabilities which are chronic, long term, or permanent in character. As a consequence, there is comparatively little analysis of experiences of people with degenerative, episodic, and progressive disabilities. Policy-related research literature in Canada on Aboriginal peoples with disabilities is fairly sparse. Compounding this limitation is that many social surveys exclude people living in the three territories and people on the six hundred plus First Nation reserves. While researchers are addressing some of these issues, Aboriginal peoples with disabilities remain invisible in most policy-related research. Furthermore, the life circumstances and experiences of ethno-racial people with disabilities in Canadian society is understudied and an issue of increasing significance.

An Overall Assessment

Canadians with disabilities have long been disadvantaged: culturally stigmatized, economically deprived, politically marginalized, and frequently overlooked in social theory and research. While important advances have occurred over the last twenty-five years – including some program reforms recently introduced at both the federal and provincial/territorial levels – there also have been many setbacks and erosions in supports, as well as continued challenges in everyday living and barriers to participation in schools, work, community activities, public services, and facilities. Research and experience show that both generic and disability specific community services are inadequate in meeting existing needs. Social work scholar Andrew Armitage (2003: 74) similarly concludes that action to deal with the inadequacies of Canadian policies for people with disabilities has not followed from the brave words of the intergovernmental vision. A recent statement by a large coalition of groups in the Canadian disability movement declares:

> Many Canadians with disabilities and their families continue to experience daily barriers to their full and equal participation in Canadian society. The personal, social and economic costs of exclusion are too high to be ignored. Immediate action is needed to address the high rates of poverty facing Canadians with disabilities and its causes and the lack of access to disability supports that perpetuate barriers and exclusion and keep people with disabilities and their families invisible and marginalized. (End Exclusion 2007: 2)

Not all Canadians with disabilities are invisible and marginalized. Even among those regarded as absent citizens, the nature of experiencing barriers to participation in society is varied. Nonetheless, as a social group, persons with disabilities in Canada, are more likely to be marginalized than non-disabled Canadians; and there are consistent patterns of marginalization in the form of under-representation in employment, mass media, or political office or the over-representation of the disabled in welfare, non-standard work, and institutions. A critical need exists for improved and enhanced supports and services. Today, services and supports are fragmented, often unavailable or unaffordable, not portable across life transitions or place, and all too often disempowering or stigmatizing to those seeking a modicum of assistance to live in dignity and to be active citizens. The needs of Canadians for disability supports and for more inclusive general services will grow and change due to Canada's aging population, smaller sized families being less available to provide informal care, public expectations of more flexible service provision, and labour market needs for well-educated and skilled people.

Advocating Reform Ideas

A number of possible reforms have been identified in previous chapters – some general and some more specific to the study and practice of disability politics and policy. These are reviewed briefly here.

Canadians with disabilities are a symbolically disadvantaged social group. Chapters in part 1 suggested the need to widen and deepen both public understanding and academic interest in disability. The Government of Canada speaks of promoting 'a culture of inclusiveness' (Canada 2006: 10), though federal activities are few in number and limited in scope. So far, the federal government has sponsored just one nationwide public opinion survey to ascertain Canadian beliefs and values toward people with disabilities and issues of inclusion/exclusion. It follows that one reform direction involves additional 'cultural work' in shifting attitudes about disability and the need for accessibility and social inclusion. Among other tasks, this cultural work involves casting public light on prejudicial beliefs in order to facilitate understanding and acknowledgment, acting to dismantle such discriminatory beliefs through sustained policy measures, and assembling new ideas and belief systems (Lord and Hutchison 2007). Playing a lead role in re-creating the image of citizenship in Canada is the disability community; it is an image of citizenship against which social absences are identifiable and towards which aspirations and actions mobilize for a fuller measure of equality.

The recently formed Mental Health Commission of Canada, headed by former senator Michael Kirby, is undertaking a ten-year campaign against stigma and discrimination faced by persons with mental disorder and mental health problems. This work could entail identifying and dissecting ableist assumptions embedded in public thinking, language, and behaviour, including the 'reactions of well-meaning people' (Young 1990: 42). It should involve exploring, both theoretically and empirically, connections among disability, human rights, and public policy (Rioux and Valentine 2006). It furthermore entails examining the textual depiction of disabled people and embodied differences in radio and television programming, print media, policy reports, and other written materials (Canada 2006: 31–2; Titchkosky 2007). The more activist side of this work, cultural politics really, involves contesting established norms and symbols, and common stereotypes about disablement that devalue people with disabilities in the workplace (Burge, Ouellette-Kuntz, and Lysaght 2007) and other social settings.

A second, related reform idea is the need for more systematic consideration of disability in studies of social stratification. This social inquiry would benefit greatly from intersectional analyses that examine disability in relation to other social divisions, plus examine differences among people with different disabilities and life experiences.[4] Thus, for some people with disabilities, it is the interplay of their impairments with social structures and environmental barriers that are the primary basis for determining their social status. For other people with disabilities, features such as age, sexual orientation, or race may be as significant or more profound in shaping a sense of self, who they are seen to be by others, and how they experience social interactions. Future research should focus also on linkages between ableism and other forms of discrimination, such as ageism, and other social phenomenon such as urbanism (Andrew et al. 2002; Frug 2001).

Mainstreaming disability into public policy and administration suggests a further set of reforms in relation to national statistics and an inclusion index; impact assessments with use of a disability or inclusion lens; and budget statements that commit to improving the lives of people with disabilities and also report on implications for people with disabilities and families, and wider economic and social conditions. A leading disability policy specialist sees the applicability of these reforms to governments in Canada: 'A high-level mechanism could be designated within each jurisdiction to take responsibility for incorporating an inclusion lens within all government activities' (Torjman 2001: 192). Public reports on disability, such as the federal government's *Advancing the Inclusion*, must go beyond being inventories of existing programs and policies. They could be robust accountability documents by including evaluations of results against objectives, over time, and by engaging interested publics of the disability community around possible new initiatives and/or reforms to current programs and delivery systems, through online consultations, roundtable meetings, and other processes.

Another reform area concerns organizational and service practices, fundamentally shifting power to individuals, families, and local communities (Bach 2002; Lord and Hutchison 2007; Wharf 1992). Foremost options here include the closure of remaining institutions that segre-

gate thousands of citizens with intellectual disabilities, public investments for building the capacity of disability consumer organizations
and local social networks, and the provision of individualized funding
(also called direct payments) to clientele as an option in lieu of direct
service provision by a government department or private organization. Experience with this approach in Manitoba, New Brunswick, and
elsewhere in Canada, and internationally, suggests it can work when
the individual entitled to funding is supported by a facilitator/broker
who assists in deciding on the desired mix of services needed, and on
how and where to obtain those services.

Canadian election offices have made strides in improving the accessibility of voting for many Canadians with disabilities. Additional
reforms are worth undertaking to assist the disabled citizen on Election Day at ordinary voting stations and, where desired, at alternative
sites. A substantial number of disability groups remain largely
unaware of the services offered to electors with disabilities. Information should be distributed widely and early enough in alternative
formats (large print, Braille, audio-cassette/diskette, plain language
and online) so that electors know what options are available. Disability groups also call for greater assistance at voting stations. This assistance takes many forms: awareness and sensitivity training for volunteers and paid staff working at polls in order to avoid biases and
humiliating situations, having sign interpreters readily available to
help, providing sufficient mobile voting stations and ensuring stations
are physically accessible and accommodating to voters with disabilities. More contentious reform ideas, where opinions seem divided, for
making it easier to vote in elections include Internet voting and telephone voting (Courtney 2004; Gidengil et al. 2004). Concerns here
relate to security, fraud, and the loss of public participation in the
process. In a similar manner, future e-consultations by governments or
legislatures must be more accessible to and inclusive of all people with
disabilities (Stienstra and Troschuk 2005).

To improve the capacity of Canada's disability community in
general, and for civic engagement in particular, reform options put
forward include federal, provincial, and urban governments hiring
more people with disabilities in their public services, governments and
legislatures consulting with the disability community on a regular
basis prior to taking action, and not only increasing the level of
funding to disability organizations but also modifying resource allocation from a year-to-year to a multi-year funding approach in order to

improve the stability and planning of organizations (Canadian Centre
for Disability Studies (CCDS) 2002). To renew organizations and
strengthen the movement, more needs doing to involve activists and
agencies across all the regions of the country (Hutchison et al. 2007a,
2007b). Where they do not currently exist, legislative committees with
designated responsibility for issues of disability and inclusion should
be established; such parliamentary bodies offer an important democratic and public space for disability policy deliberation. Disability
advisory councils appointed by governments and linked to government departments have a mixed record of effectiveness. For the disability movement, such councils are not meant to be disinterested
agencies; they are looked to not as councils *on* disability issues, but
rather expected to be councils *for* disability issues, actively dedicated
to tackling barriers and advancing inclusion through public policy
processes.

The rise and fall, then revival and demise once again, of the Court
Challenges Program shows how citizenship rights 'are not static but
are always open to reinterpretation and negotiation' (Lister 1997: 35).
In this case, such rights are also subject to contestation and termination
by the federal state. For most of the past twenty-five years, the Court
Challenges Program offered resources to disability organizations
enabling these groups to be more effective participants in fundamental legal cases dealing with equality rights and constitutional questions
of the relationship between citizens and the state, and between the
Charter of Rights and governments. Disability associations made considerable use of this program for augmenting their modest influence
on public policy and government politics, and as a way of giving
meaning to the rights of Canadians living with disabilities in a society
marked by systemic barriers and ambivalent public culture of pride
and prejudice. It seems obvious that this program should rise again
and be reinstated by the federal government and Parliament.

Two other significant reforms in advancing social citizenship for
persons with disabilities are the idea of a federal disability act promised by federal political parties and a national action plan formulated
by a coalition of groups in the disability community.

A Federal Disability Act

A symbol of disability becoming a major area of policy attention is 'the
recent introduction in many liberal democratic societies of some form

of anti-discrimination legislation to protect disabled people from unjustifiable treatment and overt discrimination' (Barnes, Mercer, and Shakespeare 1999: 153). Such legislation usually follows political action by disability coalitions for full rights. In the Canadian context, proposals for such legislation have emerged since the introduction of the Americans with Disabilities Act in 1990, and frustrations over the limited success with human rights laws and reforms to other legislation. Canada's disability movement acutely feels the costs and other limits of litigating barriers one at a time through antidiscrimination laws, with enforcement often slow or inconsistent; another consequence of reform through litigation is the support the process lends to the social construction of people with disabilities as victims.

A federal government task force on disability issues in 1996 called for comprehensive legislation for Canadians with disabilities, and Quebec and Ontario, as noted earlier, have wide-ranging accessibility laws for persons with disabilities. In addition to the limits of the human rights laws, and examples of legislative reforms in these provinces and in other countries, the persistent social exclusion, poverty, and stigma experienced by Canadians with disabilities also spurs interest in a federal disability act. This sort of legislation fits Canadian political practice of formulating group-conscious policies, as for Aboriginal peoples, veterans, official language communities, women, seniors, and visible minority communities.

In Canada's case, the idea of a federal disability act is usually seen in terms of 'positive action' legislation. This is in contrast to antidiscrimination legislation that relies on complaints, the investigation of individual cases, possibly litigation, and court or tribunal orders. Canadian jurisdictions already have such legal remedies and mechanisms in human rights codes and related legislation. Positive action legislation, by comparison, is proactive and systemic in design with a focus on accessibility, mainstreaming, reducing inequalities, and promoting universal design. Core tools of positive action include public awareness, procurement and contract policies, and development of standards, timelines for implementation and compliance, and enforcement.

For the 2006 federal general election, for the first time political parties put forward promises on a disability act. The Green Party supported the idea of a Disabilities Act, the Liberal Party expressed intentions to strengthen existing laws and to consider a Canadian Inclusion and Accessibility Act, the New Democratic Party proposed a Canadi-

ans with Disabilities Act, and the Conservative Party pledged to intro-
duce a National Disability Act 'to promote reasonable access to
medical care, medical equipment, education, employment, transportation and housing for Canadians with disabilities' (Conservative Party
of Canada 2005: 16). Upon their election, the Conservative minority
government of Stephen Harper reaffirmed the party platform to intro-
duce a disability law and, over the next three years (2006–2008),
federal government officials worked on such a law, with plans to
consult eventually with community groups and parliamentarians.

Activists and groups within the disability movement respond to the
idea of a federal disability act in three ways. One response is that such
legislation is unnecessary and, more seriously, holds certain legal and
political risks (McCallum 2006). Critical concerns are that rather than
mainstream, such legislation may ghettoize disability as a social policy
area, that the Conservative's promise ignores jurisdictional issues of
the division of responsibilities between federal and provincial orders
of government, that such a law risks sidestepping Charter of Rights
and human rights guarantees, that disability groups have higher priorities and this legislation reform process detracts from mobilizing
efforts to achieve other concrete social program reforms, and that,
since this legislation is limited to federal jurisdictions, it risks ignoring
more pressing needs or objectives of certain groups in the disability
community. For example, the Deaf community is seeking to have
American Sign Language (ASL) and Langue des Signes Québécoise
(LSQ) included in the Official Languages Act.

A second response is a mix of mild support and mild concerns.
Ambivalent supporters express a qualified yes to this reform option,
seeing it as somewhat useful for people with disabilities although tan-
gential to the core priorities of the disability movement (Gordon and
Hecht 2006). They may worry that government might regard such a
legislative initiative as their major response to the needs of Canadians
with disabilities, letting the governing party off the hook for other
needed initiatives and moving on to the claims of other social groups.
If carefully designed, and in close consultation with disability groups
across the country, a disability act could be a modest contribution to
advancing access and inclusion. Not an end in itself, a federal disability act should be a beginning in federal leadership on a wider disability agenda. No doubt, negative sentiments toward the government
proposing this reform influence adherents to both the first and second
viewpoints.

A third response is favourable, even enthusiastic in some parts of the movement, with strong commitment to the idea of a federal disability act. Here, people positively identify with the idea of disability legislation, believing it can energize the movement, raise public awareness, and help forge alliances through an inclusive policy development process (Lepofsky 2004). Enthusiastic supporters may also see a federal disability act as an opportunity to formulate a modern definition of disability informed by a social model, thereby supplementing the Charter of Rights and human rights codes.

These differing reactions to a federal disability law pose challenges for the disability movement in building a consensus, bringing various groups together to communicate a message to government officials, and in raising public understanding of disability issues. Until more details are forthcoming from the Harper government, the Conservative promise is vague, somewhat muddled, and incomplete. The party's promise is unclear as to what reasonable access means; it is muddled in including some federal service areas, but not others, and some provincial service areas, but not others; and, there is no mention of processes for tackling systemic barriers. This has prompted disability organizations and associations to articulate some 'bottom lines' in supporting such legislation at the federal level: it must be cross-disability in scope, have mandatory standards, strong enforcement provisions, and adequate funding for improving access and inclusion. If not, then disability groups are not interested in the reform.

The Council of Canadians with Disabilities (CCD) – which brings together both provincial and territorial cross disability organizations and national advocacy organizations – has taken leadership in commissioning a research paper, by legal specialists on disability issues, on the challenges and opportunities surrounding a federal disability act (Gordon and Hecht 2006). The approach is pragmatic: if the Harper government is developing an act, then the disability community needs to engage in that process, otherwise the government will set the agenda and drive the process. The potential scope of a federal act includes telecommunications, inter-provincial and international transportation, broadcasting, banking, justice, immigration, First Nations, employment in the federal public service and federally regulated sectors (about 10 per cent of the overall Canadian labour force), and various other federal programs, services, institutions, and tax measures.

Depending on political will of federal parties, the state of intergovernmental relations, and the prevailing public mood, a federal disability act could extend into areas of provincial jurisdiction through the mechanisms of access standards attached to infrastructure programs, health transfer programs, post-secondary education agreements, and social transfer arrangements.

The rationale for a continued federal role in this field through intergovernmental transfers includes several ideas. One reason is to address the core mandate and underlying mission of the Department of Human Resources and Skills Development Canada. A second is to support the portability of services and the mobility rights of Canadians with disabilities within and across jurisdictions and life situations. While a third reason is to encourage the further development and enhancement of the current patchwork of disability-related supports across the country (Crawford 2005a; Torjman 2001). A fourth reason relates to the obvious disparities among provinces and is to assist provinces and territories, with their varying degrees of fiscal capacity, to undertake the provision of a range of accessible and responsive supports. A fifth reason for a sustained federal role in this field is to advance equality rights under the Canadian Charter of Rights by sponsoring programs and activities that aim to improve conditions of disadvantaged individuals because of mental or physical disability. By increasing the size and nature of transfers to the provinces for disability supports, the federal government can directly contribute to closing the gaps between needs and services and thus truly advance the economic inclusion and social citizenship of Canadians with disabilities.

A federal disability act, to be effective and acceptable to the disability community, requires a framework of organizational structures and policy tools (Gordon and Hecht 2006). These include: a minister of disability issues named in the legislation with specific duties and powers; a commissioner of disability and inclusion, an independent officer that would report to Parliament annually on the progress of federal public bodies in complying with standards and policies related to disability; an accessibility design centre that would give the federal government capacity to develop and promote universal design standards for facilities, services, and technologies; and a full inclusion policy centre located in the Canadian Human Rights Commission in order to supply proactive advice on removing and preventing barriers. Certain items are not without controversy: some leaders in the movement view the idea of a minister's council or prime minister's advisory group as a threat to the role of national disability organizations. Hence, a key feature of a federal disability act is the creation of a set of roles and agencies linked to Parliament that could not unilaterally change at the whim of a government.

All too well, the disability movement knows federal legislation is just one item on the policy agenda of advancing equality and full citizenship.

Canadians with disabilities will support a Federal Disability Act that moves forward quickly, encompasses the issues identified, allocates significant resources for improving access and inclusion and ensures a mechanism for strong enforcement of access and inclusion. The development of a Federal Disability Act cannot preclude action in other areas nor can Canadians with disabilities and their families wait for a Federal Disability Act to implement reforms that are desperately needed now. (End Exclusion 2007: 4)

To propel action on improving access and inclusion, Canadian disability groups articulate a number of reform measures in key policy areas.

National Action Plan

For some years now, national and provincial disability organizations have been developing an overarching agenda for policy reforms and social change (Canadian Association for Independent Living Centres 2002; CCD 1999; Roeher 2001). In 2005, leading advocacy organizations called on the federal and provincial/territorial governments to put into action a national framework of the 1998 *In Unison* vision of full citizenship for Canadians with disabilities. A joint statement by the Council of Canadians with Disabilities (CCD) and Canadian Association for Community Living (CACL) urged governments to combat the poverty and exclusion of persons with disabilities by investing in aids and devices, personal assistance, and environmental accommodations (CCD and CACL 2005a). In consultation with various disability organizations, experts, and government officials, CCD and CACL proposed a national agenda.

As short-term strategies, CCD and CACL recommended the federal government commit to (i) a framework for investment in disability supports with transfer payments to the provinces and territories; (ii) a 'disability dimension' in new initiatives of caregivers, child care, infrastructure measures, and so forth; (iii) a study on poverty and disability, especially the income needs of persons with disabilities; and (iv) engagement with the disability community and other governments in developing the agenda. Over the medium term of three to five years, CCD and CACL called on the federal government to explore addressing poverty by meeting individual costs of disability through an expenditure program, perhaps modelled after the National Child Benefit. Woven together here is a set of citizenship claims that address redistribution of income, goods, and services; recognition of disability as a social issue and social group; and representation of the voices of people with disabilities in political, policy, and administrative processes.

In a subsequent open letter to federal, provincial, and territorial ministers of social services, the CCD national chairperson and the CACL president elaborated their thinking on federal investments in disability supports. Objectives to guide bilateral agreements should include enhancing disability supports across the lifespan to enable participation and inclusion, assisting governments to expand the supply of community-based supports, and transitioning from institutional services to community supports. As the two leaders stated in their open letter: 'Our priority has been, and remains, an investment in disability-related supports that assist Canadians with disabilities to participate in early learning and childcare, get an education, become employed, look after their families and enjoy the opportunities non-disabled Canadians expect as a right of citizenship' (CCD and CACL 2005b: 2). Attached to the letter were signatures from more than fifty organizations endorsing this call for addressing the unmet needs of Canadians with disabilities.

To ensure accountability of this agenda, CCD and CACL proposed quantitative targets for measuring results and encouraging success. Over five to ten years, the targets are to reduce by half the annual income gap between Canadians with and without disabilities, to reduce by half the poverty rate of adults with disabilities (which at that time was 15 per cent for working age people with disabilities), to reduce by half the non-reimbursed costs faced by persons with disabilities, and to reduce by half the labour force market participation gap between Canadians with and without disabilities, which would mean increasing the employment rate for persons with disabilities from the average of 44 per cent to 61 per cent (CCD and CACL 2005a: 4). From the standpoint of movement leaders, these are central tests of whether an agenda of action on disability is successful over the coming decade.

These reform ideas were refined in processes associated with national conferences called End Exclusion, held in Ottawa in 2006 and 2007, where hundreds of self-advocates, family members, activists, and allies gathered, and some federal politicians attended. The first of these meetings focused on marking the twenty-five years since the landmark 1981 *Obstacles* report by a federal parliamentary task force, and endorsing a vision for building an inclusive society, while the second conference developed a national action plan on disability. This plan seeks to provide a road map to help policy makers, politicians, and interested civil society groups in moving from vision to action. The national plan displays openness to the multiple dimensions and differences in the lives of Canadians with disabilities. The action plan specifically makes reference to the social markers of age, gender, ethnicity, geographical place, indigenous status, residential mode, socioeconomic class, and type of disability (End Exclusion 2007: 3–4). This illustrates the disability community acting like a new social movement – acknowledging and consciously reaching out to the diverse social identities and divisions in contemporary Canadian life. Recognizing such multiplicities in ways of life inserts additional interests and aspirations into the movement's agenda, raising further possibilities for reforms. It also shows the disability community acting like an interest group, in the Canadian tradition (Kwavnick 1972), of seeking to influence government policy by demonstration of a broad representation of interests at these national conferences.

This national action plan comprises actions in four areas centred in federal leadership, but linked to provincial responsibilities and thus intergovernmental collaboration. In brief, the four areas are new investments in disability-related supports, new initiatives to alleviate poverty, new supports to increase access to labour force participation, and new initiatives to promote access, inclusion, and full citizenship.

Targeted investments by the federal government for disability supports was again highlighted in the 2007 action plan as the top priority of the disability community, essential for improving access and the array of supports available across the country. On the poverty of Canadians with disabilities, described as 'a national disgrace,' the action plan sets out a series of short-term and long-term reforms. Short-term steps identified include making the Disability Tax Credit refundable, making CPP Disability benefits non-taxable, and expanding the Employment Insurance Sick Benefits to a full year from the present limit of fifteen weeks (Prince 2008b). Long term, the disability community sees an expanded federal role in income security for Canadians with disabilities (End Exclusion 2007: 6).

To increase access to training, education, and labour force participation, the action plan proposes two measures: first, establishing specific targets for persons with disabilities in labour market agreements between the federal and provincial/territorial governments, and second, expanding federal funds to federal programs that support innovation in labour force inclusion by disabled Canadians. Finally, the action plan recommends a bundle of actions by the federal government, some substantive in nature and others process oriented, to promote access and participation in transportation, elections, accessible technology, a universal design centre, as well as recognizing ASL and LSQ as official languages and re-establishing a parliamentary committee on the status of Canadians with disabilities (End Exclusion 2007: 7–8).

In the longer term, the disability community foresees a new relationship between income security provision and disability supports programming between the federal and provincial/territorial governments. This idea fits with prevailing trends in Canadian federalism as to respecting the division of roles while recognizing the provinces as the primary order of government for education, health, labour markets, and social services. An expanded federal role in providing a basic income for adults with severe disabilities would free up significant financial resources at provincial and territorial levels for persons presently on social assistance caseloads, and for reinvestment in disability-related supports and services. Once again, the federal condition is at the heart of Canadian politics and policy making (Cameron and Valentine 2001; Prince 2002d; Puttee 2002; Smiley 1987).[5]

Conclusion

For many persons with disabilities there is a substantial contradiction between political expressions of full citizenship and their personal experiences of social inequality. This contradiction may well be unending given fundamental differences in the interests and power resources between capitalism and democracy, never mind the tendency, in our media age, of federal and provincial political parties to employ rhetoric of a better tomorrow for all. In fact, the country's record of reform is not a series of progressive measures consistently moving toward higher levels of access and inclusion. Nor is the record one of complete disappointment. Canada's record on disability reform includes policy successes and setbacks, political spin and program substance. Activists speak of the indifferent responses from governments, at times tokenistic actions, on occasion active state resistance to disability movement claims, and all too often incremental steps. A significant gap therefore exists between the rhetoric of inclusion and the lived realities for many persons with disabilities. Yet voicing claims for essential services and basic income support in the language of citizenship is central to Canadian disability politics, and reveals social liberalism as the major ideological thread of this community. A discourse of citizenship seeks to legitimate claims using a familiar set of concepts around equality and opportunity, and to connect with the wider political community on aspirations of belonging and participation.

Disability activism is a politics of economic redistribution, accompanied by political claims for societal recognition and democratic representation. Fair access to existing services, programs, benefits, and policy processes is crucial, yet only a partial solution, to realizing full membership of Canadians with disabilities. Many of these services, programs, benefits, and processes need reviewing and altering to ensure systemic biases are not reproduced. Social justice for persons with disabilities requires a robust agenda of equity and equality measures. It means addressing differences without unwanted segregation, within a mix of general and specific measures that are accessible, affordable, and accountable.

A Canadian disability act (depending, of course, on the statutory details and implementation systems) could serve as a useful addition to the policy repertoire for lowering obstacles, mainstreaming disability, and enforcing public accountability for improving access and social inclusion. Admittedly, a new federal disability act is unlikely to tackle issues of poverty, literacy, and the lack of personal supports, issues largely within provincial jurisdiction. For these major social issues, a new spirit of cooperative intergovernmental relations devoted to advancing inclusion and equality is essential. At the same time, a national act could strengthen enforcement of activities within areas of federal jurisdiction such as telecommunications, employment equity, and human rights. It is these sorts of political actions and public commitments that form the foundation for tackling the social absences of and for enriching citizenship for all Canadians with disabilities.

Notes

Preface

1 In October 1993, Robert Latimer murdered his daughter, Tracy, who had severe cerebral palsy, at their Saskatchewan farm, weeks before her thirteenth birthday. In February 2008 the National Parole Board granted Robert Latimer, who was serving a ten-year jail sentence, day parole on two conditions. First, Latimer is to not have responsibility for, or make decisions for, any individuals who are severely disabled; and, second, Latimer is to participate in psychological counselling in order to address emotional issues and to develop stress management strategies to assist him in reintegrating into the community. For details on Tracy's life, the court trials of Robert Latimer, and larger issues of stigma and support for people with disabilities, see the book by Ruth Enns (1999).

Introduction: Disability, Politics, and Citizenship

1 For a fascinating exploration of the presence of absence and the absence of presence as it pertains to space and identity in everyday lives of women with chronic illness, see Moss and Dyck (2002). The concept of 'absent citizens' as used in this book suggests that the social position of people with disabilities imparts fewer resources, entitlements, and privileges than for most other groups in society; that persons with disabilities experience socially organized practices of exclusion and stigma; and that their claims for full membership in society are questioned and resisted. Dominant groups and dominant ways of thinking about citizenship still view persons with disabilities as 'other.' Thus, absent citizens are members of society who regularly and systematically encounter attitudi-

nal and material barriers, non-recognition in public spaces, institutions, and policies (Taylor 1992), as well as theories of citizenship and disconnections with the economic and social mainstream. Related terms are 'outcasts' (Charlton 1998: 23) and 'civic outsiders' referring to those who are 'sidelined, ignored and unheard' (James 2006: 64).

1. Pride and Prejudice: Canadian Ambivalence towards Inclusion

1 In terms of the composition of focus group workshops, in each group and across all eight groups there was a range of age groups of adults over eighteen, family incomes, household structures, and men and women. With the Lethbridge focus groups, several participants were First Nations persons (Environics Research Group 2004b: 5–6).

2 Respondents were asked if they or anyone else in their household had 'any difficulty hearing, seeing, communicating, walking, climbing stairs, bending, learning or doing any similar activities.' They were also asked if 'a physical or mental condition or health problem reduce[d] the amount or kind of activity you or anyone else in your household can do' at home, at work, or at school, or in other activities (Environics Research Group 2004a: 1). The sample was stratified across the provinces and territories to enable regional analyses, as well as by age group and disability status. The sampling error is 2.3 per cent with a confidence interval of 95 per cent; that is, that 95 per cent of all samples taken from the same population using the same questions at the same time would be within plus or minus 2.3 per cent (Mendelshon and Brent 2001).

3 There may be a linguistic/cultural wrinkle to neo-liberalism here which merits further research. In the national survey, there is a fascinating difference in opinions about the importance of families and of persons with disabilities in supporting needs between English-speaking and French-speaking respondents. Except for the areas of stable employment and recreation, French-speaking respondents were far more likely to say that the individual person with disabilities rather than their family is responsible for addressing these aspects of their lives. In comparison, English-speaking Canadians were more likely to express the belief that families have more of a responsibility than the individual person with the disability (Environics Research Group 2004c: 34).

4 The supporting organizations, which encompass national, provincial, territorial, Aboriginal, and foundations among other organizations, are listed in CCD and CACL (2005b: 4).

2. City Life and the Politics of Strangers

1 T.S. Eliot, 'Choruses from "The Rock."'
2 Space limitations do not allow a fuller examination of the strengths and
  weaknesses of each of these four perspectives in normative, theoretical, or
  empirical terms. Examples of this kind of assessment are in urban sociology and urban political science, among other fields of literature.
3 As with any theorizing, this classification unavoidably simplifies complexities of urban settings and stresses agreements rather than differences
  within each perspective. To be sure, there are ranges of emphasis among
  the writers in each of these perspectives.
4 Peter Leonard (1997: 22) notes a debate in postmodernist writings between
  what he calls optimists and pessimists, which he describes this way:
  'Should we look to the *benefits* of this contemporary shift in the culture of
  late capitalism: the new emphasis on difference, the challenge to authority,
  the increased choice in individual identity, the disapproval of ethnic arro-
  gance? Or should we focus, rather, on the detriments of the way we live
  now: the mind-deadening impact of mass-produced culture, the manufac-
  ture of desire, the increase in poverty and uncertainty, the collapse of mass
  class politics?' On balance, Leonard himself is an optimist who seeks to
  understand and confront 'the contradictory consequences of living in
  "New Times"' and imagine possibilities for a new emancipatory welfare
  project.
5 The following discussion is not an exhaustive literature survey, but I do
  rest it on a focused review of works in disability studies. Sources consulted
  include key journals such as *Disability and Society*, British and Canadian
  texts and readers such as Barnes, Mercer, and Shakespeare (1999), Barnes,
  Oliver, and Barton (2002), and Stienstra and Wight-Felske (2003).

3. Social Stratification, the State, and Disability

1 John Myles (2003) and Bernd Baldus (2004) both argue that Canadian sociologists are not examining economic inequality in as vigorous a manner,
  empirically or theoretically, as some in the discipline did some decades
  ago.
2 A welcome exception in Canadian social policy is Boychuk's (1998) book
  on provincial social assistance regimes with extensive attention to stratifying effects of welfare programs, an analysis directly influenced by the
  work of Esping-Andersen among others. Another is Margaret Hillyard

Little's (2005) study on retraining and welfare policy for low-income women, including Aboriginal women, struggling in the face of racism, sexism, and poverty.

3 From the 1940s into the 1980s, British sociologist T.H. Marshall wrote about social stratification and the welfare state. For Marshall, citizenship was a constantly developing institution in contemporary societies, and itself, in certain aspects, 'the architect of social inequality.' Marshall saw the Elizabethan Poor Laws (spanning the 1590s to the 1790s) as a system of workhouses and poorhouses that planned for and legitimated inequalities in society. While modifying rigid class and cultural divisions, Marshall claimed that the modern welfare state did preserve and ought to make legitimate a measure of economic inequality so as to provide incentives for personal responsibility, work, and other efforts (Marshall 1964: 235–55).

4 Social policy and feminist analyst, Diane Sainsbury (1996: 198–9), describes several potential strategies of disentitlement: reducing present or future benefits explicitly or by stealth, tightening eligibility requirements, interpreting and enforcing existing rules more stringently, shortening the duration available for benefits or services, eliminating outright particular benefits or services, and substituting one policy instrument with another (for example, from direct service provision to a tax credit), which has the effect of disadvantaging certain individuals and groups, such as low-income workers, single mothers, and the unemployed.

5 I agree with Naiman (2004: 138) that 'the term social stratification leads us to conceive of inequalities in social positions, or statuses.' However, I do not accept that status is a fixed phenomenon and not at all political in nature. I am persuaded by a Weberian viewpoint, in which status is a relational identity characterized by political struggles by social movements and interest groups and political parties; and, being connected to membership and participation as well as legally sanctioned entitlements, status is directly relevant to debates about citizenship (Marshall 1964; Turner 1986, 1988 and 2001).

5. The Canadian Disability Community: Five Arenas of Social Action and Capacity

1 This chapter, which expands on earlier work published in a disability and social policy text by McColl and Jongbloed (Prince 2006), presents a conceptual framework of five arenas for understanding the major activities and structures of the disability community. For Canadian case studies on specific disability organizations, groups, or campaigns, see Boyce et al.

(2001), Driedger (1989), Enns and Neufeldt (2003), Enns (1999), Lord and Hutchison (2007), Panitch (2007), Reaume (2000), and Stienstra and Wight-Felske (2003).

6. From Barriers to Ballots: Participating in Electoral Systems

1 See *Eldridge v. British Columbia (Attorney General)* [1997] 3 SCR 624.
2 Adopting quotas for increasing the number of persons with disabilities as candidates and elected members is an idea largely absent in Canada. Reasons may well include that the issue lies outside the mandates of elections offices; that political parties still struggle over the issue of gender quotas for candidates, as do some feminist scholars (Squires 2007); and that most Canadian disability organizations pursue other reforms, including widening access to the ballot box.

7. Engaging in Policy Development Processes

1 The following organizations endorsed this document: Council of Canadians with Disabilities, Canadian Association of Independent Living Centres, Canadian Association for Community Living, Canadian Paraplegic Association, Canadian National Institute for the Blind, Canadian Hard of Hearing Association, Aboriginal Reference Group on Disabilities, Neil Squire Foundation, Canadian Council on Rehabilitation and Work, Disabled Women's Network, Assembly of Manitoba Chiefs, Learning Disabilities Association of Canada, and National Educational Association of Disabled Students.
2 For information on the Saskatchewan Disability Income Support Coalition, see their web site www.saskdisc.ca. In October 2008, the government of Saskatchewan announced a Disability Income Strategy with plans for a new basic income support for persons with disabilities. The new income benefit will be separate from the province's social assistance program. Over 2009–10, community consultations will inform the design and delivery of this new program.
3 Other examples of the use of the Internet by governments in engaging Canadians with disabilities include the Persons with Disabilities Online site for the Government of Canada (www.pwd-online.ca) and the Disability Web Links site (www.disabilityweblinks.ca) that supplies information about federal, provincial, and territorial programs of interest to persons with disabilities. See also the Disability Information Technologies Research Alliance (www.dis-it.ca) work around e-Democracy.

8. Politicizing Citizenship: Towards a Fuller Measure of Equality

1 On the debate over 'reformism' as a strategy for social change in capitalist societies, Turner (1986) offers a concise and readable account, one that ultimately defends reformism as a legitimate approach to expanding citizenship. In brief, the critique asserts that extended freedoms and social securities afforded by rights of citizenship leave the basic nature of capitalism society unaltered. Moreover, such social reforms incorporate marginal groups and working classes into this unequal exploitative system of economics. In response, Turner contends that taking a long term view shows that citizenship rights are not illusory or inevitably ineffectual, but rather represent real improvements in the lives of millions of people in industrial societies. Most people with disabilities who wish to work and are not at present – a number estimated at over 600,000 in Canada – understand participation in the market economy as an intended consequence of their pursuit of full citizenship. A final conceptual observation is that the terms of debate over reformism need to widen beyond economic class relationships to include other fundamental features of society, namely, that Canada is a colonial settler society, a liberal democracy, and federalist country. These characteristics all contain power relations and interests that interact with capitalism and citizenship in multiple and contested ways.

2 The influence of neo-liberalism is evident in political discourse, public documents, social policy design choices, and government budgetary decisions (Armitage 2003; Bashevkin 2002; Bonnett 2003; Crooks 2004; Young and Everitt 2004). Social liberalism and neo-liberalism overlap in certain key respects. Both speak of the importance of individual rights, personal choices, and self-care, along with accountability as a positive organizational practice. Both subscribe to the central importance of material well-being and both, to a degree, contain critiques of professional power and therapeutic knowledge. Notable differences in these two forms of liberal beliefs are over the scope of citizenship as a bundle of rights and duties, on the validity of group identities in social policy and democratic politics, and on their respective interpretation of the meaning of entitlements and obligations. In these ways, social liberalism and neo-liberalism are distinctive projects for constructing community membership and civic participation.

9. The Policy Record and Reform Agenda

1 On the Quebec legislation, see RSQ, chapter E-20.1. This law applies to provincial government departments and their networks, municipalities, edu-

cational institutions, and any other public bodies and private agencies in the province. Most of these organizations are required to produce and publish each year an action plan on behalf of handicapped persons as regards workplace integration, equal access, and general social inclusion into Quebec society. The central oversight body is the Office des personnes handicapées du Québec, which has an advisory and coordinating role. The Accessibility for Ontarians with Disabilities Act, 2005, S.O. 2005, c.11, applies to both the private and public sectors within the province. The ultimate aim of improving access for people with disabilities is through the development, implementation, and enforcement of accessibility standards for the removal and prevention of barriers. Mandatory standards are be phased in over many years and will cover accommodation, buildings, employment, facilities, goods, and services. Standards, formulated by standards development committees with multiple groups represented, will address physical, sensory, hearing, mental health, developmental, and learning disabilities. To advise the responsible Ontario cabinet minister, there is a standards advisory council, of which most members are persons with disabilities.

2 Further information on the Mental Health Commission of Canada is available at www.mentalhealthcommission.ca. On the senate report that shaped the formation of this commission, see Kirby (2006).

3 At its core, the United Nations Convention ensures persons with disabilities enjoy the same human rights as everyone else, and are able to lead their lives as fully fledged citizens who can make valuable contributions to society if given the same opportunities. It covers rights such as equality, non-discrimination, and equal recognition before the law; liberty and security of the person; accessibility, personal mobility, and independent living; right to health, work, and education; and participation in political and cultural life. For more on the Convention, see http://www.un.org/disabilities/convention/index.shtml.

4 Sophisticated studies of disability and stratification could look, in turn, at how disability interacts with (a) other ascribed dimensions of status such as age, ethnicity, and gender, (b) achieved statuses such as education, occupation, and income, (c) how various ascribed and achieved dimensions interact at a given point in time, (d) and, over time, through key transitions of life events, (e) the effect of policy and program provisions on social inequalities and change.

5 For the 2008 Canadian general election, the NDP's platform essentially endorsed the full End Exclusion action plan as put forward by the disability movement, while the Liberal Party committed to making the Disability Tax Credit a refundable benefit for low-income Canadians with disabilities.

References

Alexander, Mary Lee. (2001). 'Democracy, Diversity, and Disability.' Background paper for the panel discussion, 'Utilizing a Consultative Process to Advance the Disability Policy Agenda in Canada.' Winnipeg: Society for Disability Studies, 14th Annual Meeting.

Allahar, Anton L., and James E. Cote. (1998). *Richer and Poorer: The Structure of Inequality in Canada.* Toronto: Lorimer.

Anderson, Karen I. (1996). *Sociology: A Critical Introduction.* Toronto: Nelson Canada.

Andrew, Caroline, Katherine Graham, and Susan D. Phillips, eds. (2002). *Urban Affairs: Back on the Policy Agenda.* Montreal and Kingston: McGill-Queen's Univ. Press.

Anspach, Renee R. (1979). 'From Stigma to Identity Politics: Political Activism among the Physically Disabled and Former Mental Patients.' *Social Science and Medicine* 13A:765–73.

Armitage, Andrew. (2003). *Social Welfare in Canada.* (4th ed.). Toronto: Oxford Univ. Press.

Armstrong, B. (1976). 'The Mentally Disabled and the Right to Vote.' *Hospital and Community Psychiatry* 27(2):577–82.

Aronson, Jane, and Sheila M. Neysmith. (2001). 'Manufacturing Social Exclusion in the Home Care Market.' *Canadian Public Policy* 27(2):151–65.

Bach, Michael. (2002). 'Governance Regimes in Disability-Related Policy and Programs: A Focus on Community Support Systems.' In Alan Puttee, ed., *Federalism, Democracy and Disability Policy in Canada*, 153–74. Montreal and Kingston: McGill-Queen's Univ. Press.

Bach, Michael, and Marcia H. Rioux. (1996). 'Social Policy, Devolution and Disability: Back to Notions of the Worthy Poor?' In Jane Pulkingham and Gordon Ternowetsky, eds., *Remaking Canadian Social Policy: Social Security in the Late 1990s*, 317–26. Halifax: Fernwood Publishing.

Bakker, Isabella, and Katherine Scott. (1997). 'From the Postwar to the Post-Liberal Keynesian Welfare State.' In Wallace Clement, ed., *Understanding Canada: Building on the New Canadian Political Economy*, 286–310. Montreal and Kingston: McGill-Queen's Univ. Press.

Baldus, Bernd. (2004). '... To Race and Gender, Everyone? Some Thoughts on the Future of Research on Social Equality.' *Canadian Journal of Sociology* 29:577–82.

Barnes, Colin, and Geof Mercer. (2003). *Disability*. Cambridge: Polity Press.

Barnes, Colin, Geof Mercer, and Tom Shakespeare. (1999). *Exploring Disability: A Sociological Introduction*. Cambridge: Polity Press.

Barnes, Colin, Mike Oliver, and Len Barton, eds. (2002). *Disability Studies Today*. Cambridge: Polity Press.

Bashevkin, Sylvia. (2002). *Welfare Hot Buttons: Women, Work and Social Policy Reform*. Toronto: Univ. of Toronto Press.

Baubock, Rainer. (2003). 'Reinventing Urban Citizenship.' *Citizenship Studies* 7(2):139–60.

Beall, Jo. (1997). 'Valuing Difference and Working with Diversity.' In J. Beall, ed., *A City for All: Valuing Difference and Working with Diversity*, 2–37. London: Zed Books.

Beatty, Harry. (2003). *Advancing the Inclusion of Persons with Disabilities: A Critical Analysis and Recommendations*. A Report Prepared for the Council of Canadians with Disabilities (CCD) and approved by CCD National Council.

Beauvais, Caroline, and Jane Jenson. (2002). *Social Cohesion: Updating the State of the Research*. Ottawa: Canadian Policy Research Networks Discussion Paper No. F/22.

Bell, Dorothy M., Colin McKay, and Kathryn J. Phillips. (2001). 'Overcoming the Barriers to Voting Experienced by People with Learning Disabilities.' *British Journal of Learning Disabilities* 29:122–7.

Berman, Marshall. (1982). *All That Is Solid Melts Into Air: The Experience of Modernity*. New York: Simon and Schuster.

Bernard, Daniella, and Nicole Bernard. (2005). 'Letters to the Editor: To all Elected Levels of Government.' *Total Access* Winter:5.

Bickenbach, Jerome. (1993). *Physical Disability and Social Policy*. Toronto: Univ. of Toronto Press.

Blackwell, Tom. (1992). 'Improved Access for Disabled: Human Rights Commission Tribunal Decision Seen as Major Advance.' *The Ottawa Citizen*, Ottawa: Feb. 19, A4.

Blais, André, Louis Massicotte, and Antoine Yoshinaka. (2001). 'Deciding Who Has the Right to Vote: A Comparative Analysis of Election Laws.' *Electoral Studies* 20(1):41–62.

Boles, Janet K., ed. (1986). *The Egalitarian City: Issues of Rights, Distribution, Access, and Power*. Toronto: Praeger.

Bonnett, Laura. (2003). 'Citizenship and People with Disabilities: The Invisible Frontier.' In Janine Brodie and Linda Trimble, eds., *Reinventing Canada: Politics of the 21st Century*, 151–63. Toronto: Pearson Education.

Boyce, William, Kari Krogh, and Emily Boyce. (2006). 'Policy Shifts and Challenges: Coping Strategies of Disability Organizations.' In Mary Ann McColl and Lyn Jongbloed, eds., *Disability and Social Policy in Canada*, 188–209 (2nd ed.). Concord, ON: Captus Univ. Press.

Boyce, William, Mary Tremblay, Mary Anne McColl, Jerome Bickenbach, Anne Crichton, Steven Andrews, Nancy Gerein, and April D'Aubin. (2001). *A Seat at the Table: Persons with Disabilities and Policy Making*. Montreal and Kingston: McGill-Queen's Univ. Press.

Boychuk, Gerald W. (1998). *Patchworks of Purpose: The Development of Provincial Social Assistance Regimes in Canada*. Montreal and Kingston: McGill-Queen's Univ. Press.

Bradford, Neil. (2004). 'Place Matters and Multi-Level Governance: Perspectives on a New Urban Policy Paradigm.' *Policy Options* Feb.:39–44.

Breton, Raymond. (1984). 'The Production and Allocation of Symbolic Resources: An Analysis of the Linguistic and Ethnocultural Fields in Canada.' *Canadian Review of Sociology and Anthropology* 21:123–44.

Broadbent, Alan. (2008). *Urban Nation: Why We Need to Give Power Back to the Cities to Make Canada Strong*. Toronto: HarperCollins.

Brooks, Stephen. (2000). *Canadian Democracy: An Introduction*. (3rd ed.). Toronto: Oxford Univ. Press.

Bryson, Lois. (1992). *Welfare and the State: Who Benefits?* London: Macmillan.

Budlender, Debbie, Diane Elson, Guy Hewitt, and Tanni Mukhopadhyay. (2002). *Gender Budgets Make Cents*. London: Gender Affairs Department, Commonwealth Secretariat.

Bulmer, Martin. (1984). *The Chicago School of Sociology*. Chicago: Univ. of Chicago Press.

Burge, Philip, Hélène Ouellette-Kuntz, and Rosemary Lysaght. (2007). 'Public Views on Employment of People with Intellectual Disabilities.' *Journal of Vocational Rehabilitation* 26(1):29–37.

Burt, Sandra, and Sonya L. Hardman. (2001). 'The Case of Disappearing Targets: The Liberals and Gender Equality.' In Leslie A. Pal, ed., *How Ottawa Spends 2001–2002: Power in Transition*, 201–22. Toronto: Oxford Univ. Press.

Cairns, Alan C. (1995). *Reconfigurations: Canadian Citizenship and Constitutional Change*. (Ed. by Doug Williams). Toronto: McClelland and Stewart.

Callahan, Marilyn, and Chris McNiven. (1988). 'British Columbia.' In Jacqueline S. Ismael and Yves Vaillancourt, eds., *Privatization and Provincial Social Services: Policy, Administration and Service Delivery*. Edmonton: Univ. of Alberta Press.

Cameron, David, and Fraser Valentine. (2001). 'Comparing Policy-Making in Federal Systems: The Case of Disability Policy and Programs – An Introduction.' In D. Cameron and F. Valentine, eds., *Disability and Federalism: Comparing Different Approaches to Full Participation*, 1–44. Montreal and Kingston: McGill-Queen's Univ. Press.

Campaign 2000. 'Early Childhood Education and Care Community Indicators Project.' Available online http://www.campaign2000.ca.

Campeau, Georges, (2004). *From UI to EI: Waging War on the Welfare State*. (Trans. by Richard Howard). Vancouver: Univ. of British Columbia Press.

Canada. (1981). *Obstacles*. Report of the Special Parliamentary Committee on the Disabled and Handicapped. Ottawa: Supply and Services Canada.

– (1993). *Pathway to Integration: Final Report, Mainstream 1992*. Report to Ministers of Social Services, Federal/Provincial/Territorial Review of Services Affecting Canadians with Disabilities. Ottawa: Supply and Services Canada.

– (1996a). *Equal Citizenship: Canadians with Disabilities: The Will to Act*. Final Report of the Federal Task Force on Disability. Ottawa: Supply and Services Canada. Available online http://www.hrdc-drhc.gc.ca.

– (1996b). *Gender-Based Analysis: A Guide for Policy-making*. Ottawa: Status of Women.

– (1998). *In Unison: A Canadian Approach to Disability Issues*. Report by the Federal/Provincial/Territorial Ministers Responsible for Social Services. Ottawa: Supply and Services Canada. Available online http://www.hrdc-drhc.gc.ca.

– (1999). *Government of Canada Response to 'Reflecting Interdependence: Disability, Parliament, Government and the Community*. Sixth Report of the Standing Committee on Human Resources Development and the Status of Persons with Disabilities. Ottawa.

– (2000a). *Canadian Human Rights Act Review, Promoting Equality*. Ottawa: Supply and Services Canada. Available online http://www.chareview.org.frp/frp-c17e.html.

– (2000b). *A Federal Accountability Framework on Disability: Access and Inclusion Lenses*. Ottawa: Social Policy Development, Human Resources Development Canada.

– (2001). *In Unison 2000: Persons with Disabilities in Canada*. Report by the Federal/Provincial/Territorial Ministers Responsible for Social Services. Ottawa: Supply and Services Canada. Available online http://www.hrdc-drhc.gc.ca.

– (2002a). *Advancing the Inclusion of Persons with Disabilities: A Government of Canada Report*. December. Ottawa: Human Resources Development Canada. Available online http://www.hrdc-drhc.gc.ca.

– (2002b). Sub-Committee on the Status of Persons with Disabilities. *Sub-Committee on the Status of Persons with Disabilities Roundtable on the Canada Pension Plan (Disability)*. Available online http://www.parl.gc.ca/dosability/whats_new/round_table_e.asp.

– (2003a). *Defining Disability: A Complex Issue*. Gatineau: Office for Disability Issues, Human Resources Development Canada.

– (2003b). Finance 'Ministers Manley and Caplan Announce Appointments to Technical Advisory Committee on Tax Measures for Persons with Disabilities.' Ottawa, Ap. 29. News Release. Available online http://www.fin.gc.ca/news03/04-026e.html.

– (2003c). National Library. 'Council on Access to Information For Print-disabled Canadians.' Available online http://www.nlc-bnc.ca.

– (2003d). Sub-Committee on the Status of Persons with Disabilities. *Canada Pension Plan- Disability: Consultations with Canadians*. Available online http://www.parl.gc.ca/disability/Home/index_e.asp?Language=E.

– (2004). *Advancing the Inclusion of Persons with Disabilities: A Government of Canada Report*. Social Development Canada.

– (2006). *Advancing the Inclusion of Persons with Disabilities: A Government of Canada Report*. Ottawa: Human Resources and Social Development Canada. Available online http://www.hrsdc.gc.ca.

Canadian Abilities Foundation. (2007). *Directory of Disability Organizations in Canada*. Sixth Edition. Toronto: CAF.

Canadian Association of Independent Living Centres. (2002). 'A Work in Progress: A Framework for a National Disability Supports Plan.' Available online http://www.cailc.ca/aworkinprogress/htm.

Canadian Broadcasting Corporation (CBC). (2005). 'Lifting Restrictions on Mental Patients.' *CBC Archives*, clip originally broadcast November 16, 1988. Available online http://archives.cbc.ca.

Canadian Centre on Disability Studies. (2002). 'Disability Community Capacity: A Framework for Preliminary Assessment.' Available online http://www.disabilitystudies.ca.

Canadian Council on Social Development (CCSD). (2000). *Social Cohesion in Canada: Possible Indicators*. For the Social Cohesion Network, Heritage Canada and Justice Canada.

– (2002). *CCSD's Disability Information Sheets*. Ottawa: CCSD. Available online www.ccsc.ca/drip.

– (2003). *Personal Security Index, 2003: A Reflection of How Canadians Feel Five Years Later*. Ottawa: CCSD. Available online http://www.ccsd.ca.

– (2004). *Supports and Services for Adults and Children Age 5–14 with Disabilities in Canada' An Analysis of Needs and Gaps.* Ottawa: CCSD.

Capponi, Pat. (1992). *Upstairs in the Crazy House: The Life of a Psychiatric Survivor.* Toronto: Viking.

Carroll, Michael, and Jerry P. White, eds. (2005). *Images of Society: Readings that Inspire and Inform Sociology.* Toronto: Thomson Nelson.

Chappell, Rosalie. (2006). *Social Welfare in Canadian Society.* (3rd ed.). Toronto: Thomas Nelson.

Charlton, James I. (1998). *Nothing about Us without Us: Disability, Oppression and Empowerment.* Berkeley: Univ. of California Press.

Chivers, Sally. (2008). 'Barrier by Barrier: The Canadian Disability Movement and the Fight for Equal Rights.' In Miriam Smith, ed., *Group Politics and Social Movements in Canada,* 307–28. Peterborough, ON: Broadview Press.

Chouinard, Vera. (1999). 'Life at the Margins: Disabled Women's Explorations of Ableist Spaces.' In E. Teather, ed., *Embodied Geographies: Spaces, Bodies, Rites of Passage,* 142–56. London: Routledge.

Chouinard, Vera, and Valorie A. Crooks. (2005) '"Because *They* Have All the Power and I Have None": State Restructuring of Income and Employment Supports and Disabled Women.' *Disability and Society* 20(1):19–32.

Church, Kathryn. (1995). *Forbidden Narratives: Critical Autobiography as Social Science.* London: Routledge.

Church, Kathryn, Catherine Frazee, Melanie Panitch, Theresa Luciani, and Victoria Bowman. (2007). *Doing Disability at the Bank: Discovering the Work of Learning/Teaching done by Disabled Bank Employees.* Toronto: RBC Foundation Institute for Disability Studies, Ryerson Univ.

Coleman, William D., and Grace Skogstad, eds. (1990). *Policy Communities and Public Policy in Canada: A Structural Approach.* Toronto: Copp Clark Pitman.

Conservative Party of Canada (CPC). (2005). *Stand Up for Canada: 2006 Election Platform.* Ottawa: CPC.

Council of Canadians with Disabilities (CCD). (1999). *A National Strategy for Persons with Disabilities: The Community Definition.* Available online http://www.pcs.mb.ca~ccd/nation~4.htm.

– (2005). *A Voice of Our Own: CCD Election Challenge,* Winnipeg: CCD Publications, Special Edition. Available online http://www.ccdonline.ca.

Council of Canadians with Disabilities (CCD) and Canadian Association for Community Living (CACL). (2005a). 'A Call to Combat Poverty and Exclusion of Canadians with Disabilities by Investing in Disability Supports.' Available online www.ccdonline.ca or www.cacl.ca.

– (2005b). 'Advancing Citizenship: Moving Forward a National Disability Agenda.' Available online www.ccdonline.ca or www.cacl.ca.

Council of Europe. (2001). *Promoting the Policy Debate on Social Cohesion from a Policy Perspective*. Trends in Social Cohesion, No. 1. Strasbourg: Council of Europe Publishing.

Courtney, John C. (2004). *Elections*. Vancouver: Univ. of British Columbia Press.

CQ Researcher. (2001). 'Disabled Voters Demand Equal Rights.' *CQ Researcher* 11(38):908.

Crawford, Cam. (2005a). *Doing Without: Unmet Needs for Disability Supports in Canada – Scope and Implications*. Toronto: L'Institut Roeher Institute.

– (2005b). *Non-Reimbursed Costs of Disability-Specific Supports: Technical Paper*. Toronto: L'Institut Roeher Institute.

Crooks, Valorie A. (2004). 'Income Assistance (the ODSP) and Disabled Women in Ontario, Canada: Limited Program Information, Restrictive Incomes and the Impacts Upon Socio-Spatial Life.' *Disability Studies Quarterly* 24(3). Available online www.dsq-sds.org.

– (2007). 'Women's Experiences of Developing Musculoskeletal Diseases: Employment Challenges and Policy Recommendations,' *Disability and Rehabilitation*, 29(14):1107–16.

Curtis, James, Edward Grabb, and Neil Guppy, eds. (2004). *Social Inequality in Canada: Patterns, Problems, and Policies*. (4th ed.). Toronto: Pearson Prentice Hall.

Dale, Ann, and Lenore Newman. (2005). 'The Role of Online Dialogue in the Creation of Policy Alternatives.' *Canadian Review of Social Policy*, 55:99–103.

Dale-Stone, Sharon. (2007). *A Change of Plans: Women's Stories of Hemorrhagic Stroke*. Toronto: Sumach Press.

Danermark, Berth, and Lotta Coniavitis Gellerstedt. (2004). 'Social Justice: Redistribution and Recognition – A Non-Reductionist Perspective on Disability.' *Disability and Society* 19(4):339–53.

D'Aubin, April, and Deborah Stienstra. (2004). 'Access to Electoral Success: Challenges and Opportunities for Candidates with Disabilities in Canada.' *Electoral Insight* 6(1):8–14.

Davidson, Diane R., and Miriam Lapp. (2004). 'The Evolution of Federal Voting Rights for Canadians with Disabilities.' *Electoral Insight* 6(1):15–21.

Davies, Jonathan S. (2005). 'The Social Exclusion Debate: Strategies, Controversies and Dilemmas.' *Policy Studies* 26:3–27.

De Jong, G. (1979). 'Independent Living: From Social Movement to Analytic Paradigm.' *Archives of Physical Medicine and Rehabilitation* 66:435–46.

Devlin, Richard, and Dianne Pothier. (2006). 'Introduction: Toward a Critical Theory of Dis-Citizenship.' In Dianne Pothier and Richard Devlin, eds.,

Critical Disability Theory: Essays in Philosophy, Politics, Policy, and Law, 1–22. Vancouver: Univ. of British Columbia Press.

Doe, Tanis. (2003). *Studying Disability: Connecting People, Programs and Policies.* Victoria: Island Blue Press.

Doern, G. Bruce, Allan M.Maslove, and Michael J. Prince. (1988). *Public Budgeting in Canada: Politics, Economics and Management.* Ottawa: Carleton Univ. Press.

Dossa, Parin. (2005). 'Racialized Bodies, Disabling Worlds: 'They [service providers] Always Saw Me as a Client, not as a Worker.' *Social Science and Medicine* 60(11):2527–36.

– (2008). 'Creating Alternative and Demedicalized Spaces: Testimonial Narrative on Disability, Culture, and Racialization.' *Journal of International Women's Studies* 9(3):79–98.

Driedger, Diane. (1989). *The Last Civil Rights Movement: Disabled Peoples' International.* New York: St. Martin's Press.

Driedger, Diane, and Michelle Owen. eds. (2008). *Dissonant Disabilities: Women with Chronic Illnesses Explore Their Lives.* Toronto: Women's Press.

Driedger, S. Michelle, Valorie A. Crooks, and David Bennett. (2004). 'Engaging in the Disablement Process over Space and Time: Narratives of Persons with Multiple Sclerosis in Ottawa, Canada,' *Canadian Geographer* 48(2): 119–36.

Duckworth, K., S.J. Kingsburg, N. Kass, R. Goisman, C. Wellington, and M. Etheridge. (1994). 'Voting Behavior and Attitudes of Chronically Mentally Ill Outpatients.' *Hospital and Community Psychiatry* 45(6):608–9.

Duffy, Ann, and Nancy Mandell. (2001). 'The Growth in Poverty and Social Inequality: Losing Faith in Social Justice.' In Dan Glenday and Ann Duffy, eds., *Canadian Society: Meeting the Challenge of the Twenty-First Century*, 77–114. Toronto: Oxford Univ. Press.

Eadie, Ross. (2000). 'A Politician Wanna Be.' *Canadian Blind Monitor* (summer):26–9. Available online www.blindcanadians.ca.

Echenberg, Havi, with Fraser Valentine. (2001). *Access and Inclusion Lens: A Discussion Paper for the Federal/Provincial/Territorial Governments of Canada.* Ottawa: Prepared for Human Resources Development Canada.

EKOS Research Associates Inc. (1998). *The Use of Social Indicators as Evaluation Instruments.* Ottawa: Final Report for Human Resources Development Canada.

Elections Canada (2001). *Special Needs Associations, Post-Mortem Studies of 37th General Election.* Unpublished report prepared by Ipsos-Reid.

– (2003). *Compendium of Election Administration in Canada 2003.* Prepared for the Conference of Canadian Election Officials. Available online http://www.elections.ca.

Ellis, Angele, and M. Llewellyn. (1997). *Dealing with Differences: Taking Action On Class, Race, Gender and Disability.* Thousand Oaks, Calif.: Cowrin.

Elson, Diane. (2006). *Budgeting for Women's Rights.* New York: United Nations Fund for Women.

End Exclusion. (2007). *National Action Plan 2007.* A National Initiative of CACL, CCD and Other Partners. Available online www.endexclusion.ca.

Enns, Ruth. (1999). *A Voice Unheard: The Latimer Case and People with Disabilities.* Halifax: Fernwood Publishing.

Enns, Henry, and Aldred H. Neufeldt, eds. (2003). *In Pursuit of Participation: Canada and Disability at Home and Abroad.* Concord, ON: Captus Press.

Environics Research Group. (2004a). *Government of Canada, Canadian Attitudes towards Disability Issues: Final Questionnaire.*

– (2004b). *Canadian Attitudes toward Disability Issues, A Qualitative Study, Final Report.* Prepared for Government of Canada, the Office for Disability Issues.

– (2004c). *Canadian Attitudes toward Disability Issues: 2004 Benchmark Survey, Final Report.* Prepared for the Office for Disability Issues, Social Development Canada.

Esping-Andersen, Gösta. (1990). *The Three Worlds of Capitalism.* Cambridge: Polity Press.

– (1993). *Changing Classes: Stratification and Mobility in Post-Industrial Societies.* London: Sage.

Fagan, Tony, and Phil Lee. (1997). '"New" Social Movements and Social Policy: A Case Study of the Disability Movement.' In Michael Lavalette and Alan Pratt, eds., *Social Policy: A Conceptual and Theoretical Introduction,* 140–60. London: Sage.

Fawcett, Gail, Coryse Ciceri, Spyridoula Tsoukalas, and Angela Gibson-Kierstead. (2004). *Support and Services for Adults and Children Aged 5–14 with Disabilities in Canada: An Analysis of Data on Needs and Gaps.* Ottawa: Canadian Council on Social Development.

Feld, John. (1997). 'Sam Savona: What a Candidate! What a Campaign.' *Abilities* Fall:14.

Finkel, Alvin. (2004). *Social Policy and Practice in Canada: A History.* Waterloo: Wilfrid Laurier Univ. Press.

Foucault, Michel. (1984). *The Foucault Reader.* New York: Pantheon.

Fraser, Nancy. (1989). *Unruly Practices: Power, Discourse and Gender in Contemporary Social Theory.* Minneapolis: Univ. of Minneapolis Press.

– (2000). 'Rethinking Recognition.' *New Left Review* 3:107–20.

– (2005). 'Reframing Justice in a Globalizing World.' *New Left Review* 36:69–88.

Frazee, Catherine (2006). 'Toward Robust Citizenship.' Notes for Remarks at End Exclusion Forum. Ottawa: Nov. 2.

Frazee, Catherine, Joan Gilmour, and Roxanne Mykitiuk. (2006). 'Now You See Her, Now You Don't: How Law Shapes Disabled Women's Experience of Exposure, Surveillance, and Assessment in the Clinical Encounter.' In Dianne Pothier and Richard Devlin, eds., *Critical Disability Theory: Essays in Philosophy, Politics, Policy, and Law,* 223–47. Vancouver: Univ. of British Columbia Press.

Frug, Gerald E. (2001). *City Making: Building Communities without Building Walls.* Princeton: Princeton Univ. Press.

Gerometta, Julia, Hartmut Haussermann, and Giulia Longo. (2005). 'Social Innovation and Civil Society in Urban Governance: Strategies for an Inclusive City.' *Urban Studies* 42(11):2007–21.

Gidengil, Elisabeth, André Blais, Neil Nevitte, and Richard Nadeau. (2004). *Citizens.* Vancouver: Univ. of British Columbia Press.

Gleeson, B. (1999). 'Can Technology Overcome the Disabling City?' In R. Butler and H. Parr, eds., *Mind and Body Spaces: Geographies of Illness, Impairment and Disability,* 98–118. London: Routledge.

Gold, Marta. (1993). 'Campaign Aims to Motivate Disabled Voters,' *Edmonton Journal,* Edmonton: Sept. 22, A4.

Gordon, Phyllis, and Mark Hecht. (2006). *Considerations Regarding a Federal Disability Act.* Toronto: Interim Report Prepared for the Council of Canadians with Disabilities.

Gorham, Eric. (1995). 'Social Citizenship and its Fetters.' *Polity* 28:25–47.

Grace, Joan. (1997). 'Sending Mixed Messages: Gender-based Analysis and the Status of Women.' *Canadian Public Administration* 40(4):582–98.

Graham, John R., Karen J. Swift, and Roger Delaney. (2003). *Canadian Social Policy: An Introduction* (2nd ed.). Toronto: Prentice Hall.

Graham, Katherine A., and Susan D. Phillips. (1997). 'Citizen Engagement: Beyond the Customer Revolution.' *Canadian Public Administration* 40(2):255–73.

Graham, Katherine A., Susan D. Phillips, and Allan M. Maslove. (1998). *Urban Governance in Canada: Representation, Resources, and Restructuring.* Toronto: Harcourt Canada.

Greer, Scott. (1989). 'Urbanism and Urbanity: Cities in an Urban-Dominated Society.' *Urban Affairs Quarterly* 24(3):341–52.

Guest, Dennis. (2003). *The Emergence of Social Security in Canada* (3rd ed.). Vancouver: Univ. of British Columbia Press.

Haluza-Delay, Randolph. (2003). 'Community-Based Research, Movement Intellectuals and the "Knowledge Council."' *Canadian Review of Social Policy.* 52:133–8.

Hankivsky, Olga. (2007). 'Gender Mainstreaming in the Canadian Context:

One Step Forward and Two Steps Back.' In Michael Orsini and Miriam Smith. eds., *Critical Policy Studies*, 111–35. Vancouver: Univ. of British Columbia Press.

Hardina, Donna. (2003). 'What Social Workers Need to Know about the Right to Vote.' *The Social Policy Journal* 2(4):53–70.

Harrison, Trevor W., and John W. Friesen. (2004). *Canadian Society in the Twenty-First Century: A Historical-Sociological Approach.* Toronto: Pearson Prentice Hall.

Henderson, Helen. (2006). 'Truly Accessible Meetings at Last.' *Toronto Star,* Toronto: Jan. 7, L6.

Higgins, P.C. (1992). *Making Disability: Exploring the Social Transformation of Human Variation.* Illinois: Charles C. Thomas.

Hiller, Harry H., ed. (2005). *Urban Canada: Sociological Perspectives.* Don Mills: Oxford Univ. Press.

Hogg, Peter W. (2007). *Constitutional Law of Canada.* Toronto: Thomson Carswell.

Holston, James, and Arjun Appadurai. (1999). 'Cities and Citizenship.' In J. Holston, ed., *Cities and Citizenship*, 1–18. Durham: Duke Univ. Press.

Howard, G., and R. Anthony. (1977). 'The Right to Vote and Voting Patterns of Hospitalized Psychiatric Patients.' *Psychiatric Quarterly* 49(2):124–32.

Hughes, Bill. (2002). 'Bauman's Strangers: Impairment and the Invalidation of Disabled People on Modern and Post-modern Cultures.' *Disability and Society* 17(5):571–84.

Human Resources Development Canada. (1997). 'Social Indicators: What Are They All About?' *Applied Research Bulletin.* Winter/Spring, vol. 3, no. 1.

Hummon, David M. (1986). 'Urban Views: Popular Perspectives on City Life.' *Urban Life* 15(1):3–36.

Hutchison, Peggy, Susan Arai, Alison Pedlar, John Lord, and Colleen Whyte. (2007b). 'Leadership in the Canadian Consumer Disability Movement: Hopes and Challenges.' *International Journal of Disability, Community and Rehabilitation* 6(1). Available online www.ijdcr.ca.

Hutchison, Peggy, Susan Arai, Alison Pedlar, John Lord, and Felice Yuen. (2007a). 'Role of Canadian User-led Disability Organizations in the Non-profit Sector.' *Disability and Society* 22(7):701–16.

Ignatieff, Michael. (1984). *The Needs of Strangers: An Essay on Privacy, Solidarity, and the Politics of Being Human.* London: Penguin Books.

Imrie, Rob. (1996). *Disability and the City: International Perspectives.* London: Paul Chapman Publishing.

– (2000). 'Disabling Environments and the Geography of Access Policies and Programs.' *Disability and Society* 15(1):5–24.

– (2001). 'Barriered and Bounded Places and the Spatialities of Disability.' *Urban Studies* 38(2):231–7.

Isin, Engin F. (1992). *Cities Without Citizens: Modernity of the City as a Corporation*. Montreal: Black Rose Books.

Jacobs, Jane. (1961). *The Death and Life of Great American Cities*. New York: Random House.

James, Matt. (2006). *Misrecognized Materialists: Social Movements in Canadian Constitutional Politics*. Vancouver: Univ. of British Columbia Press.

Jenkins, Richard. (1991). 'Disability and Social Stratification.' *British Journal of Sociology* 42(4):577–80.

Jennissen, Therese, Michael J. Prince, and Saul Schwartz. (2000). 'Workers' Compensation in Canada: A Case for Greater Public Accountability.' *Canadian Public Administration* 43(1):23–45.

Keung, Nicholas. (2006). 'Candidates Asked to Listen Up.' *Toronto Star*, Toronto: Jan. 11, B5.

Kingsley, Jean-Pierre. (2004). 'Blind Solution Sought.' *Langley Advance*, Langley, BC: Jul. 16, 41.

Kirby, Michael J. L., Chair. (2006). *Out of the Shadows at Last: Transforming Mental Health, Mental Illness and Addiction Services in Canada*. Ottawa: The Standing Senate Committee on Social Affairs, Science and Technology. Available online http://www.parl.gc.ca/39/1/parlbus/commbus/senate/com-e/soci-e/rep-e/rep02may06-e.htm.

Kivisto, Peter, and Thomas Faist. (2007). *Citizenship: Discourse, Theory, and Transnational Prospects*. Oxford: Blackwell.

Kjellberg, Anette. (2002). 'Being a Citizen.' *Disability and Society* 17(2):187–203.

Klein, M., and Grossman, S. (1971). 'Voting Competence and Mental Illness.' *American Journal of Psychiatry* 127(11):1562–5.

Kleiss, Karen. (2004). 'Ballot Machine Boon for Blind Voters.' *Edmonton Journal*, Edmonton: Sept. 22, B1.

Krause, Carol, ed. (2005). *Between Myself and Them: Stories of Disability and Difference*. Toronto: Second Story Press.

Krogh, Kari, and Jon Johnson. (2006). 'A Life without Living: Challenging Medical and Economic Reductionism in Home Support Policy for People with Disabilities.' In Dianne Pothier and Richard Devlin, eds., *Critical Disability Theory: Essays in Philosophy, Politics, Policy, and Law*, 151–76. Vancouver: Univ. of British Columbia Press.

Kruse, Douglas L., Kay Schriner, Lisa Schur, and Todd Shields. (1999). *Empowerment through Civic Participation: A Study of the Political Behavior of People with Disabilities*. Final Report to the Disability Research Consortium,

Bureau of Economic Research, Rutgers Univ. and New Jersey Developmental Disabilities Council.

Kwavnick, David (1972). *Organized Labour and Pressure Politics.* Montreal and London: McGill-Queen's Univ. Press.

Laforest, Rachel, and Susan Phillips. (2007). 'Citizen Engagement: Rewiring the Policy Process.' In Michael Orsini and Miriam Smith, eds., *Critical Policy Studies,* 67–90. Vancouver: Univ. of British Columbia Press.

Leclerc, Michel. (2004). 'The Evolution of Access to Voting for People with Disabilities in Quebec.' *Electoral Insight* 6(1):22–5.

Leonard, Peter. (1997). *Postmodern Welfare: Reconstructing an Emancipatory Project.* London: Sage.

Lepofsky, David M. (2004). 'The Long Arduous Road to a Barrier-Free Ontario for People with Disabilities: The History of the Ontarians with Disabilities Act – The First Chapter.' *National Journal of Constitutional Law* 15(2):125–33.

Lian, Jason Z., and David Ralph Matthews. (1998). 'Does the Vertical Mosaic Still Exist? Ethnicity and Income in Canada, 1991.' *Canadian Review of Sociology and Anthropology* 35:461–81.

Lightman, Ernie. (2003). *Social Policy in Canada.* Toronto: Oxford Univ. Press.

Lister, Ruth. (1997). *Citizenship: Feminist Perspectives.* London: Macmillan.

Little, Margaret Hillyard. (2005). *If I Had a Hammer: Retraining that Really Works.* Vancouver: Univ. of British Columbia Press.

Lofland, Lyn H. (1973). *A World of Strangers: Order and Action in Urban Public Spaces.* New York: Basic Books.

Lord, John, and Peggy Hutchison. (2007). *Pathways to Inclusion: Building a New Story with People and Communities.* Concord, ON: Captus Press.

Lorinc, John. (2006). *The New City: How the Crisis of Canada's Urban Centres is Reshaping the Nation.* Toronto: Penguin Canada.

Lunman, Kim. (1993). 'Lack of Access to Polls Shocks Disabled Voters.' *Calgary Herald,* Calgary: Jun. 16, A2.

Macionis, John, J., Jansson, S. Mikael, and Benoit, Cecelia. (2005). *Society: The Basics* (3rd ed.). Toronto: Pearson Prentice Hall.

Macpherson, C.B. (1977). *The Life and Times of Liberal Democracy.* Oxford: Oxford Univ. Press.

Malkowski, Gary. (1997). 'Running in the Federal Election.' *CCD Election Monitor,* 1(2), Ap. 25, 1–2.

Man Ling Lee, Theresa. (2006). 'Multicultural Citizenship: The Case of the Disabled,' In Dianne Pothier and Richard Devlin, eds., *Critical Disability*

Theory: Essays in Philosophy, Politics, Policy, and Law, 87–105. Vancouver: Univ. of British Columbia Press.

Marshall, T.H. (1964). *Class, Citizenship, and Social Development.* Westport, Conn.: Greenwood Press.

Martin, Edward J., and Rodolfo D. Torres. (2004). *Savage State: Welfare Capitalism and Inequality.* Toronto: Rowman & Littlefield.

Matthews, Gwyneth Ferguson. (1983). *Voices from the Shadows: Women with Disabilities Speak Out.* Toronto: Women's Educational Press.

Matyas, Joe. (2005). 'Ruling on Disabled Fought.' *London Free Press,* London, ON: June 1, B3.

McAllister, Mary Louise. (2004). *Governing Ourselves? The Politics of Canadian Communities.* Vancouver: Univ. of British Columbia Press.

McCallum, Dulcie. (2006). 'CACL Analysis of the NDP Private Member's Proposed Bill on Disability.' Report prepared for the Canadian Association for Community Living. Toronto.

McColl, Mary Ann. (2006a). 'Electoral Participation among Disabled People.' In Mary Ann McColl and Lyn Jongbloed, eds., *Disability and Social Policy in Canada* (2nd ed.), 230–8. Concord, ON: Captus Univ. Press.

– (2006b). 'Structural Determinants of Access to Health Care for People with Disabilities,' In Mary Ann McColl and Lyn Jongbloed, eds., *Disability and Social Policy in Canada* (2nd ed.), 293–313. Concord, ON: Captus Univ. Press.

McColl, Mary Ann, Alison James, William Boyce, and Sam Shortt. (2006). 'Disability Policy Making: Evaluating the Evidence Base.' In Dianne Pothier and Richard Devlin, eds., *Critical Disability Theory: Essays in Philosophy, Politics, Policy, and Law,* 25–45. Vancouver: Univ. of British Columbia Press.

McColl, Mary Ann, and Lyn Jongbloed, eds. (2006). *Disability and Social Policy in Canada* (2nd ed). Concord, ON: Captus Univ. Press.

McDaniel, Susan A. (2002). 'Women's Changing Relations to the State and Citizenship: Caring and Intergenerational Relations in Globalizing Western Democracies.' *Canadian Review of Sociology and Anthropology* 39:125–50.

McQuaig, Linda. (1999). *The Cult of Impotence: Selling the Myth of Powerlessness in the Global Economy.* Toronto: Penguin.

Meekosha, Helen. (2001). 'Virtual Activists? Women and the Making of Identities of Disability.' *Hypatia: Journal of Feminist Philosophy* 17(3):67–88.

Mendelshon, M., and J. Brent. (2001). 'Understanding Polling Methodology.' *The ISUMA Canadian Journal of Policy Research* Autumn:131–6.

Michalko, Rod. (1999). *The Two in One: Walking with Smokie, Walking with Blindness.* Philadelphia: Temple Univ. Press.

– (2002). *The Difference that Disability Makes.* Philadelphia: Temple Univ. Press.

Mitchell, Don. (2003). *The Right to the City: Social Justice and the Fight for Public Space*. New York: Guilford Press.

Moffatt, Ken. (1999). 'Surveillance and Government of the Welfare Recipient.' In Adrienne S. Chambers, Allan Irving, and Laura Epstein, eds., *Reading Foucault for Social Work*. New York: Columbia Univ. Press.

Moss, Pamela, and Isabella Dyck. (2002). *Women, Body, Illness: Space and Identity in the Everyday Lives of Women with Chronic Illness*. Toronto: Rowman & Littlefield.

Moss, Pamela, and Katherine Teghtsoonian, eds. (2008). *Contesting Illness: Processes and Practices*. Toronto: Univ. of Toronto Press.

Mulvale, James P. (2001). *Reimagining Social Welfare: Beyond the Keynesian Welfare State*. Aurora, ON: Garamond Press.

Myles, John. (2003). 'Where have All the Sociologists Gone? Explaining Economic Inequality.' *Canadian Journal of Sociology* 28:551–9.

Naiman, Joanne. (2004). *How Societies Work: Class, Power, and Change in a Canadian Context* (3rd ed.). Toronto: Thomson Nelson.

Nash, Michael. (2002). 'Voting as a Means of Social Inclusion for People with a Mental Illness.' *Journal of Psychiatric and Mental Health Nursing* 9:697–703.

Noll, Heinz-Herbert. (1996). 'Social Indicators and Social Reporting: The International Experience.' Available online http://www.ccsd.ca/noll 1.htm.

Organisation for Economic Co-operation and Development (OECD). (2001). 'Engaging Citizens in Policy-Making: Information, Consultation and Public Participation.' Public Management Policy Brief No. 10. Available online http://www.oecd.org.

– (2003). 'Engaging Citizens Online for Better Policy-making.' Available online http://www.oecd.org.

Orsini, Michael, and Miriam Smith, eds. (2007a). *Critical Policy Studies*. Vancouver: Univ. of British Columbia Press.

Orsini, Michael, and Miriam Smith. (2007b) 'Critical Policy Studies,' In Michael Orsini and Miriam Smith, eds., *Critical Policy Studies*, 1–16. Vancouver: Univ. of British Columbia Press.

Osberg, Lars. (2001). 'Needs and Wants: What Is Social Progress and How Should It Be Measured?' *The Review of Economic Performance and Social Progress*, 23–41.

Osberg, Lars, and Andrew Sharpe. (2003). *Human Well-being and Economic Well-being: What Values Are Implicit in Current Indices?* Ottawa: Centre for the Study of Living Standards. Available online http://www.csls.ca.

Otto, Mary. (2004). 'Advocates Encourage, Protect Disabled Voters.' *The Washington Post*, Washington, DC: Jan. 31, C4.

Overboe, James. (2007). 'Disability and Genetics: Affirming the Bare Life (the State of Exception).' *Canadian Review of Sociology and Anthropology* 44(2):219–35.

Packard, Vance. (1974). *A Nation of Strangers*. New York Pocket Books.

Pal, Leslie A. (1997). *Beyond Policy Analysis: Public Issue Management in Turbulent Times*. Scarborough: Nelson.

Panitch, Leo, ed. (1977). *The Canadian State: Political Economy and Political Power*. Toronto: Univ. of Toronto Press.

Panitch, Melanie. (2007). *Disability, Mothers, and Organization: Accidental Activists*. London: Routledge.

Peters, Yvonne. (2003). 'From Charity to Equality: Canadians with Disabilities Take Their Rightful Place in Canada's Constitution.' In D. Stienstra and A. Wight-Felske, eds., *Making Equality: History of Advocacy and Persons with Disabilities in Canada*, 119–36. Concord, ON: Captus Press.

Phillips, Susan D., with Michael Orsini. (2002). *Mapping the Links: Citizen Involvement in Policy Processes*. Canadian Policy Research Networks Discussion Paper No.F/21. Ottawa. Available online http://www.cprn.org.

Porter, John. (1965). *The Vertical Mosaic: An Analysis of Social Class and Power in Canada*. Toronto: Univ. of Toronto Press.

Pothier, Dianne, and Richard Devlin, eds. (2006). *Critical Disability Theory: Essays in Philosophy, Politics, Policy, and Law*. Vancouver: Univ. of British Columbia Press.

Prince, Michael J. (1992). 'Touching Us All: International Context, National Policies, and the Integration of Canadians with Disabilities.' In Frances Abele, ed., *How Ottawa Spends: 1992–93: The Politics of Competitiveness*, 191–239. Ottawa: Carleton Univ. Press.

– (2000). 'Battling for Remembrance: The Politics of Veterans Affairs Canada.' In Leslie A. Pal, ed., *How Ottawa Spends 2000–2001: Past Imperfect, Future Tense*, 131–59. Toronto: Oxford Univ. Press.

– (2001a). 'Tax Policy as Social Policy: Canadian Tax Assistance for People with Disabilities.' *Canadian Public Policy*, 27(4):487–501.

– (2001b). 'Citizenship by Instalments: Federal Policies for Canadians with Disabilities.' In Leslie A. Pal, ed., *How Ottawa Spends 2001–2002, Power in Transition*, 177–200. Toronto: Oxford Univ. Press.

– (2001c). *Governing in an Integrated Fashion: Lessons from the Disability Domain*. CPRN Discussion paper No.F/14. Ottawa: Canadian Policy Research Networks. Available online http://www.cprn.org.

– (2001d). 'Canadian Federalism and Disability Policy Making.' *Canadian Journal of Political Science* 34(4):791–817.

– (2002a). *Wrestling with the Poor Cousin: Canada Pension Plan Disability Policy and Practice, 1964–2001.* Research paper for the Office of the Commissioner of Review Tribunals Canada Pension Plan/Old Age Security, Government of Canada. Available online http://ocrt-bctr.gc.ca/pubs/prince/index_e.html.

– (2002b). 'The Return of Directed Incrementalism: Innovating Social Policy the Canadian Way.' In G. Bruce Doern, ed., *How Ottawa Spends 2002–2003: The Security Aftermath and National Priorities,* 176–95. Toronto: Oxford Univ. Press.

– (2002c). 'The Governance of Children with Disabilities and Their Families: Charting the Public-Sector Regime in Canada.' *Canadian Public Administration* 45(3):389–409.

– (2002d). 'Designing Disability Policy in Canada: The Nature and Impact of Federalism on Policy Development.' In A. Puttee, ed., *Federalism, Democracy and Disability in Canada,* 29–77. Montreal and Kingston: McGill-Queen's Univ. Press.

– (2004a). 'Persons with Disabilities and Canada's Electoral System: Gradually Advancing the Democratic Right to Vote.' *Electoral Insight* 6(1):2–7.

– (2004b). 'Canadian Disability Policy: Still a Hit-and-Miss Affair.' *Canadian Journal of Sociology* 29(1):59–82.

– (2006). 'Who Are We? The Disability Community in Canada.' In Mary Ann McColl and Lyn Jongbloed, eds., *Disability and Social Policy in Canada* (2nd ed.), 160–75. Concord, ON: Captus Univ. Press.

– (2008a). 'Claiming a Disability Benefit as Contesting Social Citizenship.' In Pamela Moss and Katherine Teghtsoonian, eds., *Contesting Illness: Processes and Practices,* 28–46. Toronto: Univ. of Toronto Press.

– (2008b). *Canadians Need a Medium-Term Sickness/Disability Income Benefit.* Ottawa: Caledon Institute of Social Policy. Available online http://www.caledoninst.org/.

Proulx, Jean, Lucie Dumais, and Yves Vaillancourt. (2006). *Les services aux personnes ayant des incapacités au Québec: Rôle des acteurs et dynamiques régionales.* Montréal : Cahier du LAREPPS 06-12/UQUAM.

Pupo, Norene. (2001). 'The Role of the State in a Restructured Economy.' In Dan Glenday and Ann Duffy, eds., *Canadian Society: Meeting the Challenge of the Twenty-First Century,* 117–44. Toronto: Oxford Univ. Press.

Puttee, Alan, ed. (2002). *Federalism, Democracy and Disability Policy in Canada.* Montreal and Kingston: McGill-Queen's Univ. Press.

Rahder, Barbara, and Richard Milgrom. (2004). 'The Uncertain City: Making Space(s) For Difference.' *Canadian Journal of Urban Research* 13(1)Supplement:27–45.

Raoul, Valerie, Connie Canam, Angela D. Henderson, and Carla Paterson, eds. (2007). *Unfitting Stories: Narrative Approaches to Disease, Disability, and Trauma.* Waterloo: Wilfrid Laurier Univ. Press.

Reaume, Geoffrey. (2000). *Patients Past: Patient Life at the Toronto Hospital for the Insane, 1870–1940.* Toronto: Oxford Univ. Press.

Reichl, Alexander J. (2005). 'Rescaling Urban Politics: Structure and Agency in the Global Era.' *Polity* 37(1):149–66.

Rice, James J., and Michael J. Prince. (2000). *Changing Politics of Canadian Social Policy.* Toronto: Univ. of Toronto Press.

Riesman, David, with Nathan Glazer, and Reuel Denney. (1955). *The Lonely Crowd: A Study of the Changing American Character.* New York: Doubleday Anchor Books.

Rioux, Marcia H., and Michael Bach, eds. (1994). *Disability is not Measles: New Research Paradigms in Disability.* North York, ON: The Roeher Institute.

Rioux, Marcia H., and Michael J. Prince. (2002). 'The Canadian Political Landscape of Disability: Policy Perspectives, Social Status, Interest Groups and the Rights Movement.' In Alan Puttee, ed., *Federalism, Democracy and Disability Policy in Canada,* 11–28. Montreal and Kingston: McGill-Queen's Univ. Press.

Rioux, Marcia H., and Rita M. Samson. (2006). 'Trends Impacting Disability: National and International Perspectives.' In Mary Ann McColl and Lyn Jongbloed, eds., *Disability and Social Policy in Canada* (2nd ed.), 112–42. Concord, ON: Captus Univ. Press.

Rioux, Marcia H., and Fraser Valentine. (2006). 'Does Theory Matter? Exploring the Nexus between Disability, Human Rights, and Public Policy.' In Dianne Pothier and Richard Devlin, eds., *Critical Disability Theory: Essays in Philosophy, Politics, Policy, and Law,* 47–69. Vancouver: Univ. of British Columbia Press.

Roeher Institute. (1997). *Disability, Community and Society: Exploring the Links.* North York: L'Institut Roeher Institute.

– (2001). *Striking a New Balance: Proposal for a Joint Federal-Provincial/Territorial Disability Supports Initiative.* North York: L'Institut Roeher Institute.

Room, Graham. (1979). *Sociology of Welfare: Social Policy, Stratification, and Political Order.* Oxford: Blackwell.

Ross, Jonathon, and Kyle P. Nelson. (2005). 'The Accessible and Inclusive City.' An Academic Paper Submitted to the World Urban Forum.

Sadava, Mike. (2006). 'Deaf Voters Feel Left Out at Forums, Interpreting Meetings Would Only Cost $200, Advocate Says.' *Edmonton Journal,* Edmonton: Jan. 18.

Sainsbury Diane. (1996). *Gender, Equality, and Welfare States.* Cambridge: Cambridge Univ. Press.

Saul, John Ralston. (2005). *The Collapse of Globalism. And the Reinvention of the World*. Toronto: Viking Canada.

Schaefer, Richard T., and Edith Smith. (2005). *Sociology: First Canadian Edition*. New York: McGraw-Hill Ryerson.

Schriner, Kay, and Andrew Batavia. (2001). 'The Americans with Disabilities Act: Does It Secure the Fundamental Right to Vote?' *Policy Studies Journal* 29(4):663–73.

Schriner, K., L. Ochs, and T. Shields. (1997). 'The Last Suffrage Movement: Voting Rights for People with Cognitive and Emotional Disabilities.' *Publius* 27(3):75–96.

Schriner, K., and T. Shields. (1998). 'Empowerment of the Political Kind: The Role of Disability Service Organizations in Encouraging People with Disabilities to Vote ... the Motor Voter Bill.' *Journal of Rehabilitation* 64(2):33–7.

Schur, Lisa A. (1998). 'Disability and Psychology of Political Participation.' *Journal of Disability Policy Studies* 9(2):3–31.

Schur, Lisa A., and D.L. Kruse. (2000). 'What Determines Voter Turnout? Lessons from Citizens with Disabilities.' *Social Science Quarterly* 81(2):571–87.

Scope. (2005). *Polls Apart 4: Campaigning for Accessible Democracy*. London. Available online www.pollsapart.org/uk.

Seymour, Ron. (2004). 'Blind Voters Want Ballots in Braille.' *Kelowna Daily Courier,* Kelowna: Jun. 11.

Sheedy, Amanda. In collaboration with Mary Pat MacKinnon, Sonia Pitre, and Judy Watling. (2008). *Handbook on Citizen Engagement: Beyond Consultation*. Ottawa: Canadian Policy Research Networks.

Shields, Todd, K.F. Schriner, and K. Schriner. (1998). 'The Disability Voice in American Politics: The Participation of People with Disabilities in the 1994 Election.' *Journal of Disability Policy Studies* 9(2):33–52.

Shields, T. G., Kay Schriner, K.F. Schriner, and L. Ochs. (2000). 'Disenfranchised: People with Disabilities in American Electoral Politics.' In B.M. Altman and S.N. Barnartt, eds., *Expanding the Scope of Social Science Research on Disability*, 177–203. Stanford Connecticut: Jai Press.

Shimrat, Irit. (1997). *Call Me Crazy: Stories from the Mad Movement*. Vancouver: Press Gang.

Short, John R. (1989). *The Humane City: Cities as if People Mattered*. Oxford: Basil Blackwell.

Smiley, Donald V. (1987). *The Federal Condition in Canada*. Toronto: McGraw-Hill Ryerson.

Smith, H., and M. Humphreys. (1997). 'Changes in the Law are Necessary to

Allow Patients Detained under the Mental Health Act to Vote.' *British Medical Journal* 315:431.

Smith, Miriam, ed. (2008). *Group Politics and Social Movements in Canada.* Peterborough, ON: Broadview Press.

Söder, Martin. (1990). 'Prejudice or Ambivalence? Attitudes toward Persons with Disabilities.' *Disability and Society* 5(3):227–41.

Spicker, Paul. (1996). *Social Policy: Themes and Approaches.* London: Prentice Hall.

Squires, Judith. (2007). *The New Politics of Gender Equality.* Basingstoke: Palgrave.

Staggenborg, Suzanne. (2008). *Social Movements.* Toronto: Oxford Univ. Press.

Statistics Canada. (2002). *Profile of Disability in Canada 2001.* Ottawa. Available online www.statcan.ca.

– (2003). *Children with Disabilities and Their Families.* Ottawa. Available online www.statcan.ca.

– (2007). *Participation and Activity Limitation Survey, 2006.* Ottawa: Available online www.statscan.

Status of Women Canada. (1997). *Economic Gender Equality Indicators.* Report for the Federal-Provincial/Territorial Ministers Responsible for the Status of Women. Ottawa: Status of Women Canada.

Stienstra, Deborah, and April D'Aubin. (2006). 'People with Disabilities and Political Participation.' In Mary Ann McColl and Lyn Jongbloed, eds., *Disability and Social Policy in Canada* (2nd ed.), 210–29. Concord, ON: Captus Univ. Publications.

Stienstra, Deborah, and Lindsey Troschuk. (2005). 'Engaging Citizens with Disabilities in eDemocracy.' *Disability Studies Quarterly* 25(2). Available online at www.dsq-sds.org.

Stienstra, Deborah, and A. Wight-Felske, eds. (2003). *Making Equality: History of Advocacy and Persons with Disabilities in Canada.* Concord, ON: Captus Press.

Taylor, Charles. (1992). *Multiculturalism and the Politics of Recognition.* Princeton: Princeton Univ. Press.

Taylor, David. (1996). 'Introduction.' In David Taylor, ed., *Critical Social Policy: A Reader*, 1–12. London: Sage.

Teevan, James J., and W.E. Hewitt, eds. (2005). *Introduction to Sociology: A Canadian Focus* (8th ed.). Toronto: Pearson Prentice Hall.

Teghtsoonian, Katherine. (2000). 'Gendering Policy Analysis in the Government of British Columbia: Strategies, Possibilities and Constraints.' *Studies in Political Economy* 61:105–27.

– (2004). 'Neoliberalism and Gender Analysis Mainstreaming in Aotearoa/New Zealand.' *Australian Journal of Political Science* 39(2):267–84.

Tepperman, Lorne, and James Curtis, eds. (2002). *Sociology: A Canadian Perspective.* Toronto: Oxford Univ. Press.

Titchkosky, Tanya. (2001). '"Disability" A Rose by Any Other Name? "People-First" Language in Canadian Society.' *Canadian Review of Sociology and Anthropology* 38(2):125–40.

– (2003a). *Disability, Self, and Society.* Toronto: Univ. of Toronto Press.

– (2003b). 'Governing Embodiment: Technologies of Constituting Citizens with Disabilities.' *Canadian Journal of Sociology* 28:517–42.

– (2007). *Reading and Writing Disability Differently: The Textured Life of Embodiment.* Toronto: Univ. of Toronto Press.

Titmuss, Richard. (1958). *Essays on the Welfare State.* London: Allen & Unwin.

Torjman, Sherri. (1999). *Are Outcomes the Best Outcome?* Ottawa: Caledon Institute of Social Policy.

– (2001). 'Canada's Federal Regime and Persons with Disabilities.' In D. Cameron and F. Valentine, eds., *Disability and Federalism: Comparing Different Approaches to Full Participation,* 151–96. Montreal and Kingston: McGill-Queen's Univ. Press.

Touraine, Alain. (2001). *Beyond Neoliberalism.* Cambridge: Polity.

Tremain, Shelley, ed., (2005). *Foucault and the Government of Disability.* Ann Arbor: Univ. of Michigan Press.

Tremblay, Mary, Audrey Campbell, and Geoffrey L. Hudson. (2005). 'When Elevators Were for Pianos: An Oral History Account of the Civilian Experience of Using Wheelchairs in Canadian Society. The First Twenty-Five Years: 1945–1970.' *Disability and Society* 20(2):103–16.

Turner, Bryan S. (1986). *Citizenship and Capitalism: The Debate over Reformism.* London: Allen & Unwin.

– (1988). *Status.* Minneapolis: Univ. of Minnesota Press.

– (2001). 'The Erosion of Citizenship.' *British Journal of Sociology* 52:189–209.

Turner, R.S. (2002). 'The Politics of Design and Development in the Postmodern Downtown.' *Journal of Urban Affairs* 24(5):533–48.

Tyjewski, Carolyn. (2006). 'Ghosts in the Machine: Civil Rights Law and the Hybrid "Invisible Other."' In Dianne Pothier and Richard Devlin, eds., *Critical Disability Theory: Essays in Philosophy, Politics, Policy, and Law,* 106–27. Vancouver: Univ. of British Columbia Press.

United Nations. (2002). *Human Development Report, 2002.* New York: Oxford Univ. Press.

– (2008). *Mainstreaming Disability in the Development Agenda.* New York: Economic and Social Council, Commission for Social Development. Available online http://www.un.org/disabilities/documents/reports/e-cu5-2008-06.doc.

United States. (2001). General Accounting Office. *Voters with Disabilities:*

Access to Polling Places and Alternative Voting Methods, Washington, DC: United States General Accounting Office, Report GAO-02-107. Available online http://www.gao.gov.special.pubs/d02107.txt.

Valentine, Fraser, and Jill Vickers. (1996). 'Released from the Yoke of Paternalism and Charity: Citizenship and the Rights of Canadians with Disabilities.' *International Journal of Canadian Studies* 14(fall):155–77.

Vernon, Richard. (2006). *Friends, Citizens, Strangers: Essays on Where We Belong.* Toronto: Univ. of Toronto Press.

Westhues, Anne, ed. (2003). *Canadian Social Policy: Issues and Perspectives* (3rd ed.). Waterloo: Wilfrid Laurier Univ. Press.

Wharf, Brian. (1992). *Communities and Social Policy in Canada.* Toronto: McClelland and Stewart.

Wharf, Brain, and Brad McKenzie. (2004). *Connecting Policy to Practice in the Human Services* (2nd ed.). Toronto: Oxford Univ. Press.

Wickman, Percy. (1987). *Wheels in the Fast Lane ... A Blessing in Disguise.* Edmonton: Triwicky Enterprises.

Williams, Fiona. (1989). *Social Policy: A Critical Introduction.* Cambridge: Polity Press.

Wilton, Robert D. (2006). 'Working at the Margins: Disabled People and the Growth of Precarious Employment.' In Dianne Pothier and Richard Devlin, eds., *Critical Disability Theory: Essays in Philosophy, Politics, Policy, and Law,* 129–50. Vancouver: Univ. of British Columbia Press.

Young, Iris Marion. (1990). *Justice and the Politics of Difference.* Princeton: Princeton Univ. Press.

– (1997). 'Unruly Categories: A Critique of Nancy Fraser's Dual Systems Theory.' *New Left Review* 222:147–60.

Young, Lisa, and Joanne Everitt. (2004). *Advocacy Groups.* Vancouver: Univ. of British Columbia Press.

Index

ability: bio-medical/cultural con-
structions of, 80, 192, 194–5; and
normalcy, 71, 145, 183; as organizational capacity, 128–30; to participate, 176; as personal mobility,
59, 60; restricted, 5, 69, 105, 108,
186; to vote, 136, 146, 148, 150,
153
ableism, 14, 17, 87, 202, 214
ableist, 109, 129, 181, 187, 213
Aboriginal peoples, xii, 16, 102, 114,
161, 211, 217. *See also* First
Nations; indigenous; Inuit; Métis
absence: of barriers, 8; of policies,
39; of presence, 227–8n1; of recognition, 31; of social supports, 34;
of studies, 150
absent citizens: analytical approach,
10–14 passim; concept of,
227–8n1; as excluded Others, 66;
institutionalization, 209; persons
with disabilities, viii, 3, 15, 188;
persons in mainstream, 13; production of, 48; varied experiences, 212
access: attitudes toward, 11, 189; to
benefits and services, 8, 19, 46, 74,
81, 85, 116, 196, 208, 225; Conservative Party promise, 218–19; disability movement goal, 10, 158,
163, 180, 183, 194, 207, 221; to
electoral systems, 21, 142–3,
146–53 passim, 231n2; to employment, 40, 182, 223; health care,
190; to information/research, 127,
169, 205; to intergovernmental
relations, 170; lack of, 4, 25, 64,
138, 184, 212; to legal resources,
56, 130; to opportunities, 99, 140;
to participation, 62; physical, 34;
policy perspective on, 95, 100–1,
107–10, 161; to policy processes,
92, 167, 173; to public spaces, 63,
109; requirements to programs, 9,
119, 204; social, 60; standards,
142, 220, 233n1; to training, 23,
224; to transportation, 40
accessibility: architectural, 21;
design centre, 220; differences in,
77; to facilities, 41, 84; laws, 92,
143, 206, 217, 233n1, 233n3; as
objective, 63, 124, 184, 192, 217; of
Toronto, 64; of voting processes,
135, 142, 205, 215

197, 205; shifting, 205; social
liberal, 181, 184; social movement, 121; in urban policy, 54
discrimination: ableist, 214; anti-,
92, 109, 217; adverse effect, 19;
against persons with disabilities,
34, 36, 38, 40, 45–6, 64, 85, 111;
cause of inequality, 163; challenge
to citizenship, 15, 45, 183; direct,
19; double, 36; equality rights, 20;
on genetic predisposition, 19;
intentional, 69; mental illness, 48,
206, 213; positive, 73; rights
analysis, 123, 125, 168–9, 207;
shared, 120; solutions to stop, 34,
40–1, 110, 129, 187; unconscious,
69
Doern, G. Bruce, 97, 102
domination, 56, 63, 69, 121
Dossa, Parin, ix, 189–90
Driedger, Diane, ix, xiii, 49, 66, 116,
120, 122, 128, 230–1n1
Duffy, Ann, 70, 83
Dumais, Lucie, 116
duties: citizenship, xi, 18, 179, 180,
232n1; differential, 181, 186, 196;
to others, 180
Dyck, Isabella, ix, 56, 117, 190,
227–8n1

Echenberg, Havi, 95, 101
Edmonton, 139–41
education: accessible, 122, 218; and
attitudes to disability, 35; barriers,
3, 45, 48, 68, 163; children and
youth, 91, 96, 222; citizenship, 17,
195, 233n3; civic, 137; as disability
policy, 192; disability studies, vii,
128, 211; federalism, 224; inclu-
sive/mainstream, 37, 49, 91, 208;

institutions, 169; post-secondary,
230; to raise awareness, 36, 40, 85,
115, 149, 184, 205; responsibility
for, 42–3, 46–7, 210, 224; self, 207;
social status, 96, 98, 233n4; stratification, 86; tax system, 22. *See
also* schools; students
*Eldridge v. British Columbia (Attorney
General)*, 231
elections: access problems, 139;
campaigns, 149; candidates in,
149; city/municipal, 140, 153;
federal, 140, 142, 146–7, 150; laws
and procedures, 145–7, 151–2;
outreach activities, 145, 149;
provincial/territorial, 141, 145–7;
reform ideas, 215, 224; role of
election officers, 141–2, 149,
231n2; role of media in, 148; role
of parties in, 184
Elections Canada, 21, 136, 139, 142,
145–8
electoral participation: accessibility
of polling stations, 136; exclusions, 139; international experiences, 141; marginal voices in, 13;
of people with disabilities, 21,
134–5, 141; as political citizenship, 145, 149; satisfaction with
services, 205; turnout rates, 135,
144, 150, 152, 200. *See also* voter
turnout; voting
electoral systems, 21, 134–54
passim; informal/official, 151–2;
involvement in, 26
Eliot, T.S., 52, 229n1
elites, 10, 51, 104, 124, 165
employment: access to, 40, 182, 218;
active measures for, 9, 22, 32,
41–2, 110, 182, 204, 219; and citi-

Saskatchewan Disability Income
Support Coalition, 163, 231n3
schools, viii; accommodation in,
41, 168, 180, 191; awareness
efforts in, 40; discrimination in,
36, 60, 212; special, 15. *See also*
education
Schriner, Kay, 142–4
Schur, Lisa A., 142–4
self, x, 214; conceptions, 121, 151;
control, 197; dignity, 186; education, 207; embodied, ix; identity,
122; loss of in cities, 60; valued,
viii
self-advocacy/self-advocates, xiii,
111, 155, 223
self-confidence, 40–1; -defined as
disabled, 34; -esteem, 39; -respect,
promoted by the mad movement,
122; -worth, 158
self-determination, xii, 17, 20, 83,
116–17, 132, 155, 192, 194, 201,
208; expression, 153
self-development, 26, 58, 186, 192,
197
self-help/organization, 113–14,
121–2
self-managed care, 208, 232n2
self-reliance, 74, 150, 186; and neo-
liberalism, 24
seniors, 102, 114, 130, 161, 217
sexuality, 87, 107, 190, 202
sexual orientation, 69, 190, 214
Shakespeare, Tom, 59–60, 83, 217,
229n5
sheltered workshops, 182, 195
Shields, Todd, 142–4
Shimrat, Irit, ix, 120
sign language, 132, 140, 149, 151,
205. *See also* American Sign Lan-

guage (ASL); interpreters; Langue
des Signes des Québécoise (LSQ)
Skogstad, Grace, 10, 119
Smiley, Donald V., 44, 224
Smith, Edith, 68, 81
Smith, H., 145
Smith, Miriam, 10–11, 95, 120, 186
social class, 9, 54, 68, 71, 86, 135,
190, 202. *See also* social stratification
social construction, 12, 64, 217. *See
also* social model of disability
social economy, 58, 211
social exclusion: in city life, 52, 69;
faced by people with disabilities,
13, 217; manufacturing in programs, 185, 188; and social policy
texts, 72; not in the spotlight, 13.
See also marginalization; oppression; othering
social group: differences, 62; and
disability policy lens, 93; people
with disabilities as, 3, 10, 135,
173, 199, 200, 212–13, 222; privileged, 76
social inclusion: agenda, xiii, 72,
109; and city life, 53, 65; as flagship concept, 91; inclusion/exclu-
sion, 53, 83, 126, 189–90, 213;
national index of, 14, 26, 91–9,
109–10; of people with disabilities, 116, 181, 184; public attitudes
on, 14, 31, 40, 213; responsibility
for, 41; as rhetorical device, 8; role
of the state, 4, 102, 203, 225,
233n1; voting as a means, 145;
and the welfare state, 80
social inequalities: absences created
by, 14; actions to address, 70;
aggravated by cutbacks, 72; of